Principles of American Journalism

Designed to engage, inspire and challenge students while laying out the fundamentals of the craft, *Principles of American Journalism* introduces readers to the core values of journalism and its singular role in a democracy. From the First Amendment to Facebook, the new and revised edition of this popular textbook provides a comprehensive exploration of the guiding principles of journalism and what makes it unique:

- ▶ the profession's ethical and legal foundations;

- ▶ its historical and modern precepts;

- ▶ the economic landscape of journalism;

- ▶ the relationships among journalism and other social institutions;

- ▶ the key issues and challenges that contemporary journalists face.

Case studies, exercises and an interactive companion website encourage critical thinking about journalism and its role in society, making students more mindful practitioners of journalism and more informed media consumers.

Stephanie Craft is Associate Professor of Journalism at the University of Illinois at Urbana-Champaign. Before earning a doctorate in Communication from Stanford University, she worked as a newspaper journalist in California, Arkansas and Washington.

Charles N. Davis is the Dean of Grady College at the University of Georgia, and is the former executive director for the National Freedom of Information Coalition (NFOIC), headquartered at the Missouri School of Journalism. In 2008, Davis was named the Scripps Howard Foundation National Journalism Teacher of the Year.

Principles of American Journalism

An Introduction

2nd edition

Stephanie Craft

Charles N. Davis

Routledge
Taylor & Francis Group

NEW YORK AND LONDON

Please visit the companion website at www.routledge.com/cw/craft

This edition published 2016
by Routledge
711 Third Avenue, New York, NY 10017

and by Routledge
2 Park Square, Milton Park, Abingdon, Oxon OX14 4RN

Routledge is an imprint of the Taylor & Francis Group, an informa business

© 2016 Taylor & Francis

First edition published 2013 by Routledge

Library of Congress Cataloging-in-Publication Data
Names: Craft, Stephanie. | Davis, Charles N.
Title: Principles of American journalism : an introduction / Stephanie Craft
    and Charles N. Davis.
Description: 2nd edition. | New York : Routledge, 2016. | Includes bibliographical
    references and index.
Identifiers: LCCN 2015038721| ISBN 9781138910300 (hardback) |
    ISBN 9781138910317 (pbk.) | ISBN 9781315693484 (ebook)
Subjects: LCSH: Journalism—United States. | Press—United States.
Classification: LCC PN4855.C84 2016 | DDC 071/.3—dc23
LC record available at http://lccn.loc.gov/2015038721

ISBN: 978-1-138-91030-0 (hbk)
ISBN: 978-1-138-91031-7 (pbk)
ISBN: 978-1-315-69348-4 (ebk)

Typeset in Warnock Pro, Neutraface and Syntax
by Apex CoVantage, LLC

Editor: Erica Wetter
Editorial Assistant: Simon Jacobs
Production Editor: Sarah Thomas
Copy Editor: Andy Soutter
Proofreader: Deborah Blake
Cover Design: Gareth Toye

Dedicated to
Principles of American Journalism *students past, present and future.*

Contents

7 The Foundations of Free Expression   179

8 A Declaration of Journalistic Independence   207

Preface

This book results from the process of co-teaching the Principles of American Journalism course at the Missouri School of Journalism—the task we were hired for and the course that challenged us and changed our thinking on so many issues, day after day.

In our daily conversations as we took turns teaching the course, we concluded that the many fine "Introduction to Mass Media" texts on the market did not meet the needs of a course designed to introduce students not to the entire world of mass communication, but to the central role that journalism plays within that broader world. What if we created a text that not only introduced students to journalism as a practice, but also highlighted its values and the many forces promoting and hindering journalism's ability to act in accordance with them? What if, in other words, we could teach students why journalism matters?

We, like so many others, were deeply influenced by *The Elements of Journalism*, Bill Kovach and Tom Rosenstiel's elegant testament to what makes journalism unique and important. It fundamentally changed the way we thought about teaching the course, and underscored the importance of a course that focuses singularly on the news media.

Of course, much has changed and continues to change since we began teaching the course and since Kovach and Rosenstiel published *The Elements*. We both have moved on to other universities for one thing. But we believe that much of what Kovach and Rosenstiel set forth has stood the test of time—indeed, the ferocity and pace of change make taking a clear stance about journalism's values all the more important. We hope this book does credit to Kovach and Rosenstiel's work and pursues, even if it never quite reaches, the goal of making the case for journalism's essential role. In the end, we do feel we have a text that matches the goals of the course.

Chapters 1 and 2 trace journalism's role in democracy and ways of defining journalism that have implications for what we expect journalism to do. Chapter 3 takes a look at the changing tides of journalism, making the argument that while tools change, the principles underlying journalism don't (or at least shouldn't). Chapters 4 and 5 attempt to make sense of the economic context for journalism and the ever-present tension between profit and public service that has new urgency with the collapse of traditional revenue models. Chapters 6 and 7 address the ethical and legal underpinnings of journalism practice as well as offering practical information to help students understand what they *can* do and whether they *ought* to do it. Finally, Chapter 8 concludes the book with a spirited discussion of independence, the element of journalism that is central to journalism's ability to fulfill its democratic function.

Acknowledgments

A book is a collective effort reflecting the labors of many people. We'd be remiss if we failed to recognize the many fine colleagues, former students and friends who have added their expertise to the book through the many sidebar features you'll read. They add a depth and breadth to the text, as well as a fresh new voice.

We also would like to thank the thousands of students who marched in and out of Principles of American Journalism in the 13 years we taught it. To say that we could not have done it without you all is trite, maybe, yet so true. Your feedback, your questions in class, your responses to the discussions we've had are all reflected in this book. Likewise, we owe a huge debt of gratitude to the many wonderful graduate students who worked with us at Missouri. Many appear in these pages as contributors to the sidebars, but many, many others played a role in this book through discussions, comments and occasional cajoling. We thank you all.

And finally, we thank our families and friends and colleagues, who have made countless adjustments to their own lives so we could get this book written and now revised. As for the Davis side of the writing partnership: thanks to my dear wife Julie, and my kids, Charlie, and Mamie Davis—your father does nothing without you in mind. And from the Craft side, heartfelt thanks to my husband, Kevin, for his encouragement and good humor.

1

The Mirror, the Watchdog and the Marketplace

Navigating the rush-hour traffic on his way to work in January 2009, Sri Lankan newspaper editor Lasantha Wickramatunga was gunned down by two assassins on motorcycles.

He knew it was coming.

For years his newspaper, the *Sunday Leader*, had exposed government corruption and questioned its conduct of the war against the separatist Tamil Tigers—reporting that had already subjected Wickramatunga and his family to beatings and no-holds-barred intimidation. Just days before his murder, he received a message scrawled in red ink on a page of his newspaper: "If you write you will be killed."

So why did he do it? Why did he keep writing in the face of such threats? In an editorial he wrote anticipating his assassination and published three days after his death, Wickramatunga offers a compelling answer, describing how he saw his role as a journalist and the role of a free press in society:

LEARNING OBJECTIVES

▼

Develop an understanding of the essential role journalism plays in democracy;

▼

Explore the specific functions the press performs to fulfill democratic needs;

▼

Consider the factors that influence whether and how well journalism can perform those functions.

1

> The free media serve as a mirror in which the public can see itself sans mascara and styling gel. From us you learn the state of your nation, and especially its management by the people you elected to give your children a better future. Sometimes the image you see in that mirror is not a pleasant one. But while you may grumble in the privacy of your armchair, the journalists who hold the mirror up to you do so publicly and at great risk to themselves. That is our calling, and we do not shirk it . . . We have espoused unpopular causes, stood up for those too feeble to stand up for themselves, locked horns with the high and mighty so swollen with power that they have forgotten their roots, exposed corruption and the waste of your hard-earned tax rupees, and made sure that whatever the propaganda of the day, you were allowed to hear a contrary view.

That Wickramatunga would put himself in harm's way—and ultimately pay with his life—for the "calling" of journalism demonstrates a singular kind of courage. But the very idea that simply doing journalism put him at risk might be a little difficult to understand from the vantage point of the United States, where journalists can generally report on and even criticize the actions of government without fear of violence. That freedom is easy for us to take for granted, but was grimly elusive for Wickramatunga. In that final editorial, he offered this blunt prediction: "When finally I am killed, it will be the government that kills me."

What can we, separated by thousands of miles and great historical and cultural differences, learn about American journalism from the assassination of an editor in Sri Lanka? A lot. In fact, if you substitute "pounds" for "rupees" in the quotation above, you could easily believe you were reading something penned by a patriot during the American Revolution. (OK, so you'd have to substitute "powdered wigs" or something for "styling gel" too. But you get the idea.) Why do these ideas sound so familiar to us? Because they echo a widely shared understanding of what democracy requires of journalism, and of the kind of freedom necessary for journalism to do what democracy requires.

▶ THE HISTORICAL BACKDROP

In America, that widely shared understanding has its roots in American colonial experience and the subsequent revolution, particularly in the background and mindsets of the group of men who would become the framers of the U.S. Constitution. The colonists' reasons for revolt largely centered on what was considered to be the tyranny—economic and political—of their British rulers. An ocean away from the Crown, the colonies wanted to shake off the inequity of taxation without representation and the indignity of being forced, after a long period in which the government practiced a "hands-off" policy toward them and they began to develop a distinct, "American" identity, to re-submit to British authority. (We are skipping over a ton of really interesting history here in the name of brevity. Promise us you'll read up on press history on your own.) But once they managed to successfully break free, they would still need to come up with a system of government to manage their affairs. What would it look like? Something completely different.

FIGURE 1.1 English philosopher John Locke (1632–1704) was a key Enlightenment figure whose ideas were very influential on the Founding Fathers of the United States.
Source: Georgios Kollidas/ Shutterstock.

In addition to their personal experiences as colonists, the framers of the U.S. Constitution also were steeped in Enlightenment philosophy, particularly that of John Locke, which emphasized the power and authority of individual reason over other— arbitrary— sources of authority, such as the state. In very over-simplified terms, this emphasis assumes that individuals are free to exercise reason and that reason is the source of truth. Perhaps you can begin to see where all this is heading: A basic idea that people, exercising reason, are best equipped to govern themselves, to make sense of the competing "truths" in the marketplace of ideas, and the related conclusion that government power must be harnessed in the service of the people, not the other way around.

So, how might a free press assist in that self-governance? By acting as a check on government power and by creating a space in which claims about truth could be debated. This notion of the press contradicts a tenet of English common law during colonial times that sounds, well, tyrannical. It's called "seditious libel." A libel is a statement that harms someone's

▶ **DEMOCRACY:**
A system of government in which the people govern themselves. Typically characterized by free elections in which every adult can participate, freedom of expression, and an independent judiciary, this kind of self-governance stands in contrast to monarchies, dictatorships, theocracies and other forms in which an unelected person or small group of people hold power.

reputation. The "seditious" part refers to a libel about government authority. In England, this was a crime punishable by life imprisonment.

It gets better. (Or worse.)

"The greater the truth, the greater the libel." This feature of the law essentially said that the truth of whatever libelous thing you dared to say against the government didn't matter. In fact, the more true the criticism, the bigger trouble you would be in for voicing it. Imagine what a law like that can do to the marketplace of ideas. Shut it down altogether, that's what.

When the framers turned their attention to drafting the founding documents of the United States, they saw vestiges of English law such as seditious libel to be contrary to what their experiment in democratic government would require. Not only did it violate Enlightenment notions of reason, but it also ran contrary to more practical concerns about how to check tyranny and discuss and debate public affairs. (Seditious libel, sadly, crops up again and again in American history, typically during times of war. You can take some comfort in the fact that it has been repeatedly beaten back.)

Among those founding documents is the Bill of Rights, drafted by James Madison, which declares freedom of speech and of the press to be basic rights. (You'll learn much more about the First Amendment in Chapter 7.) The need—or lack of need—for a document to enumerate such basic rights was the topic of much debate. In fact, some colonists didn't want to ratify the U.S. Constitution without such a list. Nevertheless, if a list were to be drawn up, certainly freedom of expression would have to be on it. As Madison later wrote, "A popular Government, without popular information, or the means of acquiring it, is but a Prologue to a Farce or a Tragedy; or, perhaps both."

In his overview of the twists and turns the discussion about the Bill of Rights took, scholar Rodney Smolla gives us a sense of the magnitude of the framers' accomplishments:

> America had, for the first time in world history, put the people before
> the state. [. . .] In the Declaration of Independence and the
> grandiloquent opening of the Preamble to the Constitution, in which "We

the People" asserted their ultimate authority, America reversed the
flow of power.

(p. 39)

▶ WHAT DEMOCRACY NEEDS FROM JOURNALISM

Now that we've got some background into why a free press is so intertwined
with democracy, we will delve more deeply into just what, specifically, the
press can or ought to do to support democratic governance. Interesting that
the ideas of 18th Century American revolutionaries are echoed in the thinking of a 21st Century Sri Lankan newspaper editor, isn't it?

Notice the three metaphors for the role of the press that Wickramatunga's
editorial contains: First, the mirror, where society can see itself, warts and
all. Second, the watchdog that is supposed to start barking when those in
power become corrupt, forget their roots and waste the people's hard-
earned money. Third, the marketplace of ideas, the space where even unpopular causes and contrary views can get a hearing. These metaphors for
the press come up again and again, so it's worth spending time here to examine them in some depth.

First, let's compare those metaphors with how scholars talk about what
democracy needs from the press. Five commonly discussed needs are: information dissemination, accountability, representation, deliberation and
conflict resolution. *Information dissemination* is probably the easiest one to
understand: Democracy requires some method for distributing all the information people need to make decisions and govern themselves. That means
the press has to make decisions about what we need to know to do our jobs
as citizens in a democracy, decisions that require exercising editorial judgment. Not all information is necessary for democracy to function, but without access to the essential information about governance, we can't begin
to make decisions in a complex global marketplace of ideas. *Accountability*
refers to democracy's need for some way to hold those in power responsible
for their actions—actions that can affect all members of society. The value of
accountability is as a corrective influence on government, which on its own
is loath to revisit mistakes and concede error. *Representation* means that
in a democratic system, all people, not just those with the most education,
money or influence, are visible to others and have the chance to be heard.

The news media have a responsibility to ensure that those without an army of spokespeople still have a voice, that they can counter the voices of institutional power that might otherwise crowd them out of the marketplace of ideas. *Deliberation and conflict resolution* address democracy's need for a forum in which the interests of the public can be aired and debated and conclusions can be reached. The press exists, at least in part, so that a diversity of ideas find their way to the public conversation about the best course of action on the issues of the day.

What Wickramatunga knew—and what everyone from the framers and their Enlightenment philosophical forebears to 21st Century press critics have understood—is that when those needs go unfulfilled, democratic life is jeopardized. A free press is at the vanguard of all other liberties people in democracies enjoy. Without it, it's difficult to have freedom of pretty much anything else. The 1947 Commission on Freedom of the Press (known as the Hutchins Commission) put it this way:

> Freedom of the press is essential to political liberty. Where men can-
> not freely convey their thoughts to one another, no freedom is secure.
> Where freedom of expression exists, the beginnings of a free society and

---

WHO AND WHAT
WAS THE HUTCHINS COMMISSION?

Officially known as the Commission on Freedom of the Press, this group of 13 leading public intellectuals (but no journalists) was launched in 1942 "to examine areas and circumstances under which the press in the United States is succeeding or failing, to discover where free expression is or is not limited, whether by governmental censorship, pressures of readers or advertisers, the unwisdom of its own proprietors or the timidity of its managers," its chair, University of Chicago president Robert Maynard Hutchins, told the *New York Times*.

The group met several times over the course of a couple years, interviewed many witnesses, and read lots of reports and documents. They didn't like what they saw.

Freedom of the press was in danger of failing, the Commission concluded. But that danger was largely due to the press' own poor performance and not some threat of government censorship. The evidence? Sensationalism, an emphasis on the trivial and stereotypical, the "scoop" mentality, the blurring of lines between advertising and news, and (significantly, as you'll see in later chapters) increased concentration of media ownership.

Commission members wrangled over the final report, some wanting to offer rather shocking prescriptions for government regulation of the press, others preferring to focus on improving the press by voluntary means. In the end, the 1947 report cautioned the press that, unless it ramped up its own accountability, regulation of some kind would come.

The report was a call to journalists to consider themselves "professionals." It also marked the birth of what is known as "social responsibility theory" in journalism. That theory is based on the idea that with freedom comes responsibility. So, while journalism must be free from constraints on its actions, it still must act in ways that serve the public.

Journalists at the time hated the Commission report. No surprise there. But it has had an enduring influence on how people think about the role of journalism in society. That's why you'll see it pop up again and again throughout this and other books on American journalism.

Read more:

Stephen Bates, *Realigning Journalism with Democracy: The Hutchins Commission, Its Times, and Ours* (Washington, D.C.: The Annenberg Washington Program in Communications Policy Studies of Northwestern University, 1995). www.annenberg.northwestern.edu/pubs/hutchins/default.htm

a means for every extension of liberty are already present. Free expression is therefore unique among liberties: it promotes and protects all the rest.

(p. 6)

So where do those metaphors fit in? The mirror, watchdog and marketplace of ideas metaphors describe the functions a press performs to meet those democratic needs. We can match up the mirror metaphor with the needs for information dissemination and representation. The watchdog is all about accountability—monitoring power—and includes information dissemination as well. And the marketplace of ideas metaphor addresses representation, deliberation and, ideally, conflict resolution.

Taken together, these functions and the metaphors often used to describe them paint a picture of the press as a key player in democratic life. How can people be self-governing if they lack the information to make good decisions or a public forum in which to debate their options or a way of figuring out if their leaders are doing what they're supposed to be doing? The answer seems to be that without the press (and, importantly, a *free* press, which we'll discuss later), they can't. If that sounds like an awful lot of responsibility to place on the press, well, it is. And whether and how well the press performs those functions is the subject of thousands of books, editorial columns and shouting matches on television.

Take Scott Pelley of CBS News, for example. Pelley is a correspondent on *60 Minutes*, a veritable journalistic institution that pioneered the television news magazine format. Over its history, *60 Minutes* has aired everything from hard-hitting interviews with heads of state, to investigations of criminal wrongdoing, to celebrity fluff. (It also has been the target of hard-hitting interviews and investigations when its own correspondents' work has been called into question. Go look it up—but only after you finish this chapter.) Even though *60 Minutes* is old, Pelley and his producers are doing state-of-the-art journalism employing new, digital tools alongside the traditional ones. And they needed the entire toolbox for their 2015 report on a sarin

FIGURE 1.2 Arrests of journalists highlight the tenuous nature of press freedom in many parts of the world.
Source: Courtesy of Sedat Suna/EPA/LANDOV.

gas attack during the Syrian civil war that was estimated to have killed more than 1,400 civilians, almost a third of them children. Given that even the worst governmental regimes on Earth prohibit the use of nerve gas like sarin, the idea that the Syrian government might have used sarin at all, much less against civilians, clearly warranted investigation. It was a story that needed to be told—and told in a way befitting the immensity and ghastliness of the allegations.

Pelley and his team spent months locating eyewitnesses to the attack in refugee camps, as well as amassing information from weapons inspectors, doctors, government and United Nations officials and so on. But it was the survivors' cellphone video, which had shown up on YouTube as early as 2013, that really captured the horror and presented a challenge to the *60 Minutes* team: Could they—should they—show graphic video of people gasping for air, foaming at the mouth, convulsing . . . dying? Would doing so cross the line from corroborating the video and lending weight to their own reporting to sensationalizing it? CBS considered those questions and ultimately decided to include the video in its report, "A Crime Against Humanity," along with lots and lots of warnings to viewers. Here's Scott Pelley explaining the decision:

> These kinds of things happen in the world too often because people don't see them and don't know why sarin, of all the weapons in the world, why sarin is banned by almost every country on earth. We wanted to just stop and show it to the world so that people could understand the hideousness of this weapon. If you don't see it, I don't believe the impact truly hits you.

Riveting television. And it certainly looks like the mirror and the watchdog in all their glory. But was it good journalism? Was it the kind of reporting democracy needs? In discussing how CBS handled the story, Pelley linked it to broader changes in the protection of human rights made possible "by the fact that everybody has a video camera and a way to publish that video. We've never seen anything like these sarin gas attacks in Damascus. And I use the word 'seen' with great emphasis," Pelley said. "These things have happened and they keep happening because we don't see them."

Demanding answers and action by those we elect to do our business at home and represent our values and interests abroad is the cornerstone of what makes journalism, well, journalism. Whatever controversy "A Crime

Against Humanity" might have generated centered on the graphic content of the video and how Pelley in some ways saw himself as an advocate for human rights, for the victims—just like Wickramatunga.

None of these metaphors—the mirror, the watchdog or the marketplace— makes mention of a specific medium such as print, broadcast or online, so let's separate out the practice of journalism from the final form it might take. And it's not all public officials and government meetings, either—not by a long shot. One of the amazing things about the rapidly changing media landscape is that wherever those with questions in need of answers gather to demand those answers, something akin to journalism emerges. It could be a website dedicated to a medical condition, a dog breed or a football team, but once its proprietor begins asking questions and posting the results on behalf of a readership, seeks and demonstrates independence, and exhibits transparency of method, it's hard to call it anything but journalism.

FIGURE 1.3 While the tools of early 20th Century journalism are a bit different from today's, much of the work and the values behind it remains the same.

Source: Everett Collection/Shutterstock.

Standing as we now do in the thick of a seismic shift in how people get information makes it sometimes difficult to see just how and by whom our democratic needs will be fulfilled. Partly that's because the available media have shaped our traditional understanding of the press in society. Certainly the Founding Fathers had only newspapers in mind when they thought about press freedom, and those Colonial newspapers bear little resemblance to the newspapers of today. What does seem certain is that democracy's needs don't change even though the method for delivering journalism does. In fact, as the delivery platforms change, it's more important than ever for us to have a shared understanding of the values that make journalism an indispensible part of civic life.

▶ **HOW DOES THE PRESS FULFILL THOSE DEMOCRATIC NEEDS?**

So, we've detailed five communication needs in a democracy. Let's flip those around now to examine how the press can/should/does fulfill them. The press performs at least five core functions in a democracy:

1. Journalism informs, analyzes, interprets and explains.
2. Journalism investigates.
3. Journalism creates a public conversation.
4. Journalism helps generate social empathy.
5. Journalism encourages accountability.

This is not an exhaustive list, but it's awfully close. A press that is performing these five functions is a press that improves the civic health of a democracy. We'll return to each time and again throughout the book, but a quick look at each is in order.

Journalism Informs, Analyzes, Interprets and Explains   But first, it informs.

As self-evident as this may seem, it's worth noting that while the news media's role is informational, information does not necessarily equate to news. What? Information is the stuff of life, conveyed to us in a rich stream of

◀ **THE PRESS:** Originally a term referring to printed newspapers and magazines, the term now includes journalism outlets spanning all types of media, from television and radio to the Internet. The term is often—as it is in this book—used interchangeably with "news media." Also, it is a collective noun, referring to journalism outlets as a group, or even an institution in society.

stimuli, from the conversations we have with our roommates to the apps on our phone to the billboards we pass on the highway.

When you arrive at your home tonight, you may let your roommate in on some hot piece of gossip you picked up at work. That's information, certainly, but is it news? No, it's information. We are awash in it, veritably drowning in it, and that's precisely why news is so important, so endangered, so in need of saving. News is more than mere information; it is the result of processes and judgments constructed through institutions devoted to newsgathering. These institutions matter, for they convey value, judgment and professional norms on the process of news construction.

Think the distinction between information and news doesn't matter? Let's talk about the weather. Turn on the Weather Channel—one of our favorite cable destinations—and you'll see a ton of weather-related information: temperature, humidity levels, five-day forecasts and pollen counts. If you catch an anchor doing a standup, you'll no doubt see news as well—a tornado warning in Alabama, a hurricane brewing in the Caribbean. Why those two events, and why not the gentle rain landing in Topeka at the very same moment? Decisions have been made, about that which is newsworthy—unusual, or in the matter of that hurricane, potentially threatening. The decisions were journalistic in that their impetus was to inform, but also to bring meaning and context to the information. Not to persuade anyone of anything, and not to sell anything, but to bring meaning to the day's events, as the Hutchins Commission famously said.

It's not that news doesn't sell things, or persuade people to do things. But that is not the goal. The goal of the news is to share that information with others under the assumption that when citizens are properly informed, they will make sound decisions.

There are two concepts to take away from this information-versus-news discussion. First, news is a product, created by journalists, who happen to be human beings with all the promise and pitfalls of the species. Second, because news is a product, it is constructed. Its value lies in the fact that it is created to inform, first and foremost, by bringing meaning and context to what happened today. No similar institution exists in democracies.

1.1 THE VIEW FROM THE PROS: JOURNALISM INFORMS

A Tip, a Document and a Mountain

The call came in sometime on the afternoon of July 23, 2001, from a contact on my beat—science and the environment. I can't remember the exact words, but they were something like, "Check the Federal Register for Ameren."

It didn't sound like much, but in the end a major electric utility company withdrew its plan to build a huge hydroelectric facility on a pristine mountaintop in the Missouri Ozarks.

I hung up the phone and spent a few minutes on the Web searching the Federal Register, a public document in which government rules, notices and other business are published daily. Bingo. Buried in the complex language of law and technology, was a request filed by the St. Louis-based electric utility Ameren Corp. with the Federal Energy Regulatory Commission.

Ameren wanted to build its largest hydroelectric power plant ever—a $642-million, 770-megawatt facility with two dams. Filing its plan with the Commission was the first legal step.

The key detail was the "where." The plant would be built on Church Mountain, considered by outdoor-conscious Missourians one of the gems of the Ozarks' gorgeous labyrinth of green mountains and clear floating and fishing streams.

This story *had* to get in the next day's paper, and I had only three hours till deadline. After telling my editor about the story and writing a summary he could use in the budget meeting a few minutes later, I called Ameren, the Missouri Coalition for the Environment and the Missouri Department of Natural Resources.

It's important to note that I was a journalist, not an environmental advocate. And my simple, straight, hard news scoop—citing just the facts—ran the next morning on page 1 of the B section, the Metro section, with this lead:

"Ameren Corp. wants to build a hydroelectric power plant atop Church Mountain in the Ozarks, one of Missouri's most scenic areas."

What happened next? Nothing. No calls, no letters, no e-mails. I moved on. I had plenty of other stories to do.

A few weeks later I got another afternoon call. The politicians were weighing in, presumably having measured public opinion on the Ameren plan. This call came from the Missouri attorney general's press aide. The AG was announcing he planned to file suit against the company.

Another story that *had* to be in the next day's paper. I told my editor and wrote the budget line. I interviewed the AG, the Ameren spokeswoman, the governor's spokesman, the director of the environmental coalition and a few others. The AG said, "We are opposed to blowing off the top of Church Mountain and replacing it with a limestone bathtub." (You've got to love the rhetorical artistry of politicians who've figured out where they stand on an issue.)

The next day, August 30, the story ran, this time on page 1 of the A section. Here was the lead:

"Citing public opposition, Ameren Corp. on Wednesday pulled out of its plan to build a hydroelectric power plant and two dams on Church Mountain in the Ozarks. The company's announcement came shortly after Missouri Gov. Bob Holden and other state officials attacked the plan." (A governor's words generally trump an AG's.)

How did this turn of events happen? Was my first story the trigger? After all, I broke the story, and my newspaper was the most powerful and respected source of information in that region. The public was informed. Elected officials responded. The company's plans changed.

Whoa! First, I can't take credit for "breaking" this story. C'mon. A guy called me. I just did what a professional journalist does: vet and report an interesting story that was going to come out sooner or later anyway.

Nor can I take credit for bringing about that change in Ameren's plans. Yes, I reported the facts to the readers of my newspaper, and the media echo chamber magnified the story. But how can you trace back the definitive moment in that scrum of stories, ideas, influence and decision-making that lead to such changes?

Even so, there's no denying the role journalists play in shining a light on activities of the powerful is important, no matter who gets the credit.

But is it ever fun finding and chasing such stories! And participating in that sometimes awesome marketplace of ideas.

The Church Mountain episode reveals many lessons.

Lesson 1: The power of producing a simple, short news story about something way under your audience's radar.

Lesson 2: The amazing changes that can happen when the public is informed about seemingly routine events.

Lesson 3: The objective journalist's role as a reporter of straight news.

Lesson 4: The value of setting up a beat and getting to know sources who may contact you with tips.

THINK ABOUT IT: Allen lists four lessons from the series of events. Can you think of others? Could beginning reporters on other types of beats (sports, fashion, food or health) have this kind of impact? Why or why not?

—————————

Bill Allen is assistant professor of science journalism at the University of Missouri, and a former science writer for the *St. Louis Post-Dispatch*.

Journalism Investigates   It hasn't always, you know.

In fact, the investigative press we know today is a late-20th Century creation, but one with roots in its muckraking past. The "watchdog press" revered by journalists is not nearly as all encompassing as we'd like to think, but it is a vital function of journalism.

From award-winning project teams at some of America's larger news outlets looking into topics of national import to the community newspaper editor filing a public records request for the contract that the school board signed at its last meeting with a consultant, journalism's investigative function takes on many forms.

James S. Ettema and Theodore L. Glasser, in their book, *Custodians of Conscience: Investigative Journalism and Public Virtue*, put it this way: "the work of these reporters calls us, as a society, to decide what is, and what is not, an outrage to our sense of moral order and to consider our expectations for our officials, our institutions, and ultimately ourselves."

Documents, verified facts, eyewitnesses: these are the stuff of investigative journalism. Note also that there is an adversarial tone at the heart of investigative journalism, as reporters are cast as challengers to the concentrated power of government and of the corporate state. As Ettema and Glasser put it, "the notion that the press should be a relentless adversary of the powerful" has always animated American journalism.

Detached, independent observation, or impassioned adversarial watchdog: which is it? Well, a bit of both, if journalism is to flourish.

1.2 THE VIEW FROM THE PROS: JOURNALISM INVESTIGATES

Why do we investigate? We do it because power and corruption so often go hand-in-hand. We do it because we care, almost to a fault, about the people at the edge of society. We care about the little guys and want to make sure "the system," in all its incarnations, works as it should.

Doing this kind of work is antagonistic. It's oppositional. It requires you to ask questions no one wants to ask and get things people don't want to give.

Its nature dictates that investigative reporting can't be done on word of mouth alone. A good investigation can change laws. A good investigation can get people fired, freed or locked up. To put power like that in the hands of hearsay alone would be irresponsible.

For that reason, more and more reporters turn to documents. "Documents," in this sense, is a shorthand. It means traditional dusty paper records, sure. But it also means e-mails, text messages, databases and maps. It means meeting minutes, letters and forms. In short, documentation means evidence that speaks for itself.

Interviews have their place. But using documents and independent analysis as the backbone of my reporting changes the entire tenor of the interview process. Rather than a means to find information, interviews have become a way to get reactions or explanations. If I've really done my job, the interview is a time for people to give excuses.

Investigative reporting is some of the hardest, most time-consuming work we do. But it's increasingly necessary. In the new information economy, people in power increasingly have "message" people on staff. They call them "public information officers" or "spokespersons." I call them flaks. Their job is to dictate the news of the day, and they're good at what they do. Daily e-mails of story ideas, phonecalls during breaking news—if we aren't doing the independent research required by investigative reporting, we allow ourselves to be used.

Perhaps that's the best way to describe the role. Too often, journalism is reactionary and forgetful. A shooting happens, we report who got shot, where, when and what weapon was used. A person gets convicted, we answer the same basic questions.

Investigative reporting allows us to turn the tables and focus on the "Why?" and "How?" we rarely get to answer with breaking news. It allows us to tell our audience more substantive truths about the things we cover. It allows us to do what, at its best, journalism is meant to do.

LEARN MORE: To get a feel for the types of documents that can be used in reporting, go to the Public Records page of the Journalist's Toolbox, a site produced by the Society of Professional Journalists (www.journaliststoolbox.org/archive/public-records/).

Matt Wynn is a reporter at the *Omaha World-Herald*. He has worked at the *Springfield* [Mo.] *News-Leader* and *Arizona Republic* since graduating from the Missouri School of Journalism in 2007.

Journalism Creates a Public Conversation Scholars long have agreed that democracy requires a public forum where people can speak freely about government without government interference. For decades, the press together with its broadcast colleagues performed this role: people read the news, wrote their editors, and television contributed news and public affairs programming.

Today's mix of news, opinion, outright spin and the rich social conversation that is the online medium's great strength make it difficult to point to any one civic conversation as the "public sphere" deemed so crucial to the life of a democracy, yet it's clear that one of the things journalism must provide is that public sphere.

If, as Kovach and Rosenstiel explained so simply in *The Elements of Journalism*, the principles of American journalism are defined by the role of journalism in the lives of people, then the more things change, the more they stay the same: to provide citizens information in a context in which they can govern themselves. Media scholar James Carey put it this way: "The role of the press," he once said, "is simply to make sure that in the short run we don't get screwed, and it does this best not by treating us as consumers of news, but by encouraging the conditions of public discourse and life."

1.3 THE VIEW FROM THE PROS: JOURNALISM CREATES CONVERSATION

A columnist's confession: In all my years of writing columns, only one reader has told me I changed his mind about something. One!

Hundreds of readers have told me I'm wrong, and some have even suggested I'm so wrong, so often, that it would just be best if I moved away. Of course, hundreds of other smart, enlightened readers have chimed in to say I'm right, and they've often expressed their gratitude and good fortune that I'm in town.

I wouldn't want it any other way.

As an opinion journalist, one of my main goals is to foster community conversations. Whether I'm covering a mass shooting, or something as seemingly minor as whether an elephant should be kept in the zoo, my main goal is to raise questions and spark community conversation. Sure, I have a viewpoint, and an argument to make. But what really matters is engaging with readers and sparking multiple viewpoints so we can have a full, and nuanced, conversation. One that hopefully makes this world a little better.

That's opinion writing, of course. But don't think news reporting is a conversation-free zone. The best journalism is formative. In broad strokes: It raises questions, exposes corruption, highlights failure and celebrates triumph. It should spark reader reaction—and, yes, conversation. If you are writing stories that no one is talking about, something is wrong.

But wait, there is more.

As a journalist, you are uniquely positioned to reflect and shape that conversation. Not only will your stories and columns raise reader questions, but you get to ask questions. After all, you're the one who gets to grill the mayor after a controversial vote or the football coach after a tough loss. When tragedy strikes, you are first on the scene. It's the coolest thing, really. You get to ask questions for everyone else.

One last point. These days journalism sparks conversation in many forms, and more and more often journalists are part of that conversation thanks to social media. Opinions fly fast online. It can make for a lot of nastiness and even more white noise. To avoid that white noise, be interested and passionate about the beats and people you cover. The conversation, online and in real life, will naturally follow.

THINK ABOUT IT: Go online and look at the blog or column by a popular columnist for your local newspaper (hint: sports columnists usually attract large numbers of followers). Read the column and then read the comments (either at the bottom of the story, posted to Facebook or shared on Twitter). How closely do the comments follow the issues raised in the column? How often does the conversation veer off topic? Are comments informed or based solely on gut reaction? Did the columnist succeed in starting a conversation?

Josh Brodesky is an editorial writer and columnist at the *San Antonio Express-News.*

Journalism Helps Generate Social Empathy The Hutchins Commission report points to the importance of the news media as inculcators of tolerance and pluralism:

> The truth about any social group, though it should not exclude
> its weaknesses and vices, includes also recognition of its values, its
> aspirations, and its common humanity . . . If people are exposed to the
> inner truth of the life of a particular group, they will gradually build up
> respect for and understanding of it.
>
> (p. 27)

A cursory review of the media landscape today could lead one to question whether the members of the Hutchins Commission would recognize the place, until we stop and revisit the notion of democratic self-governance.

Self-governance means far more than being informed voters. It is not only about bills and laws and votes. Our democracy, after all, is a social compact in which we collectively regulate all of society through what academics call "public norms"—the formal rules of the road, sure, but also the conventions and expectations that shape everyday life. We socialize one another, in other words, and in doing so we set the boundaries of societal behavior. The news is a major engine for the creation of public norms, which, along with laws, are one of the ways in which we govern ourselves.

1.4 THE VIEW FROM THE PROS: JOURNALISM CREATES EMPATHY

In *To Kill a Mockingbird*, Atticus tells Scout, "You never really understand a person until you consider things from his point of view . . . until you climb into his skin and walk around in it" (Chapter 3). When journalism creates empathy, it is offering us a way to do that: to walk around in someone else's skin, to see things from another's perspective, to gain a greater understanding of how others live. Even though Atticus tells Scout this is a "simple trick" to getting along with people, it can be pretty difficult the less like us the other person happens to be— think of a refugee from a war-torn country, the husband or wife of someone suffering from Alzheimer's disease, or maybe a troubled teenager growing up in a chaotic, violent environment.

The journalists at *Vice News* captured the experiences of that last example in a Web series called "Last Chance High," whose "uncompromising look at school violence and . . . compassionate depiction" of Chicago's Moses Montefiore Academy earned it a 2014 Peabody Award for excellence in electronic media. Can you think of any group in society more deserving of empathy—but also more difficult to empathize with—than kids who are "one mistake away from being locked up or committed to a mental hospital"? *Vice News* lets the kids and the teachers at this therapeutic school speak for themselves in ways that shock us but also invite us to see the world as these kids see it and to recognize the humanity underneath the sometimes violent lashing out. As the Peabody jurors put it:

> Last Chance High's first episode can be so overwhelming that we want to run for the doors, as the cameras show us—without much explanation—the disruptive behavior and disrespect for their teachers these students display on a daily basis. The school's faculty and administrators spend so much time trying to maintain order that it is hard to imagine much teaching goes on. Across subsequent episodes, producers Brent and Craig Renaud take us deeper and deeper into this world. We get to know these students and the emotional carnage of their lives; we get to know their parents, some in jail, some indifferent, but some struggling to help their sons and

daughters make something good of their lives. The school's teachers and mentors burn out and break down, but some go the extra mile to provide these students life-changing experiences or simply a shoulder to cry on.

In creating empathy, or at least opportunities for empathy, journalism is doing more than telling compelling stories. It is helping all of us—subjects and consumers of news stories alike—hold up mirrors to the world. Seeing others as individuals, not just part of some nameless, faceless group, gets us one step closer to understanding others.

You can watch the series here: https://news.vice.com/show/last-chance-high. Descriptions of other Peabody award winners are here: www.peabodyawards.com/results/null/1/2014/2014/title/asc.

THINK ABOUT IT: What long-term impact might this story have on viewers? How does the absence of a narrator contribute to the power of this series to generate empathy?

Journalism Encourages Accountability

It's worth noting that accountability—the oversight of the functions of an institution—ought to be a two-way street in journalism. A central tenet of democracy is that it is a self-correcting mechanism; that is, it fixes itself on the fly. Key to that self-correction is the principle that no one is infallible and that no information is, either; that which we report as fact is always subject to validation and potential revision.

The concept of a Fourth Estate—a term borrowed from the Scottish satirist Thomas Carlyle, who saw the reporters in Parliament as a "fourth branch" of government, an independent arbiter of fact sitting just beyond the realm of government, yet very much involved in public affairs—begins with the recognition that government can't handle accountability left to its own devices. Other institutions must work to keep them honest.

Scholars write that accountability requires answerability and enforcement. In other words, there must be an obligation on the part of the institution to provide information about its decisions and actions, or answerability, and there must be some sort of sanction when the institution behaves badly.

There are two types of accountability: horizontal and vertical. Horizontal accountability refers to the capacity of institutions to check one another, such as the "checks and balances" enshrined in the Constitution or the requirement that state agencies report to the governor. It's one part of the institution checking up on another, and for that reason, it's fraught with political tension and potential cronyism and corruption.

That's where vertical accountability comes in, as citizens, non-governmental organizations and the press seek to enforce standards of performance on officials. Journalists provide vertical accountability every day, in countless ways. Sometimes simply showing up at a little-known, scarcely attended city meeting causes a bit of transparency that was about to be shoved into a dark corner. Other times, a well-timed, pointed question aimed at a candidate for public office reveals a shocking lack of knowledge on a vital topic. Journalists are key actors in what has been called the "chain of accountability."

1.5 "AN APOLOGY FOR PRINTERS" (1793), BY BENJAMIN FRANKLIN

Being frequently censur'd and condemn'd by different Persons for printing Things which they say ought not to be printed, I have sometimes thought it might be necessary to make a standing Apology for my self, and publish it once a Year, to be read upon all Occasions of that Nature. Much Business has hitherto hindered the execution of this Design; but having very lately given extraordinary Offence by printing an Advertisement with a certain N.B. at the End of it, I find an Apology more particularly requisite at this Juncture, tho' it happens when I have not yet Leisure to write such a thing in the proper Form, and can only in a loose manner throw those Considerations together which should have been the Substance of it.

I request all who are angry with me on the Account of printing things they don't like, calmly to consider these following Particulars

1. That the Opinions of Men are almost as various as their Faces; an Observation general enough to become a common Proverb, So many Men so many Minds.
2. That the Business of Printing has chiefly to do with Men's Opinions; most things that are printed tending to promote some, or oppose others.

3. That hence arises the peculiar Unhappiness of that Business, which other Callings are no way liable to; they who follow Printing being scarce able to do any thing in their way of getting a Living, which shall not probably give Offence to some, and perhaps to many; whereas the Smith, the Shoemaker, the Carpenter, or the Man of any other Trade, may work indifferently for People of all Persuasions, without offending any of them: and the merchant may buy and sell with Jews, Turks, Hereticks, and Infidels of all sorts, and get money by every one of them, without giving Offence to the most orthodox, of any sort; or suffering the least Censure or Ill-will on the Account from any Man whatever.

4. That it is as unreasonable in any one Man or Set of Men to expect to be pleas'd with every thing that is printed, as to think that nobody ought to be pleas'd but themselves.

5. Printers are educated in the Belief, that when Men differ in Opinion, both Sides ought equally to have the Advantage of being heard by the Publick; and that when Truth and Error have fair Play, the former is always an overmatch for the latter: Hence they chearfully serve all contending Writers that pay them

well, without regarding on which side they are of the Question in Dispute.

6. Being thus continually employ'd in serving all Parties, Printers naturally acquire a vast Unconcernedness as to the right or wrong Opinions contain'd in what they print; regarding it only as the Matter of their daily labour: They print things full of Spleen and Animosity, with the utmost Calmness and Indifference, and without the least Ill-will to the Persons reflected on; who nevertheless unjustly think the Printer as much their Enemy as the Author, and join both together in their resentment.

7. That it is unreasonable to imagine Printers approve of every thing they print, and to censure them on any particular thing accordingly; since in the way of their Business they print such great variety of things opposite and contradictory. It is likewise as unreasonable what some assert, That Printers ought not to print any Thing but what they approve; since if all of that Business should make such a Resolution, and abide by it, an End would thereby be put to Free Writing, and the World would afterwards have nothing to read but what happen'd to be the Opinions of Printers.

8. That if all Printers were determin'd not to print any thing till they were sure it would offend no body, there would be very little printed.

9. That if they sometimes print vicious or silly things not worth reading, it may not be because the People are so viciously and corruptly educated that good things are not encouraged. I have known a very numerous Impression of Robin Hood's Songs go off in this Province at 2s. per Book, in less than a Twelvemonth; when a small Quantity of David's Psalms (an excellent Version) have lain upon my Hands above twice the Time.

10. That notwithstanding what might be urg'd in behalf of a Man's being allow'd to do in the Way of his Business whatever he is paid for, yet Printers do continually discourage the Printing of great Numbers of bad things, and stifle them in the Birth. I my self have constantly refused to print any thing that might countenance Vice, or promote Immorality; tho' by complying in such Cases with the corrupt Taste of the Majority, I might have got much Money. I have also always refus'd to print such things as might do real Injury to any Person, how much soever I have been solicited, and tempted with Offers of great Pay; and how much soever I have by refusing got the Ill-will of those who would have employ'd me. I have heretofore fallen under the Resentment of large Bodies of Men, for refusing absolutely to print any of their Party or Personal Reflections. In this Manner I have made my self many Enemies, and the constant Fatigue of denying is almost insupportable. But the Publick being unacquainted with all this, whenever the poor Printer happens either through Ignorance or much Persuasion, to do any thing that is generally thought worthy of Blame, he meets with no more Friendship or Favour on the above Account, than if there were no Merit in't at all. Thus, as Waller says,

Poets lose half the Praise they would have got
Were it but known what they discreetly blot;
Yet are censur'd for every bad Line found in their
Works with the utmost Severity . . .

I take leave to conclude with an old Fable, which some of my Readers have heard before, and some have not.

"A certain well-meaning Man and his Son, were traveling towards a Market Town, with an Ass which they had to sell. The Road was bad; and the old Man therefore rid, but the Son went a-foot. The first Passenger they met, asked the Father if he was not ashamed to ride by himself, and suffer the poor Lad to wade along thro' the Mire; this induced him to take up his Son behind him: He had not travelled far when he met other, who said, they were two unmerciful Lubbers to get both on the Back of that poor Ass, in such a deep Road. Upon this the old Man gets off, and let his Son ride alone. The next they met called the Lad a graceless, rascally young Jackanapes, to ride in that Manner thro' the Dirt, while his aged Father trudged along on Foot; and they said the old Man was a Fool, for suffering it. He then bid his Son come down, and walk with him, and they travell'd on leading the Ass by the Halter; 'till they met another Company, who called them a Couple of sensless Blockheads, for going both on Foot in such a dirty Way, when they had an empty Ass with them, which they might ride upon. The old Man could bear no longer; My Son, said he, it grieves me much that we cannot please all these People: Let us throw the Ass over the next Bridge, and be no farther troubled with him."

Had the old Man been seen acting this last Resolution, he would probably have been call'd a Fool for troubling himself about the different Opinions of all that were pleas'd to find Fault with him: Therefore, tho' I have a Temper almost as complying as his, I intend not to imitate him in this last Particular. I consider the Variety of Humours among Men, and despair of pleasing every Body; yet I shall not therefore leave off Printing. I shall continue my Business. I shall not burn my Press and melt my Letters.

THINK ABOUT IT: In some ways, Franklin's apology for printers can be viewed as a description of a purpose for journalism. Which metaphor—the mirror, watchdog or marketplace of ideas—does Franklin's view seem to resonate with the most? Which metaphor isn't really represented? Also, Franklin makes frequent mention of printing as a business. Do we get a sense from the apology of how business concerns might have shaped how he saw his broader purpose as a printer?

Anything Else?   Those five functions cover quite a bit of territory. Forgive us, then, for throwing in one more function for your brief consideration. At least one scholar, Michael Schudson, might add "journalism mobilizes participation" to this list. The idea is that, beyond informing and creating conversation about the issues of the day, journalism can, and maybe even should, help people figure out how to act in response. Indeed for the 19th Century press, which was largely sponsored and funded by political parties, mobilizing people to support particular candidates and causes was the main function. There are many reasons the American press moved away from this model, as you'll learn in other chapters. But in today's increasingly crowded information landscape, there also has been increasing discussion about the role opinion and insight in journalism—what historian Mitchell Stephens calls "wisdom journalism"—might play in helping people navigate and act on all that information. As you will see, especially in Chapters 2 and 8, assigning a mobilizing function, much less a partisan function, to the press can be controversial. We bring it up here only to get you started thinking about how the purpose of journalism is shaped by the economic, political and technological context in which it operates. Our main focus will be on how and how well journalism does with the other five functions. Fulfilling those is what you might call a tall order.

▶ CAN JOURNALISM PROVIDE WHAT DEMOCRACY NEEDS?

Let's look at those democratic needs one more time, from yet another angle. Without diving too far into the deep end of democratic theory, let's just say that our views about the prospects for a robust democracy are shaped by our views of people—their nature, abilities and desires. (For now, we don't need to worry about the many specific forms democracy can take. We're just interested in the idea that in a democracy, generally speaking, the people are sovereign.) At a minimum, democracy takes as its starting point the idea that the people can and should govern themselves. That some people have been quite skeptical about the public's capacity to do so is, perhaps, not entirely surprising. And the implications of that skepticism for journalism warrant further exploration.

In the early part of the 20th Century, newspaper columnist Walter Lippmann was what we today would call a "public intellectual." More than just a journalist, Lippmann was part of the intellectual elite, an adviser to heads of state and even a player in the Treaty of Versailles negotiations. In 1922, he published the book *Public Opinion*, one of a series of three books he wrote about the relationship between democracy and the press. This one included a rather stunning and ultimately pessimistic view: People are too limited in their capacity to process the information of an increasingly complex world to effectively self-govern, and it is beyond the ability of the press, populated by similarly limited people and subject to other constraints, to help the public very much. Indeed, Lippmann seemed to express some concern that the press could make things worse. His argument wasn't that people are stupid, but that between the complexity of the information one is required to understand to be an effective democratic participant and the many "filters"—personal biases, education, background and so on—through which that information must travel, there was little or no chance of reconciling the "world outside and the pictures in our heads." If democracy depends on the "omnicompetent" citizen, it's in big trouble.

It might be understandable that Lippmann reached that conclusion, as he was writing in the aftermath of World War I, which had brought the power of propaganda and public manipulation fully into view. However, his grave prediction met with considerable resistance from John Dewey, another leading public intellectual and founder of the philosophy of pragmatism, who called Lippmann's book "perhaps the most effective indictment of democracy . . . ever penned." Dewey's 1927 book *The Public and Its Problems* responded to Lippmann's critique with an acknowledgment that, while Lippmann might be right about the limited capacity of people, he was wrong about democracy. What was missing from Lippmann's account, according to Dewey, was an understanding that democracy is more about conversation than it is about information. Dewey was a strong proponent and scholar of education, so it is understandable that he saw democracy's prospects to be intertwined with education and not just journalism. If one sees democracy as an ongoing process of education in how to deliberate and how to be a citizen, and not as the end result of the best information dissemination techniques, then the prospects for it are not so gloomy.

As Bill Kovach and Tom Rosenstiel so eloquently illustrate in *The Elements of Journalism*, Lippmann and Dewey represent not just different understandings of democracy, but different ways of thinking about journalism's role in democracy too. In terms of the metaphors and functions we've been discussing, Lippmann essentially was arguing that the press could not adequately act as a mirror or watchdog—that it would have difficulty fulfilling the informing and accountability functions. Dewey's perspective was focused more on the potential for journalism to promote the marketplace of ideas, to create conversation and generate empathy. Whose view seems to have won out in journalism? Do we see more of Dewey or of Lippmann in our current news media landscape? Perhaps these aren't really fair questions. Certainly Wickramatunga saw his newspaper performing all those functions, and he doesn't seem to have preferred or promoted one over the others. And Scott Pelley was channeling both Dewey and Lippmann, directing his watchdog "bark" to the mounting evidence of a crime against humanity in Syria while simultaneously holding a mirror up to Damascus for all to see. That Pelley happened to be holding one of the biggest microphones in the marketplace ensured public attention.

Even though journalists' self-identity is arguably more bound up in the watchdog/accountability roles—that is certainly the basis on which they defend their choice to pursue controversial stories—the range of content the news media offer suggests a broad view of the roles journalism can play in a democracy. But remember that we're talking about what democracy *requires*, not all of the functions of the press. Does the press entertain us at times? Sure, but unless you argue that democracy requires that the news entertain us, it's a bit off topic.

▶ MUST JOURNALISM PROVIDE WHAT DEMOCRACY NEEDS?

Even as they describe different functions that the press can and should perform in a society, the mirror, watchdog and marketplace metaphors share some assumptions. They all assume, for example, that the press' key allegiance is to the public, the citizens of a society, and not necessarily to those who wield power. These metaphors likewise seem to start from the premise that the press can and should act as the public's representative. Finally, the metaphors assume the press is free to act in all those ways. But free from whom and for what, exactly? The "from whom" part usually refers to the need for the press to free from government control, though as we will find out in Chapter 4, that's not the only kind of control the press needs to worry about. The "for what" part gets us back to this idea of responsibility. Some argue that because the press is uniquely positioned to be the mirror, watchdog or marketplace, it is therefore obligated to act in certain ways.

▶ **ACCOUNTABILITY:** Think of it as oversight. There are two kinds: horizontal and vertical. One of the chief functions of journalism in a democracy is vertical accountability— reporting on what the powerful do and say as a way of making them answerable to the people for their actions. Journalism that promotes such accountability is often referred to as "watchdog journalism."

Certainly the Hutchins Commission we mentioned earlier believed that. Note the title of its very influential report—*A Free and Responsible Press*— and its chief conclusions that the media should:

> (1) provide a truthful, comprehensive and intelligent account of the day's events in a context which gives them meaning; (2) serve as a forum for the exchange of comment and criticism; (3) project a representative picture of the constituent groups in the society; (4) present and clarify the goals and values of the society; and (5) provide full access to the day's intelligence.

The kicker is that the Commission believed that if the press didn't do those things, if it failed to meet its obligations, it risked losing its freedom altogether.

It might not surprise you to know that the reaction of the press to the Hutchins Commission report was, well, indignant. After all, where did the Hutchins Commission get off essentially threatening an institution whose freedom is constitutionally protected? And you might also have noticed, 60+ years later, that the press often fails to do those things, but still looks and acts pretty free. Even if the "threat" didn't amount to much, *A Free and*

Responsible Press became an important part of an ongoing conversation about journalism—what it is and, perhaps most important, what it is expected to do.

To consider journalism as entirely and solely responsible for meeting the needs of democracy is unreasonable, some scholars have argued. Such a view seems to ignore the role of other important institutions in democratic society, such as political parties, social groups and elements of civil society, like public schools, that all play a role in informing people and facilitating discussion and debate. These scholars also point to the economic pressures the news media face, pressures that can put the news media in the position of having to choose between providing a public service and producing profit. Finally, the traditional understanding of the press' democratic role seems too focused on politics and not enough on other kinds of media content, even entertainment, which can serve important democratic functions. These are important arguments to keep in mind as we explore the tension between what the press can do and what it should do that has defined the history and practice of journalism in the U.S. and will be the focus of later chapters in this book. First, though, we'll need to be clear about what we mean by "journalism" in the first place. That's the question we'll take up in the next chapter.

Chapter One Review

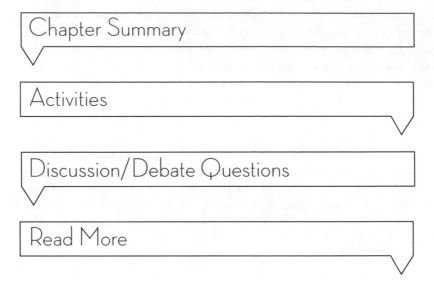

Chapter Summary

Activities

Discussion/Debate Questions

Read More

▶ CHAPTER SUMMARY

Journalism is essential to democratic self-governance, for several key reasons. First, because it serves as an essential check on power—the power of the state, the power of the corporation, and the power of the majority. The press serves society by creating a space in which claims about truth can be debated.

The press performs at least five core functions in a democracy:

1. Journalism informs, analyzes, interprets and explains.
2. Journalism investigates.

3. Journalism creates a public conversation.
4. Journalism helps generate social empathy.
5. Journalism encourages accountability.

Each is a core function of the press in America, and each can be viewed through the three metaphors for the key roles the press plays in our system: as a mirror, as a watchdog and as a marketplace. Each starts with the proposition that the press' key allegiance is to the public, the citizens of a society, and not necessarily to those who wield power.

▶ ACTIVITIES

1. To explore how the press performs its five core functions in a democracy, examine a local or national media outlet (newspaper, website, newscast, etc.) and find at least one example of content that illustrates each of the functions (Informs, analyzes, interprets and explains; Investigates; Creates a public conversation; Helps generate social empathy; Encourages accountability). You can do this in small groups or as an independent activity. Share your findings with the rest of the class. Did you find content that performed multiple functions? Was it more difficult to find examples of some functions than others?

2. Although the functions played by the press in a democracy are not dependent on delivery format, a specific medium might be better suited for one function or another. Split up into different groups in your class according to medium (print, broadcast, online/digital). Each group should examine the functions their medium is best suited for and which ones might pose more of a challenge. Discuss the following with the whole class: Will the functions change as our delivery system of news and information changes in the country?

3. Watch Associated Press officials talk about "accountability journalism" and the watchdog role of the press (www.youtube.com/watch?v=Sxf90TXThY8). How does this differ from the type of journalism that we see on a day-to-day basis? Show a clip of the first five minutes from a recent local newscast. Would any of that be "accountability journalism"? Why might local news stations and local newspapers be limited in playing this role? Next, to provide an example of how smaller news organizations can fill this role with limited resources, look at The

Cold Case Project (http://coldcases.org/). One small-town newspaper editor, Stanley Nelson of Concordia, La., has been able to work with the non-profit group to help bring unprosecuted civil rights violations to light and hold officials accountable. Click on the "cold cases" tab here to see these stories: www.hannapub.com/concordiasentinel/.

4. In an era of digital delivery of information and social networks, where everyone is a publisher and average citizens can attract tens of thousands of followers on Twitter, does American democracy need journalists to provide information dissemination, accountability, representation, deliberation and conflict resolution? Some could argue that the role of traditional journalists in fulfilling these needs has become even more important—others could argue that it's become less important. Take out a piece of paper, write down the five needs, and then write next to each whether the role of traditional news outlets has become more important, less important or stayed the same. Collect the papers and tally the results before the next class. Share the vote tallies and discuss each need, asking students to volunteer answers as to why they voted the way they did.

5. To learn more about journalism history, read the article "Early American Newspapering" from history.org (www.history.org/foundation/journal/spring03/journalism.cfm). How does the historical context relate to the roles the founders expected journalism to play in their new form of government? Using the information in the chapter about the functions of journalism in our society and the historical information from the supplemental reading, post a 350–500 word response on the class discussion board on this topic.

▶ DISCUSSION/DEBATE QUESTIONS

1. American democracy today differs in many ways from the structure laid out by the founders. For example, virtually all citizens—not just rich, White landowners—now have the right to vote. Further, those running for office appeal directly to the general public, rather than to an elite group of electors. In this new environment, is the role of journalism more or less important than it was more than two centuries ago?

2. The title of the chapter lists three ways to look at the role of American journalism: The mirror, the watchdog and the marketplace. Which do you think best characterizes the role journalism plays in our society? Does the dominant approach change based on the time period and situation we face? For example, might one approach be more appropriate in wartime and another in peacetime?

3. Legal scholars have argued that democracy needs a press that provides information dissemination, accountability, representation, deliberation and conflict resolution. Are some of these needs more important than others? Again, does the dominant need vary based on time period and state of the country?

4. Are the concerns raised by the Hutchins Commission still present today? Are they even more problematic than they were more than 60 years ago? How would you respond to people today who make threats similar to those made by the Commission—that media risk losing freedoms if they do not fulfill their functions?

▶ READ MORE

CBS News, *60 Minutes*, "A Crime Against Humanity," www.cbsnews.com/news/syria-sarin-gas-attack-in-2013–60-minutes/.

Commission on Freedom of the Press, *A Free and Responsible Press: A General Report on Mass Communication: Newspapers, Radio, Motion Pictures, Magazines, and Books*, Chicago: University of Chicago Press, 1947.

John Dewey, *The Public and Its Problems*, New York: Henry Holt, 1927.

James S. Ettema & Theodore L. Glasser, *Custodians of Conscience: Investigative Journalism and Public Virtue*, New York: Columbia University Press, 1998.

Bill Kovach & Tom Rosenstiel, *The Elements of Journalism: What Newspeople Should Know and the Public Should Expect*, New York: Three Rivers Press, 2007.

Walter Lippmann, *Public Opinion*, New York: Free Press, 1965. Originally published in 1922.

Michael Schudson, *Why Democracies Need an Unlovable Press*, Malden, Mass.: Polity, 2008.

Mitchell Stephens, *Beyond News: The Future of Journalism*, New York: Columbia University Press, 2014.

Rodney A. Smolla, *Free Speech in an Open Society*, New York: Random House, 1992.

Lasantha Wickramatunga, "And Then They Came for Me," *Sunday Leader*, January 11, 2009: www.thesundayleader.lk/archive/20090111/editorial-.htm.

World Bank Institute, "Social Accountability in the Public Sector," Washington, D.C.: WBI Working Paper no. 33641 (2005).

2

What Is Journalism?

Jackie was just starting her freshman year at the University of Virginia when she was brutally assaulted by seven men at a frat party. When she tried to hold them accountable, a whole new kind of abuse began.

So began a devastating *Rolling Stone* magazine article, "A Rape on Campus," reported and written by Sabrina Rubin Erdely. How colleges handle—or mishandle—sexual assault cases has been the subject of intense public attention since at least 2011, when the U.S. Department of Education began investigating scores of universities for possible violations of Title IX, the law relating to gender discrimination in higher education. Research indicates that 1 in 5 women experience sexual assault during college. Erdely was looking to put a human face on the issue, to find a victim whose experience would be emblematic of the problem. Her search eventually led her to Jackie.

"Jackie," a pseudonym Erdely gave the victim, had gone to the party on a date with "Drew" (also a pseudonym) a fraternity member she knew because they lifeguarded at the campus pool together. Jackie knew one of the rapists from her anthropology class. The assault happened in an upstairs bedroom where Jackie was thrown to the floor, breaking a glass table. When Jackie, bloodied from the attack, was finally able to leave and find her friends, they discouraged her from reporting the crime to the police because they were afraid such a report would ruin their social lives. Her later attempts to navigate the campus' system for handling cases of sexual misconduct revealed administrators who seemed more interested in playing down allegations than investigating them.

The story is horrifying. Indeed, when "A Rape on Campus" appeared in the magazine, readers were outraged, students protested, fraternities were suspended, administrators were called to account, legislators took action.

There's just one problem: Jackie's story is not true.

It's not false in the sense that nothing happened to "Jackie." Something terrible probably did happen to her. It's not false in the sense that sexual assault is not a problem on college campuses. It is a very big problem. It's not false that campus policies and procedures for dealing with sexual assault are a mess. They are. It IS false in the sense that too much of Jackie's account is contradicted by other known facts. Consider: The fraternity in question did not have a party the night Jackie says the rape happened. No member of that fraternity worked as a lifeguard. Her friends say Jackie told them a different story about what had happened, saw no blood or signs of injury and, because she seemed so distressed, actually offered to get help for her.

How on Earth did this happen? How on Earth do an experienced reporter and a prominent magazine get an important and explosive story so wrong?

The answers to those questions get to the heart of what separates journalism from other kinds of information: verification. Journalism is not just a process of gathering and distributing information. All kinds of people, organizations and corporations do that, but we don't—and they don't—necessarily call it journalism. What sets journalism apart is the stuff that happens between picking up on some interesting information and passing it along. It's the checking, questioning and corroborating of that information.

Establishing that it is true. Erdely and *Rolling Stone* trusted Jackie. They didn't verify.

In the midst of the public outcry when "A Rape on Campus" hit the newsstands, other news organizations, such as the *Washington Post, Slate,* and *Worth,* did try to verify. That's a bit unusual—news organizations don't typically fact-check their competitors' work. But other journalists saw too many red flags to ignore. The biggest red flag? The story relies heavily on the accounts of unnamed sources and what we might call "hearsay"—what some of those sources say other people said. Such anonymity means readers have no way of knowing how believable the sources might be—Are they who they say they are? Do we have good reason to think they know what they're talking about?—and so we have to take the reporter's word for it. Anonymity is often granted to rape victims out of concern that public attention may add to their trauma, so the mere use of unnamed sources is not a fatal flaw; however, anonymity combined with the absence of named, corroborating voices undermined Erdely's and *Rolling Stone's* credibility, making it difficult to take their word for it.

◀ **CREDIBILITY:** The combination of trustworthiness and expertise that makes us more or less likely to believe or rely on what a source of information tells us.

Other journalists' attempts to verify the story, as well as a later report into the incident conducted by faculty at the Columbia University Graduate School of Journalism, make clear that Erdely had not interviewed, or in some cases not even identified or tried to contact, key sources in the story: Drew, the anthropology classmate, the friends who discouraged her from reporting the rape. Indeed, Erdely's attempts to do such routine reporting were often thwarted by Jackie's reluctance to draw attention from the rapist and others. Erdely feared that insisting on pursuing these interviews against Jackie's wishes would push her away from cooperating with the story altogether.

Let's be clear: The reason to interview other sources is NOT because rape victims generally can't be trusted. The myth that women regularly lie about rape is just that—a myth. (Research puts the percentage of false allegations at no more than 8 percent.) The reason to at least try to corroborate someone's story is that journalism is about getting as comprehensive a version of truth as possible—especially when the stakes are this high, the story this shocking. Here's how media critic Clay Shirky explains it:

> Failure to cast a skeptical eye isn't a simple mistake. It's the dividing line between journalism and rumor. Someone who publishes an

unchecked assertion as if it had been verified has, however momentarily, abandoned the profession. For a piece like "A Rape on Campus," healthy skepticism was especially necessary because the story, meant to shine a light on a significant social ill, was going to have to survive a lot of scrutiny.

Verification would have been beneficial even if there were no problems with Jackie's account. Those sources could have shed more light on the context and circumstances of the attack, perhaps even raising additional important questions that would have made the story better.

In the end, "A Rape on Campus" turned out to be something that looked a lot like journalism, but—without the key element of verification—really wasn't journalism after all. In this chapter and throughout this book, we are interested in distinguishing journalism from all the other kinds of information, entertainment and commentary available on the Web, your smartphone, the airwaves, and at your local newsstand or coffee shop. Now would be a good time to offer a complete definition of journalism, eh? Here's something to get us started:

> Journalism is a set of transparent, independent procedures aimed at gathering, verifying and reporting truthful information of consequence to citizens in a democracy.

Many, many things look like journalism. Many of those things are imposters enabled by technological innovations that make such posing easy and that often put pressure on that definition of journalism, encouraging a focus on the gathering part while leaving the verifying part to fend for itself. We'll be thinking about those kinds of tensions throughout the book.

This chapter explains how we arrived at our definition of "journalism" from a few different directions—by examining common definitions that fall short of capturing the whole picture; by identifying activities often mistaken for journalism and explaining why they are not journalism; and by laying out what we believe are essential features of anything that can rightfully call itself "journalism."

▶ DEFINITIONS: PLENTIFUL BUT LACKING

If you enter "definitions of journalism" into Google—come on, you know you want to!—you'll discover a lot of stuff like this:

> The periodical collection and publication of current news; the business of managing, editing, or writing for, journals or newspapers; as, political journalism.
>
> (brainyquote.com)

> The collecting, writing, editing, and presenting of news or news articles in newspapers and magazines and in radio and television broadcasts.
>
> (answers.com)

And from the *Merriam-Webster Dictionary* website, you'll notice a few different meanings:

> 1a : the collection and editing of news for presentation through the media b : the public press c : an academic study concerned with the collection and editing of news or the management of a news medium

> 2a : writing designed for publication in a newspaper or magazine b : writing characterized by a direct presentation of facts or description of events without an attempt at interpretation c : writing designed to appeal to current popular taste or public interest

According to these definitions, "journalism" is an activity that involves collecting, writing, editing and publishing, and/or it is a certain kind of writing and/or an area of study. While there's nothing particularly wrong with any of these definitions—they do reflect the way people often talk about journalism—there's nothing particularly useful about them either. The first one seems to suggest that journalism happens only in newspapers and magazines. The second includes TV and radio, but doesn't have anything to say about the Internet. The third includes all media, but seems to count only writing as journalism. The definitions contain some ambiguous terms too. What is "news"? What are "facts"? What is the "public interest"? In the end, even if we had answers to these questions, these definitions still don't help us understand the difference between what *Rolling Stone* did and what it should have done—whatever it was that raised red flags about "A Rape on Campus" at other news organizations.

The question of who counts as a journalist and, therefore, what constitutes journalism has even been tackled by the courts in the United States in cases that involve things like whether a journalist must reveal the source of sensitive information included in a story. But coming up with airtight definitions is not something judges have been very excited about doing, in large part because any criteria can seem pretty arbitrary or quickly become out-dated.

The U.S. Supreme Court said as much in its 1972 decision in *Branzburg v. Hayes*:

> The administration of a constitutional newsman's privilege would present practical and conceptual difficulties of a high order. Sooner or later, it would be necessary to define those categories of newsmen who qualified for the privilege, a questionable procedure in light of the traditional doctrine that liberty of the press is the right of the lonely pamphleteer who uses carbon paper or a mimeograph just as much as of the large metropolitan publisher who utilizes the latest photocomposition methods.

Indeed, the "latest photocomposition methods" the court referred to have long been left in the dust. And things like blogging and Twitter mark a sort of return of the "lonely pamphleteer" (though without the carbon paper) the Court said has the same rights as the professional news media. So now what? As time went by, the courts, instead of creating "categories of newsmen," started to focus on the activity in which a person was engaged as the primary indicator of whether they could be called a journalist. That means journalism is mostly defined in terms of its purpose and content, and not whether the person creating or doing it makes a living at *USA Today*.

For example, in the 1993 *Shoen v. Shoen* case, the Ninth Circuit Court of Appeals said, "What makes journalism journalism is not its format but its content." The kind of content the court mostly had in mind was "investigative reporting." But what is investigative reporting? A good question, which comes up again in a case called *In re Madden* decided by the Third Circuit Court of Appeals a few years later. In that case, the court created a three-part test for whether to consider someone a journalist: the person had to be (1) engaged in investigative reporting, (2) gathering news, and (3) have had the intention from the very beginning of making that news public. Here, as in the dictionary definitions mentioned earlier, we have "journalism" (or "journalist") defined in terms of other things that need defining themselves,

FIGURE 2.1 Even though people often talk about "news" and "journalism" as meaning essentially the same thing, distinctions in their definitions do matter.

Source: Aaron Amat/ Shutterstock.

such as "news" and "investigative reporting." Also notice how the intent of the person to make the reporting *public* matters in this definition. That will be a key point, as you'll see a bit later on.

▶ DEFINITIONS HAVE CONSEQUENCES

The *Branzburg, Shoen* and *Madden* cases aren't the only ones where these issues about who counts as a journalist have been discussed. But they do offer a glimpse into the kind of thing the courts have wrestled with as well as highlighting just how difficult but important all this definitional business is. That is, thinking about what "journalism" means isn't just something people brainstorm about on long roadtrips when their mp3 player dies. The answer actually has some consequences for how free people are to do journalism and how the public interprets and responds to what they read and see.

At a time when the way "traditional" journalism has been financed is under challenge, the answer might even have consequences for the survival of journalism itself. Time.com writer James Poniewozik addressed this issue a couple years ago and almost immediately ran into the definitional problem. In the post below, he mentions what he wrote and how some people, on a journalism blog called "Romenesko," responded. Pay particular attention to the parts we've put in italics.

> You can't open a newspaper—or read a newsmagazine website—these days without seeing a report wondering if X, Y or Z "can save journalism." Maybe that's the wrong question.

Let's assume, for the sake of argument, that nothing saves journalism. "Journalism," that is, as a profession and as currently constructed: a full-time job paid for by newsgathering entities through a combination of subscriptions and advertising.

(Update: Some commenters at Romenesko argue *this is a narrow definition of journalism. Agreed. That's the point.* It is the narrow definition implicit in all those articles about "Will _____ save journalism?" But. *However you do define journalism—a term I generally hate anyway but have no substitute coinage for—it will still be practiced by human beings who need to pay rent and purchase food.* Where will they get that money? And thus, how will the activity of journalism be enabled, if not by the presently-constituated [sic] profession of "journalism"? Especially if "unnamed model that someone else will invent later" is not an allowable answer? That's the question of this post.)

Poniewozik's definition focuses on journalism as a profession, something people are not only paid to do, but paid enough to make a full-time job of it. It is, as the commenters noted, a pretty narrow definition that excludes everyone from freelance photographers to people who blog about local restaurants or what's going on in their neighborhoods. So what, if any, value is there in defining journalism this way? What Poniewozik wants to highlight is that the activity of journalism as traditionally practiced by people with full-time jobs at particular kinds of news outlets is expensive in both money and labor—but that expense is necessary if one hopes to have the kind of journalism democracy requires. He doesn't really think journalism *ought* to be defined in terms of where somebody works or how much someone is paid. He is worried about saving the practice of journalism, not necessarily the traditional news organizations that have undertaken that practice. No, he doesn't define that practice. But his distinction between practice and organizational structure is useful for our purposes here. The big picture is that the contexts—economic, as well as political and social—in which journalism is defined are critically important. We'll continue the discussion of the economics in Chapter 4.

What we might begin to conclude from these varying definitions, not to mention the sheer difficulty in defining journalism at all, is that to call something "journalism" seems to mean having some sort of expectations about it that go beyond whatever its format or distribution channel might be. As the Project for Excellence in Journalism puts it: "Journalism is storytelling with a purpose."

The Missouri School of Journalism gets us a little closer to some answers with a definition of journalism discussed in its introductory courses: "a current, reasoned reflection, in print or telecommunications, of society's events, needs and values." But even that definition is better at defining news than journalism. A reflection of society's events, needs and values describes a product of some kind, the actual content or information or "stuff" that is disseminated by the media. It says little about the process by which that reflection was produced except to say that it is "reasoned."

As it turns out, "reasoned" is pretty important. It means that the content/information/stuff that constitutes "the news" has been the subject of some kind of reasoning process, of someone thinking through things, exercising judgment, and making decisions. It's that notion of a process—and one with distinct, essential features—that's missing from most definitions of journalism.

◄ **NEWS JUDGMENT:** How journalists determine which events and information—and which aspects of those events and information—are important enough to cover as news and how to cover them.

The way we think about the difference between journalism and news in this book is that "journalism" describes the process through which "news" gets made. Pretty straightforward, right? Well, before you get too excited about how simple that sounds, consider the implications of thinking about news and journalism that way. First, it means that "news" doesn't just exist out in the world waiting for someone to trip over and report it. News is constructed by people who are selecting and confirming and explaining those things out in the world. (If this raises the notions of bias and objectivity in your mind, you're on the right track to understanding this implication. More on that later.) Second, but related to the first implication, is that "news" can mean different things in different places. That is, what's considered news in Indonesia might not be considered news in Italy or Ivory Coast. Third, it suggests that treating "news" and "information" or "journalism" and "media" as synonyms—something you'll notice happens all the time in regular conversation—is flat-out wrong. Information might be part of the raw material of news, but it's not the whole thing. And journalism might be conducted by people working in or for the media, but there are lots of media folks who don't "do" journalism at all. Finally (for now!), it means that the definition of "journalist" could apply to anyone who engages in that distinctive journalistic process of selecting, confirming and explaining. In other words, you don't have to work for the *Arkansas Democrat-Gazette*, the NBC *Nightly News* or CNN.com to do journalism.

Before we go any further with these implications, let's turn our attention to describing in detail what we argue are the essential features of the process called "journalism."

▶ THE ELEMENTS OF JOURNALISM

We—and you!—are indebted to Bill Kovach and Tom Rosenstiel for laying out a vision of journalism that highlights its distinctive features. Their book, *The Elements of Journalism*, starts from the premise that journalism really only makes sense in the context of democracy. That means journalism is defined in large part by the role it plays (or is meant to play) in aiding self-governance—all the stuff you learned about in Chapter 1. The first two "elements" Kovach and Rosenstiel describe—journalism's first obligation is to the truth and its first loyalty is to citizens—emphasize that role. Journalism treats people as *citizens* undertaking the challenging job of self-governance. To do that job, those citizens need truthful information they can rely on.

Notice that Kovach and Rosenstiel *don't* say journalism's first obligation is to facts, even though lots of people seem to think journalism is all about sticking to the facts. So what kind of truth do they have in mind? Journalists aren't necessarily looking for big, philosophical truths like the meaning of life or the nature of time as much as they are the practical truths necessary

THE ELEMENTS OF JOURNALISM

Bill Kovach and Tom Rosenstiel's *The Elements of Journalism: What Newspeople Should Know and the Public Should Expect* distills the underlying principles of journalism practice into nine elements essential to journalism fulfilling its democratic function. Those elements are:

1. Journalism's first obligation is to the truth.
2. Its first loyalty is to citizens.
3. Its essence is a discipline of verification.
4. Its practitioners must maintain an independence from those they cover.
5. It must serve as an independent monitor of power.
6. It must provide a forum for public criticism and compromise.
7. It must strive to make the significant interesting and relevant.
8. It must keep the news comprehensive and proportional.
9. Its practitioners must be allowed to exercise their personal conscience.
10. Citizens, too, have rights and responsibilities when it comes to the news.

to gaining a perspective on what's going on in the world and figuring out what, if anything, requires change or attention. This kind of truth starts with gathering facts, but it certainly doesn't stop there. Those facts have to be put in some context that gives them meaning.

Here's an example: Suppose Senator Slackjaw claims his new bill will make it easier for people to get student loans. It's certainly a fact that he introduced the bill and another fact that he claimed it will simplify getting a loan. But would the proposed law really make it easier to get a loan? Is the senator's claim actually true? That's a question the journalist might pose to bankers, people trying to get loans, people who already have loans, consumer groups, college financial aid administrators, etc. The senator's announcement about the bill is just one of many facts a journalist would gather to get at the truth. Beyond verifying those facts and claims, a journalist would seek to put the facts in context. It might be important to know, for example, that Senator Slackjaw represents a state where the largest student loan processing company is based. Or that the National Association of Really Cheap Student Loan Issuers donated a large amount of money to the senator's last election campaign. Or that his state has the lowest percentage of people who can afford to go to college. Any or all of those things might have a bearing on how the average citizen hearing about the senator's proposal interprets it. The journalistic process, then, produces a kind of actionable truth by offering citizens tools for understanding what's going on around them. That truth—unlike the immutable truths of space and time—has a way of changing and adapting as new information becomes part of the narrative.

The second important thing to notice about Kovach and Rosenstiel's description of journalism is that journalists don't seek truth just because they feel like it or it's interesting to them (though that wouldn't hurt). Kovach and Rosenstiel describe truth seeking as an obligation of journalists—an obligation they owe to *citizens*. Thinking of people as citizens instead of as, say, an audience or consumers shapes how journalists do their work, both the kinds of stories they pursue as well as how they pursue them. For example, citizens need to know if the local sewer system is failing, even though knowing that isn't particularly entertaining. And while you might, as a consumer, be happy to hear all about which store has the best price on Your Favorite Brand of soda, as a citizen you probably also need to know Your Favorite Brand has been accused of engaging in unfair trade practices that harm companies in other communities. Journalists from the Kovach and Rosenstiel perspective act in certain ways and pursue certain kinds of news and truth because they think of their readers, viewers or listeners as citizens who might need to act on the information, not merely as an audience that wants to be entertained.

So journalism is a truth-seeking endeavor, addressed to citizens. Now what? While these first two elements lay the groundwork for distinguishing journalism from other kinds of communication, such as the stuff meant primarily to entertain you or persuade you to buy something, the third element begins to describe what it is that people who practice journalism actually do. Kovach and Rosenstiel write: "The essence of journalism is a discipline of verification." This follows logically from the first element. Journalists have a basic obligation to truth; getting the truth involves engaging in a strict process of verifying evidence and claims. That process goes beyond simply repeating what others say—the kind of "he said, she said" practice that Kovach and Rosenstiel dismissively call the "journalism of assertion"—to subjecting what others say to some scrutiny. What's involved in that process? Let's have a look at an example.

FIGURE 2.2 Verifying information, not just gathering or distributing it, is a key part of what sets journalists apart from other mass media communicators.

Source: Picsfive/Shutterstock.

▶ BECAUSE I SAID SO? NOPE

In a series of articles nominated for a Pulitzer Prize in 2015, Reuters reporters Joan Biskupic, Janet Roberts and John Shiffman demonstrated how a small group of attorneys representing some of the nation's largest corporations have outsized success in getting the U.S. Supreme Court to hear their cases. As the letter nominating their work summarized it: "Although they accounted for far less than 1 percent of attorneys who sought the high court's ear, these lawyers were involved in an astonishing 43 percent of the cases the justices chose to decide" over nine Supreme Court terms.

In other words, Corporate America has a much better chance of getting its day in court than Main Street America. If that doesn't really sound like news—the rich and powerful always have it easier, don't they?—consider the implications of such a finding for the principle of equal protection under the law, not to mention the impact on how laws are interpreted and precedents are set. To publish articles asserting that the practices of the nation's highest court seem to be contrary to cherished principles in American democratic life is a pretty big deal.

Think for a second about what it takes to get to the truth of a story like this. First, Biskupic, Roberts and Shiffman had to determine whether a system that seems to overwhelmingly favor some attorneys actually exists. They couldn't just say, "Well, *everybody* knows this happens," nor could they just quote a few people who believe that to be true, though no doubt there wouldn't be any shortage of people willing to offer such an opinion. The reporters had to verify—to get some actual confirmation—that some attorneys were far more likely to gain access to the U.S. Supreme Court than others and that those attorneys with such great access were more likely to be representing corporate clients than regular people. But does that sound like something anyone—attorneys, their clients or the nine justices on the Court—would be delighted to discuss? Um, probably not.

Here's the approach the Reuters team took in the series called "The Echo Chamber" (see link to complete story at www.reuters.com/investigates/special-report/scotus/):

> To identify lawyers who enjoyed the most success before the high court, Reuters examined about 10,300 petitions for writ of certiorari, the documents that launch an appeal, filed by private attorneys during a nine-year period. Reuters excluded the large volume of appeals filed by convicts and others without a lawyer; rarely are those cases accepted by the court. The analysis also excluded petitions filed by government lawyers.

At this critical first stage of the process, justices have wide discretion to decide whether to hear a case. For a petition to be accepted—known in Supreme Court parlance as "granting cert"—four of the nine justices must vote to take the case and hear oral arguments.

Each of the 66 lawyers Reuters identified filed an average of at least one petition a year from 2004 to 2012. And each had at least three petitions that were granted in that period. Both criteria put these lawyers far above the norm.

Reuters identified about 1,500 petitions filed during those nine years in which the interests of companies were arrayed against those of customers, employees or other individuals. These appeals included employment discrimination cases, benefits disputes and antitrust cases.

In these cases, the elite lawyers were three times more likely to petition the court on behalf of businesses. And the appeals brought by a leading attorney were six times more likely to be heard than those that were not.

So, they started by gathering the facts: how many petitions were filed, who filed them and for what kind of client, and which petitions were successful. This analysis confirmed that certain attorneys and clients have better access to the court than others. The Reuters team went far beyond assertions to get to the truth. With those facts in hand, they could then start digging for answers to why and how these practices had come about and why they matter. What are the implications of what they found? For that they turned to hundreds of attorneys and experts for interviews, as well as eight of the nine sitting justices. The number of interviews is significant too: The more interviews, the more likely they were to get the widest variety of perspectives, the richest context. They didn't just rely on one or two people to defend or decry the system.

Think about any science classes you've taken in which you conducted an experiment. Let's say one experiment was meant to determine whether note-taking practices—writing class notes by hand or using a laptop computer—affect test scores. To test that claim, you would follow a set of procedures—establishing a hypothesis, recruiting subjects who would be assigned to either the "hand-written notes" or the "laptop notes" condition, having those subjects listen to a lecture and take notes, administering a test over the lecture material to all subjects, and so on. In the end, you would compare how well the subjects in each condition performed on the test. Did the subjects who took notes by hand do better or worse than those who took notes on a laptop? (Or did the note-taking practice not matter at all?) To make your results stronger and more credible, you would need to use more than one or two subjects, right? And even if you were really sure ahead of time that your hypothesis was correct, you would have to be open to the possibility that the data might not support you. Either way, you would report your experimental procedures and results so that future researchers could learn from and build on them. (P.S.: For the record, research has demonstrated that it's better to take notes by hand.)

What does that super-basic overview of the scientific method have to do with Reuters' series about the U.S. Supreme Court? More than you might think. The team started with a sort of hypothesis about who appears before the Court most often. To test that claim, they assembled all the petitions and then compared the attorneys and clients on the successful petitions with those on the unsuccessful petitions. They couldn't just rely on one or two anecdotal cases. And they had to be open to the possibility that the hypothesis wouldn't be supported by the data. Whatever this "experiment" showed, they would have to report the results.

That's what Kovach and Rosenstiel are getting at with the discipline of verification. Similar to the scientific method, the verification process in journalism is transparent. That means journalists are open about whom they talked to, what documents they consulted—all the evidence they gathered—and what that evidence says. Also similar to the scientific method, the journalism of verification doesn't just rest on what one or two "subjects" say—the journalism of assertion—without trying to determine whether what those one or two folks said is true. Are the people offering their opinions on Fox News or CNN doing journalism? Not if they aren't offering some verification along with those opinions, they're not. Verification is handy that way—it offers a clear way to think about what sets journalism apart.

One final similarity with the scientific method is that the journalistic "method" of which the discipline of verification is a key component is objective. Oh boy. Now, before your head starts to explode, notice that we've said the *method* is objective. The *method*, not the person employing that method. We'll tackle the thorny, complicated, head-exploding concept of objectivity in greater depth in Chapter 8. Right now we want to spend a moment or two underlining the importance of an objective method in helping us overcome aspects of basic human nature that otherwise can get in the way of verification.

▶ "THE STORY TOO GOOD TO CHECK"

At the beginning of this chapter, we talked about how *Rolling Stone*'s failure to engage in rigorous verification resulted in disaster and, even more important for our purposes, in an article that couldn't really be called "journalism." That's how important verification is to the very definition of journalism. So, why didn't they do it? Why didn't Erdely corroborate Jackie's story? Why weren't the editors at the magazine more skeptical in their fact-checking? Sure, verification is hard and time-consuming. But neither difficulty nor time seems to fully explain what happened with "A Rape on Campus." So what does explain it?

We are going to take yet another cue from the world of science to find the answer. And that is going to take us all the way back to the beginning of Erdely's story, even before she ever talked to Jackie.

Remember how Erdely was looking for an emblematic victim to illustrate the problems with how campuses handle rape? Well, that's a little dangerous. In searching for a "perfect" victim, Erdely was already starting with a number of assumptions about campus rape. Think: What set of circumstances would make someone's case emblematic? A perpetrator who belonged to a fraternity? Heavy drinking by the victim or perpetrator? Indifferent university officials? Once a victim whose case fit the assumptions was found, those assumptions would begin to take on the character of facts in no need of corroboration, rather than assumptions that most definitely needed it.

No person with a shred of humanity *wants* a story like Jackie's to be true, of course. But in the context of the national conversation about campus rape going on at the time, such an awful assault seemed both possible and maybe even, sadly, probable. Jackie's story appeared to confirm people's worst fears about campus sexual assault. That is, it appeared to confirm what people had already begun to believe. And once beliefs are established, they are hard to challenge.

▶ **CONFIRMATION BIAS:** The tendency for people to accept information or evidence that confirms the beliefs they already hold while rejecting information or evidence that challenges those beliefs.

Psychologists call this tendency in human nature, "confirmation bias." The idea comes from philosopher Karl Popper, who was interested in what makes a theory worthy of the label "scientific." His conclusion: That a theory is only a scientific theory if it can be tested and potentially refuted or falsified.

Here's how Judith Shulevitz, in the *Columbia Journalism Review*, explains Popper's ideas and how they relate to the *Rolling Stone* case:

> Erdely told Rosin [a *Slate* reporter looking into the story after its publication] that she'd gone all around the country looking for rape survivors and was delighted when she stumbled on Jackie. She was obviously traumatized, and her story illustrated everything Erdely knew to be true—that frat boys rape girls and universities are indifferent to rape survivors.

Erdely told Rosin that she'd based her story solely on Jackie's version because she found her "credible." Erdely's editors found her "credible" too, so much so that they let Erdely waive the usual journalistic protocols, such as getting more than one source on a story about a horrible crime. And readers found Jackie credible because everyone knows that there's an epidemic of rape on campuses around the country and women hardly ever level false rape charges, because why would they put themselves through that?

Popper would have said that Erdely and her editors were all in the grip of a myth. He'd have used that word not because rape isn't a problem in this country—obviously, it is—but because they had never subjected their beliefs to the test of falsifiability. Myths become theories only when they are tested; "Every genuine test of a theory is an attempt to falsify it, or refute it," he wrote. He went even further: He argued that evidence only corroborates a theory if it emerges out of an attempt to falsify it. Had Erdely been open to the possibility that Jackie was wrong and gone out looking for evidence to exonerate the alleged perpetrators but found instead a mountain of sleaze, then that would have been the time to deem Jackie "credible." (It would not have been the time to stop digging for corroborating facts about the crime, however.)

All this falsifiability and confirmation bias stuff is essentially a twist on an old concept in journalism: The Story Too Good To Check. This kind of "good" story is interesting and perfectly illustrates a particular narrative. It rings true; indeed you might even root for it to be true. This almost irresistible combination has the potential for confirmation bias written all over it. The

Story Too Good to Check has been around forever but has received quite a boost from the Internet and social media, which makes spreading such stories so very easy. The Story Too Good to Check rears its head in viral Internet hoaxes like the fake, live-tweeted argument between Elan Gale, a producer on *The Bachelor*, and a fellow airline passenger, and the story of a Justin Bieber ringtone scaring off an attacking bear. But it also can happen with stories of far more import, like "A Rape on Campus."

Which brings us back to the importance of an objective method incorporating a discipline of verification. It provides a way to resist the temptation of The Story Too Good to Check, to at least reduce the chance that our natural confirmation bias will lead us astray. As Clay Shirky said in the *New Republic*: "[H]ad even one person at *Rolling Stone* asked 'How do we know this is true?' the entire thing would have unraveled."

Confirmation bias is only one possible detour on the road to producing journalism worthy of the label. Along with being willing and able to challenge one's own beliefs and assumptions in pursuing a story, a journalist also

FIGURE 2.3 Media coverage of social issues often reflects broader social divisions and underscores the need for journalists to reflect the communities they cover.
Source: AP Photo/The Daily Progress, Ryan M. Kelly.

needs to be able to create some distance between herself and the beliefs, assumptions and interests of others. For example, what if the Reuters team had interviewed only those attorneys who happened to be their friends and neighbors? What if one of the reporters' cousins was an attorney at one of the elite law firms in question and the team didn't want to make him look bad?

▶ INDEPENDENCE AT THE CENTER OF IT ALL

Enter element 4: "[Journalism's] practitioners must maintain independence from those they cover." By now, you are probably starting to see how all these elements fit together. Part of what makes the discipline of verification (element #3) work is a commitment to finding the truth (element #1) that citizens (element #2) need. For verification to be the transparent and objective process necessary to meet those commitments, it can't be easily manipulated by people who might have a stake in the story—including the journalists themselves. Independence, in the way Kovach and Rosenstiel talk about it, means that journalists' loyalties cannot be divided. Nothing should come between a journalist and the truth or between a journalist and the citizens for whom she works.

2.1 THE VIEW FROM THE PROS: INDEPENDENCE

Walter Williams, founding dean of the world's first school of journalism and a newspaper publisher himself, understood the central importance of independence. He insisted that the best way to teach the principles and practices of journalism was by means of a media outlet produced by students under faculty direction that would be both editorially and commercially independent.

The school's teaching newspaper, then called the *University Missourian*, began publication on the school's first day of classes in September 1908. Within months, its independence was under assault, not from those it covered but from those who had been the school's strongest supporters: other publishers.

The objection was to the dean's decision to have the *Missourian* sell advertising, of course in competition with nearby newspapers. The objections were so strong, and the publishers' political clout so powerful, that the Missouri legislature quickly wrote into law a prohibition against the use of state funds by "any newspaper which solicits, receives or accepts paid subscriptions or which prints or publishes advertising." The university's governing body immediately translated that ban into rule.

The independence of not only the newspaper but the school, and by implication the principles it taught, appeared to be doomed.

But Williams, demonstrating his own independence from his nominal superiors, set up a nonprofit corporation, the "University Missourian Publishing Association," turned over ownership of the paper to that group and moved the publication temporarily off campus.

Advertising sales and independent coverage continued, and continue more than a century later. The *Columbia Missourian*, as the community daily is called today, is still owned by the Missourian Publishing Association, which contracts with the School of Journalism to produce it.

The continuing importance of structural separation and courageous leadership were on display again in the late 1970s, when another chancellor ordered another dean to restrict the *Missourian*'s commercial competitiveness. Dean Roy Fisher responded by enlisting prominent alumni and members of the Publishing Association board to lobby the chancellor's superiors, the university Board of Curators.

After hearing from the managing editor of the *New York Times*, the editor of Missouri's biggest newspaper and others, the curators ordered the chancellor to rescind her order.

Journalistic independence, like democracy itself, requires repeated defense. Another assault, this one directed at the school's television station, came shortly after terrorists struck America in 2001.

The news director of KOMU-TV, a member of the faculty, forbade his on-air staff, student and professional, from wearing the flag pins or ribbons that had suddenly become the popular symbol of patriotism. "Our news broadcasts are not the place for personal statements of support or any cause—no matter how deserving the cause seems to be," he wrote. "Our job is to deliver the news as free from outside influences as possible."

The television station, unlike the newspaper, is owned directly by the university, which depends on the state legislature for funding. Legislators reacted with outrage. The House of Representatives adopted a $500,000 cut in the university budget, "to send a message to the School of Journalism."

Actually, the sponsor of the cut told reporters, he'd have preferred to punch the news director in the nose.

In response, faculty colleagues sent to the state's newspapers a statement that sought to make clear what was really at stake. The statement read, in part:

"It would be easy to dismiss this latest flare-up as just another episode of the stupid legislative tricks Missourians have come to expect this time of year. However, the attitudes expressed by legislators are probably widely shared by their constituents. Certainly, university administrators appear to believe that's true.

"That's why the faculty of the Editorial Department of the School of Journalism believe it necessary—not just for the school, or even for journalism, but for the public—to emphasize that this abuse of legislative power illustrates both the importance of journalistic independence and its fragility.

"It was no accident that the First Amendment to the United States Constitution guarantees protection for our freedoms of religion, speech, press, assembly and petition. The founders, even as they launched their unprecedented experiment in democracy, understood that these freedoms were inextricably linked, that they were essential to the democracy and that they would certainly come under threat. History has demonstrated that they were right on all three counts.

"The most important moment to defend freedom is when it is most unpopular. The most important quality of a free press is that it be independent, both from the powerful whose acts it monitors and from the people to whom it reports."

In the end, the budget cut was reduced to $100,000. The "message" was received and rejected. The policy stood. Independence, one more time, was preserved.

THINK ABOUT IT: The *Columbian Missourian* is a unique community newspaper produced by the School of Journalism at the University of Missouri, but most campuses have a student newspaper, website and broadcast outlet (radio or television). What is the reporting structure of those student media outlets? Are they under the journalism program, student affairs, student government or another group? Is this transparency to readers and viewers? How might the reporting structure affect content?

George Kennedy, now a professor emeritus at the Missouri School of Journalism, was Managing Editor of the *Columbia Missourian* for nearly 12 years.

The notion of independence can apply to the press more generally, not just individual journalists. Consider, for example, a column the (now former) executive editor of the *Seattle Times*, Mike Fancher, wrote a few years back. In it, Fancher says, "Independent, as we use it, means freedom from control or influence of others. It applies whether we're talking about the relationship of the press to government or the ability of journalists to do their work without pressure from any special interest."

All those things to which someone might be loyal or have an interest in promoting or protecting are called "factions." So a political party might be a faction, but so might a church or a charitable organization or a sports team or a company or even the League of People Who Love Starbucks, for that matter. If your love of Starbucks would spur you to write or not write something about the company regardless of what's best for citizens, then you are not acting independently. You've let your factional loyalty overtake your primary loyalty, in which case you aren't doing journalism, you're doing public relations or advertising, or merely cheerleading for your favorite coffee. Independence from faction, then, helps us define journalism by specifying one way in which it is different from other information-related activities that are frequently confused with it. Someone doing journalism is loyal to citizens first; someone doing public relations is loyal to the client first. That client might be Starbucks or the Libertarian Party or the Sierra Club. Or, in the Reuters case, a faction might be Reuters' attorneys (if they are among those the story focuses on or maybe happen to be advertisers on Reuters' website). And while what's good for that client might also be good for citizens more generally, that coincidence doesn't change the basic difference in approach to gathering and reporting information that someone doing journalism and someone doing PR take. Think back to the experiment analogy, where we discussed the transparency and objectivity of the scientific method. Scientists who deviate from this by, for example, skewing the results of their experiments to please someone who might benefit from those results, are harshly criticized and their work dismissed as lacking validity. Independence, then, is necessary for the discipline of verification to work.

▶ **NEUTRALITY:**
Taking no position on an issue. While such detachment can be beneficial in journalism, it also can get in the way of journalists' truth-telling mission if it reduces journalism to merely reporting what each "side" of an issue says.

Oddly enough—at least at first glance—this doesn't mean that journalism (or journalists) should be neutral. Consider that journalism is a necessary component of democratic life, so it will always be partial in some sense— that is, non-neutral—regarding what democracy requires.

But this independent-but-not-neutral business is tricky, not just for journalism students, but for journalists too. Just consider the confusion and criticism surrounding National Public Radio's decision to prohibit its employees from attending the "Rally to Restore Sanity" (and/or the "March to Keep Fear Alive") in October 2010. Sure, the journalists *covering* the rally put on by comedians Jon Stewart and Stephen Colbert could attend. But other employees couldn't, even on their own time.

In a memo to the staff, NPR's then-senior vice president for news, Ellen Weiss, referred to the network's already established ethics code and social media guidelines. (You can find the full text of both documents here: www. npr.org/about/aboutnpr/ethics/.)

▶ NPR journalists may not run for office, endorse candidates or otherwise engage in politics. Since contributions to candidates are part of the public record, NPR journalists may not contribute to political campaigns, as doing so would call into question a journalist's impartiality.

▶ NPR journalists may not participate in marches and rallies involving causes or issues that NPR covers, nor should they sign petitions or otherwise lend their name to such causes, or contribute money to them. This restriction applies to the upcoming Jon Stewart and Stephen Colbert rallies.

▶ You must not advocate for political or other polarizing issues online. This extends to joining online groups or using social media in any form (including your Facebook page or a personal blog) to express personal views on a political or other controversial issue that you could not write for the air or post on NPR.org.

▶ NPR journalists may not serve on government boards or commissions.

These guidelines have "independence from faction" written all over them, don't they? The admonition against contributing to political campaigns or participating in rallies or advocating for causes is meant to guard against a collision of loyalties a journalist might face. We're guessing it seems rather bizarre and extreme to you that joining a Facebook group is considered just as problematic as joining an anti-war demonstration, according to NPR's guidelines. Rest assured, a lot of it seems weird to us, too. But let's not lose sight of the principle before we start nit-picking about the details of how journalists try to follow it. To call something "journalism," according to Kovach and Rosenstiel, is to say that the procedures that produced it were as free of competing interests as possible. Given the public nature of what journalists do and the transparency the verification process requires, most journalists try to avoid even the *appearance* of a conflict of interest or competing loyalties. The NPR guidelines (and the guidelines of many other news organizations) are basically saying that even if it were possible for a journalist to advocate for the League of People Who Love Starbucks on her own time and still impartially cover that league when she's on the clock as a journalist, the appearance of a conflict would raise too many questions that get in the way of the public's ability to trust her reporting.

2. 2 THE VIEW FROM THE PROS: JOURNALISM MEANS NOT TAKING "NO" FOR AN ANSWER

When I was in college, I learned from multiple professors that public records were a vital part of your reporting toolkit. I was instilled with a (rightful) sense of entitlement to those records. So when I started out in my first job after school, I pursued public records with a vengeance.

One of the first things I found out was that public employees did not actually know that much about public records law. Even city attorneys did not necessarily know their obligations under the law as much as I did by poring over the state statutes.

My first major request as a reporter was for payroll data from the city of Tempe. The paper had not requested the data for city payrolls in the area in a while and it would be my job to get us back on track.

The city attorney said they'd provide the salary ranges for specific job titles. This was the best they could do. When I pointed out that state law did not say pay information for specific employees was exempt from public record law, the city attorney replied she felt like it would be a violation of city employee privacy to provide the data I requested. I was really confused by her response. There was a mountain of case law that said payroll records were public, no exemptions. I assumed the top attorney at a city would know this kind of thing. In a fit of youthful exuberance, I told her we would probably sue the city for the data.

She said go ahead and do it.

In retrospect, I had no authority to make legal threats. Luckily, after giving me a stern lecture on how and when I can threaten public agencies, my editor agreed we should talk to the paper's attorney. We sued. We won. The judge found the city's arguments to be so weak and frivolous that they made the city pay our attorney fees.

Thanks to the Tempe data and data from other cities, we built a fairly robust searchable website of public employee pay across the Phoenix area. The value of doing your homework before you make a request? A large public payroll database and the legal fees to acquire it.

The other major thing I learned about making public records requests is never take no for an answer. Just because someone tells you no at first, doesn't mean it's the final answer. Persistence can open many closed doors.

Much later in my career, I was making a series of records requests for each county in Arizona's county assessor database. The databases I was requesting were huge. They were the property records for every parcel in each county. Each parcel would have a record that included the year it was built, what kind of property it was and more. Some counties were reluctant to give us the data without charging us thousands of dollars because these data sets were big revenue earners for these agencies. The data was essential to an important project I was working on, tying the threat of wildfires to increasing development in high-risk areas. No was not an option. I needed this data or the story was toast.

One county was dead set against providing us the data without charging us $30,000 in fees. In response, I asked them to give me an itemized list of the charges. Their response showed me they were charging us as if we were a commercial company and not a newspaper. While media outlets are absolutely commercial enterprises, most public record law treats them as non-commercial due to the value to the public in us doing our jobs as reporters. I told them they had to charge us at the non-commercial rate, which is quite a bit lower, to make sure the data is available to media outlets. After a bit of arguing about case law, I got them to drop our costs to $7,000. Still too much for my employer to dish out.

I told the county assessor some other counties already gave us their data for free because it was in the public interest. He didn't bite on that. He said he didn't care what others did. He felt he was already giving us a big discount.

I decided to wear him down. I called him every day. I told him the cost estimate seemed arbitrary since it was not based on work done. He told me it's the cost the county commissioners set for that record. I said that's not good enough. It needs to be based on the labor done. To be fair,

I wasn't entirely sure that was the truth. It was more important to me to convince the assessor it could be true. Yes, sometimes I make claims in the records negotiation process that may not be entirely true. But the goal is getting the records, not being a saint. After all, I could hear in his voice he might be wavering. So I kept calling. And kept talking. And eventually he told me he could give us everything for $220 if I'd just leave his department alone after that. I smiled, agreed and quickly told my editor what we agreed to pay.

The value of persistence in the face of a mountain of no? An award-winning story about a huge spike of properties built in the areas highest at risk for wildfires. Dollar value? About $29,000.

THINK ABOUT IT: It can be expensive to gather the data needed to do rigorous verification. How might that affect the ability of citizen journalists to do certain kinds of stories? What are alternative, and perhaps cheaper, ways of pursuing verification?

Matt Dempsey is a data reporter at the *Houston Chronicle*.

▶ SO WHAT IS JOURNALISM, ANYWAY?

If nothing else, this chapter has illustrated how difficult but important the task of defining "journalism" is. It's pretty easy—too easy—to wind up with a definition that includes or excludes too much, or that defines "journalism" using *other* terms that are also ambiguous, such as "news" or "information." Scholars Erik Ugland and Jennifer Henderson point out one further complication: People seem to assume that a question like "Who is a journalist?" is a single question, and not a number of different questions, depending on the context in which one is asking. If one is considering how to define "journalist" for the purpose of deciding who may qualify for a privilege like a White House press pass, then certain kinds of elements will be important. If, on the other hand, one is considering the definition for the purpose of distinguishing good or credible practices from less credible ones, the focus of the definition will be very different. Ugland and Henderson refer to the first context as the legal domain characterized by "an *egalitarian model* that emphasizes equal access to rights and privileges," and the second context as the professional ethics domain characterized by "an *expert model* that emphasizes the unique proficiencies and duties of media professionals" (p. 244).

> In the law domain, fundamental rights are at stake, so the consequences of defining protections for newsgathering and expression too narrowly (especially when the party drawing the line is the government) are substantially greater than in the professional ethics domain where the debate is more about virtue than freedom. In the legal domain, there is an element of coercion—the exercise of government power to restrain

> behavior. That is not true in the professional ethics domain. There, it is
> about a private dispute among communicators regarding whose work is
> more valuable.
>
> (Ugland and Henderson, 2007, p. 259)

What we learned earlier in this chapter about legal definitions is that the courts have been far happier to define journalism in terms of its content or the type of activity that produced that content than in terms of its format or mode of distribution or, even worse, where someone works. What Ugland and Henderson are suggesting refines this point further. Even if we agree that journalism ought to be defined in terms of content and practices and not format, distribution or whatever, we might still disagree about whether the definition ought to focus on *what* a person does or *how* they do it. That kind of disagreement seems to be at the heart of skepticism about "citizen journalism"—essentially, news content produced by people who don't work full-time as journalists but who might, nevertheless, engage in reporting practices that look an awful lot like the journalistic method. Columnist Leonard Pitts put it this way:

> Journalism is hours on the phone nailing down the facts or pleading
> for the interview. Journalism is obsessing over nit-picky questions of
> fairness and context. Journalism is trying to get the story and get it
> right. "Citizen journalism," we are told is supposed to democratize all
> that, the tools of new technology making each of us a journalist unto
> him or herself . . . If some guy had a wrench, would that make him a
> citizen mechanic? If some woman flashed a toy badge, would you call
> her a citizen police officer? Would you trust your health to a citizen
> doctor just because he produced a syringe?

Pitts' skepticism seems to rest, at least in part, on his view that *standards* are an important defining feature of journalism—a view that shares some similarities with the expert model Ugland and Henderson describe. Even if citizen journalists would meet the definition of a journalist put forth under the egalitarian model, Pitts is saying they wouldn't (or shouldn't) meet the definition under the expert model.

We happen to disagree with Pitts that the work of citizen journalism can be dismissed so easily. If, in fact, a citizen journalist spends "hours on the phone nailing down the facts" and engages in the kind of independent verification process aimed at offering a truthful account of events that citizens need, then how is that NOT journalism? Even so, we acknowledge the difficulty in separating "professional"—connoting adherence to a certain set of standards—from "journalism"—which we think refers to a set of procedures. What we, Kovach and Rosenstiel, and many others in journalism have in common is a tendency to slide back and forth between the egalitarian and expert models and an inclination to talk as much about what journalism *ought* to be or do as what journalism is. (Notice, for example, that elements 5–10 on Kovach and Rosenstiel's list are framed in terms of what journalism "must" do.) One thing is certain: As the opportunities and technical capabilities for more people to do journalism outside of traditional news organizations grow, standards and expectations will change in ways we can't fully anticipate. Some of those changes might even be positive.

In late 2003 and early 2004, the Anuak tribe in Ethiopia lost 425 of its members in a massacre by the Ethiopian military. No one would know about this terrible event if it weren't for The McGill Report, a website run by former *New York Times* reporter Douglas McGill. How he came upon the story and reported it is a fascinating tale (see www.mcgillreport.org for more) that begins with a student in his English as a Second Language class telling him about receiving cellphone calls from friends and family in his village in which he could hear shooting and screaming, and eventually leads to McGill traveling to Ethiopia to interview witnesses and survivors. Even with the accounts of dozens of people and a separate investigation by Genocide Watch confirming many of the details, McGill could not get more traditional news organizations to publish information about the massacre. Why not? Without the confirmation of high government officials, McGill's story didn't meet the demands of those news organizations' verification processes or, really, their definition of "journalism."

▶ ENOUGH ALREADY! WHAT'S THE ANSWER?

Ultimately, who gets to say what journalism is? The power to define is, indeed, power. Scholar Andrew Cline comes down on the side of the public, saying that who counts as a journalist "should arise primarily from the experiences of a public that uses journalism as a civically important text." That means that journalists alone don't get to decide what journalism is; the public is part of any defining process. As Cline goes on to say, "Journalists produce journalism for citizens, and citizens use journalism for public purposes" (p. 295). That relationship creates obligations for both journalists and for the public. Those obligations and the ethical issues arising from them will be discussed later. For now, let's reprise our definition of journalism:

> Journalism is a set of transparent, independent procedures aimed at gathering, verifying and reporting truthful information of consequence to citizens in a democracy.

It's not perfect, and it's only the beginning of the story. We have a lot more refining and elaborating to do in the rest of the book.

Chapter Two Review

Chapter Summary

Activities

Discussion/Debate Questions

Read More

▶ CHAPTER SUMMARY

Defining what is—and is not—journalism is a difficult task indeed, but an important one. While scholars, journalists and even the courts offer a variety of definitions, it's best to focus on the unique values that distinguish journalism from other forms of mass communication. The work of Kovach and Rosenstiel provides a great foundation for a working definition by declaring initially that journalism is a truth-seeking endeavor, addressed to citizens in a democracy. In order to perform such democratic truth seeking, journalism requires verification and independence. Each value forms a key part of a working definition of journalism:

> Journalism is a set of transparent, independent procedures aimed at gathering, verifying and reporting truthful information of consequence to citizens in a democracy.

▶ ACTIVITIES

1. Parking on campus. On virtually every campus, students think it's too expensive, too inconvenient and too limited. Gather into small groups to discuss this project. Using Kovach and Rosenstiel's elements as a guide, half of the groups should tackle this problem: How would you get at the "truth" if assigned to write this story? What facts would you gather and from whom? Which facts, if left out, would compromise the truth? The other half of the groups can examine the issue using the discipline of verification. Are the students off base in their thinking? How could you verify whether student opinion is correct? Discuss your ideas with the entire class.

2. To illustrate the confusing mix of news, punditry and advocacy, select a hot-button topic in your community (one example was a debate over a proposed "fair tax" in Missouri) and have students search online for information. This activity works well with pairs or small groups. First, make an unfiltered Google search for the information on the issue. Critically evaluate the content you find. How much of it is true journalism? How much of it masquerades as journalism, but is really advocacy? What role do social networks pay in the discussion? Next, limit your search to the "News" results from Google and then carry out a directed search on a local newspaper online archive or a news database such as Lexis/Nexis. How do the quality, tone and structure of the information they find differ based on limiting the search to established news outlets? Post your thoughts in a discussion board (online) or share with the class (group discussion).

3. Invite a journalist and a local newsmaker (politician, official, etc.) to class and interview them about how they define journalism and journalism's role in democracy. Read this chapter and prepare questions for each about journalistic independence, verification, transparency and truth-seeking. How do their perceptions of these journalistic conventions and role of the profession differ? How are they similar?

4. Find the NPR ethics guidelines at http://ethics.npr.org. Under "Impartiality," several guidelines talk about journalistic independence and the appearance of objectivity. Choose one guideline (for example: "Don't sign, don't advocate, don't donate") and discuss your reactions to it in small groups for a few minutes. Then discuss among the class whether the policy goes too far, not far enough or is just right. Why might the NPR guidelines be tougher in this area than those of other U.S. news outlets? Now consider reporters covering sports, fashion or entertainment. Should they be held to the same standards as those covering politics? Does a one-size-fits-all policy work?

5. Find a breaking news story online on a major news outlet (CNN, a national newspaper, ESPN.com). Note the attribution (sources quoted or paraphrased) used in the story. How many sources are used? What percentage of the story is attributed? Now find people writing about the same story on Twitter, Facebook or on a general blog site. Does the attribution differ on these posts from the writing for the traditional news outlets? Post your findings to the class discussion board, then examine what others have posted. Be sure to also discuss how attribution is related to the definition of journalism discussed at the start of this chapter.

▶ DISCUSSION/DEBATE QUESTIONS

1. Think back to the *Rolling Stone* example at the start of this chapter. How might the magazine's search for a "perfect" victim to be the face of the campus rape problem have shaped or skewed how they reported the story? What pressures might the journalist have felt to protect "Jackie"?

2. Unlike physicians, lawyers, teachers and electricians, journalists do not need to be licensed or pass a test to practice their profession. Is this good or bad for journalism? Good or bad for U.S. democracy? If journalists had to pass one test to enter the profession, what kinds of things

would they be required to know? What kinds of skills would they need to have?

3. What news outlets or organizations do you consider the most accurate and credible? Which do you see as lacking credibility? What drives this perception? Is it the kinds of stories they cover? Is it because you agree with their political point of view? Is it the quality of their writing/reporting?

4. What do journalists mean by "transparency"? Is it simply crediting sources or something more? Why is transparency important in journalism?

5. Are standards of journalism the same for newspapers, magazines, radio, television and the Internet? If not, should they be? What about journalists and news outlets that use Twitter—should they be held to journalistic standards of verification, transparency, accuracy, etc.? Why?

▶ READ MORE

Joan Biskupic, Janet Roberts and John Shiffman, "The Echo Chamber," Reuters.com, December 8, 2014, accessed June 22, 2015. www.reuters.com/investigates/special-report/scotus/.

Andrew R. Cline, "Death in Gambella: What Many Heard, What One Blogger Saw, and Why the Professional News Media Ignored it," *Journal of Mass Media Ethics* 22 (2007): 280–299.

Sheila Coronel, Steve Colland and Derek Kravitz, "Rolling Stone and UVA: The Columbia University Graduate School of Journalism Report: An Anatomy of a Journalistic Failure," *Rolling Stone*, April 5, 2015, accessed June 22, 2015. www.rollingstone.com/culture/features/a-rape-on-campus-what-went-wrong-20150405.

Michael Fancher, "What Independence Means to This Paper," *Seattle Times*, January 30, 2005, accessed June 21, 2012. http://seattletimes.nwsource.com/html/localnews/2002164845_fancher30.html.

Pew Research Center's Project for Excellence in Journalism, "Principles of Journalism," accessed June 21, 2012. http://www.journalism.org/resources/principles.

Leonard Pitts, Jr., "Why Citizen Journalism Doesn't Measure Up," *The Dallas Morning News*, October 6, 2010, accessed June 21, 2012. www.dallasnews.com/opinion/latest-columns/20101006-Leonard-Pitts-Why-citizen-1722.ece.

James Poniewozik, "If the Journalism Business Fails, Who Pays for Journalism?" Time.com, June 8, 2009, accessed June 21, 2012. http://entertainment.time.com/2009/06/08/if-the-journalism-business-fails-who-pays-for-journalism/.

Clay Shirky, "The Columbia Report on Rolling Stone's Rape Story is Bad for Journalism," *New Republic*, April 7, 2015, accessed June 22, 2015. www.newrepublic.com/article/121475/columbias-journalism-school-didnt-need-issue-report-rolling.

Judith Shulevitz, "What Happened at Rolling Stone Was Not Jackie's Fault," *Columbia Journalism Review*, December 6, 2014, accessed June 22, 2015. www.cjr.org/watchdog/rolling_stone_sabrina_rubin_erdely.php.

"This is NPR. And These are the Standards of Our Journalism," accessed June 21, 2012. www.npr.org/about/aboutnpr/ethics/.

Erik Ugland and Jennifer Henderson, "Who Is a Journalist and Why Does It Matter? Disentangling the Legal and Ethical Arguments," *Journal of Mass Media Ethics* 22 (2007): 241–261.

How Is News Made?

Tony Barnhart, otherwise known as "Mr. College Football," is a one-man social media wrecking crew. Barnhart, a longtime college football reporter for the *Atlanta Journal-Constitution*, currently serves as a contributing columnist for the *AJC* and for SECSports.com. He's a studio analyst for the SEC Network as well. He's hosted and co-hosted a dozen other football shows on TV and on the radio through the years. He's the author of five books on college football. He's a lifer, the sort of journalist you can build a newsroom around.

He's also a blogging, tweeting machine. His 101,000-plus followers on Twitter engage with him hundreds of times a day, as he feeds the insatiable hunger for college football news. Barnhart is a classic example of how newsgathering has changed, and how the best journalists have changed right along with it, embracing new tools while remaining true to the shoe leather reporting that fuels their best work.

Barnhart began his career in 1976 on a manual typewriter and sent copy on an old telecopier he lugged from stadium to stadium; today he lives on a laptop, a smartphone, and an iPad.

LEARNING OBJECTIVES

▼

Examine the ways news is made, and note how newsgathering is changing;

▼

Identify newsgathering in the broader world of mass communications;

▼

Think about what changes in news processes are doing to the principles of good journalism;

▼

Reconcile newsgathering with current forces shaping the media economy.

He's a one-man operation these days, having taken the leap from the *AJC* in one of its rounds of buyouts and set out on his own. He could make it largely because his was a personal brand, one built through years of reportage from across the SEC. Today, he's synonymous with college football, but Mr. College Football also offers very real life lessons for young journalists.

First, he says, "Learn how to do everything."

"You may very well start off covering a local beat, but start picking up other skills as you go," he said. "The fundamentals don't change, but the ways in which we deliver news have changed drastically. Twitter made no sense to me until I saw how I could link to my work and drive traffic to my columns, and I began to see quickly how I could go directly to the readers."

Today, you're likely to find Barnhart tweeting live from SEC football games, then filing a column for the *AJC* site and appearing later that day on the SEC Network. He uses multimedia in much the same way that he once used a reporter's notebook, compiling information that might find its way into the print edition.

"I'm still a reporter at the end of the day," Barnhart said. "Nothing changes where my reporting is concerned. I'm just taking advantage of the tools available to me to tell stories and get direct feedback from the audience."

Emerging Storytelling Forms

Nate Skid, a video production manager at *Advertising Age*, directs video strategy for one of the world's most venerable trade publications.

Skid began his career seven years ago as a reporter and multimedia editor for *Crain's Detroit Business*, where he covered restaurants, the music business and oversaw the publication's multimedia efforts before moving to *Advertising Age*.

Today, Skid works with reporters as well as the advertising staff to produce custom, sponsored and editorial videos. He tells video stories about advertising, and evangelizes about video throughout the newsroom. It's a role that didn't exist at *Advertising Age* until Skid was brought in to create it himself.

So what's a typical assignment for a video production manager? It depends on the day. Skid just returned from Rome, Bucharest and Berlin where he shot a video on one of MasterCard's "Priceless Moments" spots. ESPN had approached Skid seeking a way to spotlight winning marketing campaigns—from Frito-Lay to MasterCard.

He pitched a behind-the-scenes look at the "Priceless Moments" campaign, which surprises MasterCard cardholders with once-in-a-lifetime experiences. He maintained editorial control for *Advertising Age* throughout—this was coverage of a campaign, after all—and now that he has the footage in the can, the hunt begins by the *Ad Age* sales team for a sponsor.

"We all see the ads, we all see the work, but consumers just don't know how it all works behind the scene," he said. "MasterCard is not happy—at all—with the stuff, either. They thought it was a bit too behind-the-scenes for their taste."

Another series, "Explain It Like I'm Eight," sponsored by the Mobile Majority (an $86,000 sponsorship, at that) uses an eight-year-old kid to demystify advertising lingo.

Skid's job—a rich mix of journalism, filmmaking and deal making—came about because *Advertising Age* created the job for him. It did not exist until his skill set came to the fore. A journalist by training and inclination, he now thinks at least as much about the business side as the editorial side of video content.

"To produce video, you have to find sustainable revenue models—you have to come up with a strategy to make all the upfront costs of video production pay for itself down the road," Skid said. "Rather than do sporadic, on-off videos, I thought of *Advertising Age* in network terms. If *Advertising Age* were a network, what would we produce? And how would we get it make money for the company?"

In 2015, Skid's video unit has brought in $486,000 in new revenue from video alone. All from a Missouri School of Journalism graduate who readily admits that he never dreamt of such a job.

"I shot a little in school, but when I got to *Crain's Detroit*, I saw that I would need to get a lot better at it, so I just began to experiment, and now, here I am the go-to guy for video," he said.

Skid's day is a hodgepodge of shoots, edits, audio that is not married to video, footage needing organization and narrative in need of writing, all while he works across the newsroom with the creative director, managing editor, sale staff and reporters—getting buy-in from them for his projects and getting reporters to embrace video in their coverage areas. At the end of the day, though, Skid says he remains a writer.

"I am willing to try things that better tell the story, and that sometimes means I will grab a new tool, but when it all comes down to the story, I am practicing journalism, just like I did when all I had was a pen and paper," he says. "The questions that are asked, and the documents that are relied upon, and the sources I use, none of that changes."

Skid said that his days as a beat reporter prepared him for this moment.

"Learning how to craft a well developed, readable story is the key to it all," he said. "Starting out that's the most important thing to learn, because it all grows from that."

"I came out of school with my eyes wide open, and hungry. I did not know I would be doing what I am doing, but the business has moved this way and I have developed new skills to meet it."

▶ TOOLS CHANGE, AUDIENCES CHANGE. THE WORK DOESN'T.

OK, so Skid and Barnhart are picking up new skills and advancing their careers by embracing the newest techniques in newsgathering—and that is great. The tools of the profession do change—the School of Journalism at Missouri once had a thriving linotype program, after all—but it's important to think about where journalism has come from in order to understand where it might be headed.

In speaking with scores of journalists, young and old, tech-savvy and just learning, a few trends emerge about the way news is made these days. Journalists tell us that the more things change, the more they need the basics: persistence, enterprise, a love of fact, and the willingness to dig and to ask tough questions of those in power. Whether on Twitter or through a crowdsourcing site, on video, the Web or in print, journalism retains its first principles. In other words, even while the form of journalism changes fundamentally, the process changes only slightly—and its values don't change at all.

Recall the definition we came up with in the previous chapter:

> Journalism is a set of transparent, independent procedures aimed at gathering, verifying and reporting truthful information of consequence to citizens in a democracy.

It's comforting to think that while digital media certainly have sped up the process of newsgathering, increased opportunities for transparency and widened the possibilities as far as distributing news, those in the business of making news stress the purpose of journalism and, therefore, the

FIGURE 3.1 New ways of gathering and delivering information are threatening to take over the old. Whether and how printed newspapers will survive in the online era is a topic of great speculation and anxiety in the industry.
Source: GaudiLab/Shutterstock.

fundamental principles underlying it, haven't changed—and if they *have* changed, that should sound alarm bells. Could it be possible for an industry in the throes of such cataclysmic change to keep its soul intact?

We believe the answer is yes. And not just because we are wishful thinkers who believe it's essential to democratic society for the answer to be yes. We see "yes" in the work Barnhart and Skid and scores of other journalists are doing. We see "yes" in the way those journalists are making sense of the flood of news and information, not getting washed away by it.

▶ INFORMATION, NEWS AND JOURNALISM

Notice how we just said journalists make sense of news and information. That implies that news and information are two different things. Notice also how we describe what journalists are doing as sense making. That sounds like some sort of process, doesn't it? When we talked briefly about news in the last chapter, we pointed out that it is *constructed*; it's not just like a penny on the sidewalk waiting for someone to walk by and pick it up. We'll expand on that construction idea a bit here and throw "information"— sort of the raw material for news—into the mix for good measure. The basic idea is this: Information, news and journalism are not synonyms. News might bear a striking resemblance to information sometimes, and journalism might get talked about as though it's news. But journalism must be understood as distinct from both. That distinction is all in the process and the principles.

Let's try to begin making some distinctions through an example. Take this Al-Jazeera story that ran May 21, 2012:

> At least four explosions have hit separate areas in the Iraqi capital Baghdad, killing at least 37 people and injuring several others, police sources told Al-Jazeera. The first car bomb blast hit a crowded popular market in a predominantly Shia neighbourhood in Baghdad, killing at least 18 people, authorities said.

That's information: It gives us details about events on the ground as they happen. Back when journalists were the major providers of news, particularly about faraway events, that sort of information came almost exclusively from news organizations. In today's world of information surplus, that which we perceive as news comes from a rushing flood of sources, from our Twitter account to our Facebook page to an incoming text. And that includes information from around the world, not just around the corner.

No longer owned or even significantly controlled by media organizations, information has become a commodity—a product that news consumers don't want to pay for because they can get it free from so many different channels. Information transmission is what the Internet perfected.

◄ **COMMODITY:** A product, usually produced and/or sold by many different companies that is uniform in quality and thus driven entirely by price.

There's also a way in which that Al-Jazeera story is news. How so? Because Al-Jazeera took some facts—some information—and put them together in a specific way. They (and other news organizations) decided that what was happening in Iraq was important, so they reported it. They *decided* it was news. The journalistic process transformed the raw information into news. Decisions were made as to the newsworthiness of the material by journalists who have keenly developed news judgment, honed through years of evaluating just such stories.

Is that really necessary? Couldn't people just put all that information swirling around the Internet together for themselves? Theoretically, of course they could (and sometimes do). But practically? That's quite a lot to do, because information alone tells us very little. The Iraq story is a perfect example: these sorts of attacks have been raging in Iraq for years, but even against the backdrop of all that violence, the attacks of late have taken on a different flavor, as the story mentions:

> The violence is part of ongoing clashes between ISIL (Islamic State of Iraq and the Levant) and government forces, who have been cutting the supply lines of the armed group, isolating the cities of Ramadi and Fallujah.

The story mentions that ISIL and government forces have been stepping up combat in recent weeks. That is, the battles and suicide bombings that happened before July 22, 2015 were important context—bits of information put together in a certain way—for what happened on that day.

Let's turn to a story that made national headlines for days—the death of Sandra Bland in a Texas jail after her arrest during a traffic stop. Bland's death generated a great deal of outrage, resulting in the release of the dash-cam video of her arrest. The now-infamous video posted online by the Texas Department of Public Safety shows the trooper stopping Bland for failure to signal a lane change. After he hands her a ticket, the trooper remarks that Bland seems irritated. Bland says she is irritated because she was ticketed after changing lanes to get out of the path of the trooper's car.

The video shows a routine traffic stop that became confrontational when the officer asks Bland to put out a cigarette. She asks why, and the trooper then orders her out of the car. She tells him she doesn't have to step out, and he continues to yell at her. At one point, he pulls a stun gun and says, "I will light you up." After she finally steps out of the vehicle, the trooper orders her to the side of the road, where the confrontation continues off-camera but is still audible. The officer says in an arrest affidavit that she swung her elbows at him and kicked his shin after being handcuffed.

Police said they found the 28-year-old dead after she hanged herself with a plastic bag inside the Waller County Jail, where she was incarcerated after allegedly assaulting an officer during that traffic stop. Her family refused to believe the police and critics demanded an independent investigation.

Once the video was released, we begin to see pieces of the story added day by day, hour by hour. NBC News reported that an autopsy revealed scars consistent with cutting attempts. The Associated Press added that an assistant district attorney said preliminary tests found marijuana in Bland's system, although he said investigators had not determined how long it was there or whether it played a role in her death.

Pressure increased on the police department in Waller County, Texas, until the decision was made two days later to investigate Bland's death like a murder. Later came assessment of Bland's arrest, the suspension of the arresting officer, the level of training in mental health issues by guards in the facility—each new story adding depth and nuance to what we knew before.

See how information becomes breaking news, and those fast-moving, seemingly random events on the ground begin to take shape as the procedures of journalism are applied to information? Journalists pointed to events in Texas and Iraq as news and then gathered information—facts and context—to make sense of those events for their audiences.

In an age of information surplus—of news as commodity—journalists must become the processors of news, and in that process they must take that news flood and organize it, synthesize it, digest it and make it engaging as well as informative. Wow, that's some task! But it's always been journalism's core job to get it right, to bring meaning to the day's events. It's just that now journalists no longer need worry themselves with who got the news first, because it most likely was not a media actor at all. The origination of news, so important in the rise of the mass media, no longer matters as much. In a world in which news travels the world in the blink of an SMS message, journalism, fueled by reporting, takes on added importance.

Don't be fooled by the volume and accessibility of information. It's tempting to see a cascading Twitter feed as a substitute for journalism, but it's not. Without journalism, what we have is lots of information vying for dominance, untested, unvetted, and often coming from people wishing to persuade rather than inform. That's why it's important to think about the process of news: so you can start to understand how and why it differs from other forms of communication.

▶ SO WHERE DOES NEWS COME FROM?

There's still a missing piece in our discussion so far: How does something get called "news" in the first place? How and why did journalists "construct" the events in Iraq or Texas as news? Ask a non-journalist and you'll likely hear something sort of clichéd, like "If it bleeds, it leads," or "Sex sells." Ask a journalist the same question and you'll likely get an equally simplistic response: "Because it's news." Indeed, perhaps the greatest source of misunderstanding between journalists and their critics lies in the selection of news. Arguments abound over whether the news includes too much of this or too little of that.

Newsworthiness defies simple explanation, yet if we cannot tell our audience what constitutes news, how can we expect to defend where our news judgment takes us? We'll start by harkening back to what you learned in Chapter 1 about the functions journalism performs. Informing, investigating, creating conversation and so on suggest a set of criteria journalists use to make news judgments—the kinds of information and events that self-governing people need will (or ought to) make the cut as "news," right? But those functions don't offer a complete description of the criteria.

Scholars, critics and long-time observers of the news have identified a number of factors that seem to influence what becomes news. Journalists' reliance on these "news values," as the factors are called, offers us a way to discuss the first step in how news is made—its selection as news. It's not surprising, really, that the way journalists select news is not so different from the way the rest of us perceive and discuss the world. Keep in mind, though, that while the following list does a good job of *describing* the factors that make up news judgment, it isn't necessarily meant to *prescribe* them. In fact, a couple of the items on the list are a bit problematic, as you'll discover in later chapters. But let's not get ahead of ourselves. In no particular order, the news values are:

▶ **Timeliness** (Immediacy) News isn't news, we often are told, if it is not of recent vintage. In today's 24/7 media landscape, it's stressed more than ever before. It also underscores the tyranny of the deadline: less and less time to acquire different viewpoints from multiple sources, to verify, to fact-check.

▶ **Impact** Impact describes an issue's effect on the public. The number of people affected by a news event can be an important part of the equation, but it's more than mere numbers—it's more of a judgment call on how many members of the audience are likely to be interested in the story.

▶ **Currency** Articles with currency describe ongoing issues, using the ongoing nature of the story to maximum advantage. If it happened today, it's news. If the same thing happened last week, it's no longer interesting, unless people can't stop talking about it.

▶ **Conflict** Perhaps the most common news value, conflict appears in nearly every imaginable story as reporters question who benefits or suffers and who is involved. Conflict often provides action, villains and heroes . . . the stuff of storytelling!

▶ **Novelty/Emotions** Don't underestimate the power of human interest in news selection. An unusual aspect to a story often gets coverage. In fact, human interest stories often cause news organizations to disregard the main rules of newsworthiness: for example, they don't date as quickly, they need not affect a large number of people, and it may not matter where in the world the story takes place.

▶ **Prominence** Behold the power of fame. Prominent individuals, such as politicians, celebrities and athletes often receive coverage by virtue of their position in society.

▶ **Proximity** News events in areas close to the audience are considered to be more relevant than events further away. The emphasis on geographic proximity is being challenged by the borderless nature of online communication, but local news still drives much of the news agenda.

Just as reporters use news values to select news, editors use news values to determine where and how prominently news will be played. Typically, articles containing multiple news values are more likely to appear in more prominent roles in the news product.

This list is not used as a checklist, and journalists exercise a great deal of independent judgment when selecting news events for coverage. Still, much that appears in daily journalism ticks off one or more of these values.

▶ THE NUTS AND BOLTS OF NEWS GATHERING

Much of what becomes today's news originates with press releases, government press conferences, legislative hearings, court hearings and the like—far too often, with what the historian Daniel Boorstin called "pseudo events." In newsrooms across the country, journalists monitor these developments and select from an ever-growing pile of press releases, notices, incoming e-mails and phone calls alerting them to potential news. So journalists are culling through mountains of information, choosing the best bits and passing them along.

◀ **PSEUDO EVENTS:** A term popularized by the historian Daniel J. Boorstin, describing events or activities that serve little to no purpose other than to be reproduced through advertisements or other forms of publicity.

Journalists also produce what are called *enterprise stories*—stories that rely upon sources they have developed through their area of coverage, or beat, to keep them informed and pass along news items to create original works of journalism.

Stories—the currency of journalism—are either assigned by supervisors (editors in the print world; producers in broadcasting, although job titles are fluid these days) or originated by journalists as enterprise stories.

Assignments vary wildly according to medium, beat, reporter expertise or even the time of day, for that matter. If you're the night police reporter, and a crime suddenly hits the scanner in the newsroom, guess whose assignment it is?

▶ **BEAT:** A specific topic area of news coverage, such as the police beat or the local government beat.

The life of a story, from origination to distribution, depends as well on a number of things. If the story concerns what we call breaking news—a sudden, compelling news event such as a multi-vehicle accident on the main thoroughfare through town, a sports star's sudden departure for another franchise, or an unexpected hailstorm that tears through the city—things are moving fast and the process will be as short as a few hours.

On the other hand, enterprise stories and even some assignments require serious research and preparation, multiple interviews with several sources, time spent with a subject observing and follow-up interviews to nail the story down and get it straight.

Longer, more detailed stories may involve multiple drafts, and editors look for holes, logical problems and missing angles at each turn. Often, reporters are sent back to the field for additional reporting and fact-checking, before a story is deemed finished.

3.1 THE VIEW FROM THE PROS: THE ACTIVE AUDIENCE

At Nevada Public Radio, audience engagement is something that's always in the back of our minds. Our flagship daily program, *State of Nevada*, relies on audience participation and feedback to be successful. We invite our listeners to call into our program and ask questions of our guests, or provide some kind of counterpoint to the discussion being held on the air.

Engaging the audience in the most effective way, however, requires good judgment. For example, we choose not to open every segment up to calls. We don't really need to have people call in to a discussion with, say, someone from the health department about why rates of sexually transmitted infections are on the rise. But a debate on Common Core learning standards is enhanced by hearing our listeners—like parents who send their kids to public schools—

give their perspectives. While the decision-making process about which segments to solicit feedback for is a bit ad-hoc, you tend to develop a sort of sixth sense about which segments people will call in for and which ones they won't.

We also screen every call that comes in during the broadcast to see what the caller wants to talk about. Oftentimes, the caller will have a point that we want to bring up at some point during the conversation anyway, so we use them as a segue to get to that point. Sometimes, the caller will bring something to the table we didn't even think of, which often has us scrambling to figure out how quickly we can put them on the air. Perhaps luckily for us, it's very rare we get someone who wants simply to rant or to yell. When that does happen, we politely explain we might not get to their call during the segment and invite them to comment by going online.

Take the debate on Common Core I mentioned earlier. Because we felt there was such rancor, discord and—frankly—disinformation over Common Core, we wanted to take a big picture approach. We wanted to look at what exactly Common Core is, how it has worked in some states, why the federal government is encouraging these standards (if it actually is), and so on. Accordingly, we were pretty heavy with expert opinion in the segment, and we felt we did a good job talking about the nuts and bolts of Common Core.

Not everyone shared our pleasure. We invited groups who were steadfastly against the standards to participate in our segment, but none responded in enough time to take part. Naturally, then, we got a lot of feedback from listeners saying we didn't have enough contrary voices. And those groups who oppose the standards but didn't respond quickly enough to be on the air with us? They also called in to say we were too supportive of Common Core. Another complaint we got was that we didn't have any actual teachers on the program as guests. Of course, this is a problem when you have a show airing in the morning during the course of a school year, but the complaint had merit. We knew their voices would be ones we wanted to hear too.

All of the audience feedback helped us shape the follow-up program that we knew from the start we wanted to do, but weren't quite sure how. We got really good ideas for other potential guests, and once summertime came and teachers were out of the classroom, we were able to have them share their thoughts about Common Core and the state of education in Nevada.

We try to solicit as much feedback as possible through a number of channels. In addition to encouraging calls, we invite our listeners to tweet at us during the course of each show, and to leave comments on our website. Every story we air has an article online, so people who wish to comment on that story have an easy avenue to do so. Every couple of weeks we try to collect some of the "greatest hits" from the tweets and online comments we receive and read them on-air as part of a mailbag segment. This helps remind people of some of the stories we've covered in recent weeks, potentially driving them back to our website to listen to them if they missed them the first time out.

Although we never want to get too far into the realm of letting listeners dictate what we choose to cover—if we did that, we'd dish up the news equivalent of ice cream every day, and nobody would eat their broccoli—it's still vital to listen to what your audience has to say. Newsrooms can sometimes become very insular places, and sometimes it's easy for us to miss things out there in the rest of the world. Feedback helps keep us honest.

LEARN MORE: To get a flavor of how audiences participate in news making in your community, tune into a local radio or television program that features call-ins from listeners or viewers. What sorts of topics are covered? How engaged is the audience? How would you rate the quality of the discussion? Does the audience participate via social media in addition to calling in? If your community doesn't have such a local program, try tuning into the cable station C-SPAN instead. How does C-SPAN's call-in show compare to the one Casey Morell describes in this article?

Casey Morell is the coordinating producer at Nevada Public Radio, based in Las Vegas. He is a graduate of New College of Florida (B.A. '12) and the University of Missouri School of Journalism (M.A. '14).

But that's far from the end of the process. Copy editors then step in, reading microscopically to ensure clarity, grammatical and mechanical cleanliness and last but certainly not least, compliance with Associated Press style, the dominant style and usage guide in American newsrooms. Copy editors often also create headlines, photo captions and other news elements.

If the story concerns, say, the federal budget, there may be a need for a news artist to produce a compelling graphic representation of the budget, before the whole package is delivered to news designers, who maximize the layout of the piece within the news product.

Broadcasting's use of more extensive technology and its dependence upon a finite time period, alter the way that news is gathered and presented. Television reporters, working with producers, often spend most of the day away from the station, getting footage shot on location for the stories that will appear that night.

▶ **PACKAGE:** An edited set of video clips for a broadcast news story.

Time dictates that broadcast news be written and edited down to the second, with no room for error. That makes for a lively, and at times chaotic, work environment as producers and editors work on editing packages to fit, adding voiceovers and graphics as they go. News directors oversee the process, supervising reporters and producers and consulting with the news anchors on the upcoming show. The anchors await the completion of the packages before going on air to present the news.

We could move from broadcasting to radio and magazines, detailing the news production process, but at this point, you should know that the newsgathering process differs only in form, not in function. Sure, significant differences emerge between daily newspaper stories, radio stories and long-form magazine articles, for example, but did the process of originating the content for any of those stories vary drastically? Not really.

The process of magazine news production differs from other media forms, of course, as does radio news and online news, thanks to size and time constraints, audience segmentation, market, and a host of other variables, but we'd be remiss if we didn't instead turn our attention to the news here—because all of the various forms of news production have felt the changes ushered in by digital technologies to various degrees.

The actual process of creating news reflects many of the changes transforming the business of journalism these days. News organizations have been famously slow to grasp the extent to which digital media are changing the process, but signs clearly point to a long-awaited awakening on the part of the profession.

The question is whether it's too little, too late, and whether new technologies will strengthen or threaten traditional newsgathering. The early results are a mix of promise and peril. Much about online journalism can be seen as a beacon of hope, from its emphasis on innovation to the interactivity fostered between news consumers and audiences.

FIGURE 3.2 Mobile devices such as tablets are among the newest platforms for reporting and receiving news.
Source: Denys Prykhodov/Shutterstock.

▶ NEWS: NOT JUST LIKE ANY OTHER PRODUCT

A prevailing myth underscores much of the discussion of journalism: that because news is the product of a predictable, replicable series of processes, it is "made" just like other consumer products. This reduces a craft to a factory line, and excuses a lot of behavior damaging to journalism itself. And as journalism's production and distribution models have come under evolutionary stress in recent years, many observers have looked at all that change and concluded that if the process has changed, then the values undergirding the profession must be changing as well.

While that's certainly possible, it doesn't have to be. The *Dallas Morning News*' series (see Sidebar 3.2) is a fine example: Much was different about the way the reporters and editors on the series did their jobs, until you drill down to the reporting itself. That reporting—from the identification and interviewing of a whistleblower reluctant to talk, to battles with the hospital over documents, to scores of interviews with officials and former patients—is the way journalism is "made." The process changes daily with each story, to say nothing of each new technology. Yet its core remains the work of reporters and editors—the shoe leather reporting, the documents, finding the elusive eyewitness. Amid all the change, some things remain unchanged.

3.2 THE VIEW FROM THE PROS: CONTINUAL NEWSGATHERING

Maud Beelman is a great interviewer, and a fine example of a journalist wrestling with what all of this change means, at the end of the day. Beelman is a deputy managing editor at the *Dallas Morning News*, where she directs a team of investigative and special projects reporters on major long-term news stories.

Beelman—who, as the founding director of the International Consortium of Investigative Journalists at the Center for Public Integrity in Washington, D.C., won a George Polk, an Investigative Reporters and Editors, and a Society of Professional Journalists' award for investigative reporting—also spent 14 years reporting for Associated Press in the United States and abroad. She's covered German unification, reported from Iran and Iraq on the aftermath of the first Gulf War and spent five years covering the wars in the former Yugoslavia. In short, she's a lifer—a journalist who has worked throughout all of the changes we are discussing in this book.

In a 2010 series for the *Morning News*, "First, Do No Harm," the newspaper demonstrated its embrace of all that is new in the delivery of journalism, while also demonstrating the craft itself, strengthened, perhaps, but otherwise unchanged by technology.

The story focused on a pair of venerable Dallas institutions: the University of Texas Southwestern Medical Center and Parkland Memorial Hospital. A renowned medical campus long known for world-class research and residency programs that have turned out generations of excellent doctors, Parkland is the main training ground for the school's new doctors. As a public hospital and major trauma center, it is also a safety net for the region's most vulnerable patients. In other words, it's a sacred cow, and a pretty important one, too.

The *Morning News'* stories began as so many great journalistic projects do—with a tip from a source, pointing reporters to a lawsuit from a whistleblower inside the hospital system upset with what he was experiencing.

"Fifteen stories later, we found a system that for decades had deceived virtually all of its patients, put many at risk and, by the hospital's own estimate, seriously and often needlessly harmed on average two people a day," Beelman said.

The "stuff" of the investigation came from the lifeblood of journalism: sources and records. Reporters obtained internal records from the two institutions, sworn testimony by current and former employees and records stemming from federal inquiries. The documents led the reporters to people—patients harmed by loosely supervised residents and what the newspaper described as "a class-based culture of care."

Among the stories' findings:

- Most of the patient care at Parkland was delivered by doctors in training—first-year interns and other residents. Some patient care was even handled by students who had not yet graduated from medical school.
- Patients were harmed during surgeries by resident physicians, including a young mother whose common bile duct was severed during a gall bladder operation and a former Parkland employee who eventually had her leg amputated after knee-replacement and post-surgical care provided, in part, by medical students.

It's a heavy-hitting, serious piece of journalism. Was it altered at all by the digital arena? Sure it was. Beelman said the entire package was produced with a Web-first mentality, which affected everything from the way the stories were approached to the deadlines to story length.

"We did not handle this as a traditional investigation," Beelman said. "Before the Internet, we would have done the research, then the reporting, then the writing, and then we would have dropped a huge Sunday piece on people's doorsteps," she said.

Instead, the *Morning News'* approach was to continually research, report, and when ready, write—then publish online and in print.

"The Web places a certain discipline on you," she said.

We knew we had to publish bite-sized pieces of this stuff, and we knew we needed video and accompanying documents online as the stories broke on print. So rather than wait for the whole package to go into one giant "poodle killer," as we always called those massive Sunday papers, we saw it evolve into this continual process of newsgathering.

From this myth about the news "product," flow other misconceptions about journalism, journalists and the news, some of which have done real damage to the craft. For if news is "made" like any other consumer product, its production can be forever streamlined, tightened, its processes refined by the technology available to it, with the goal of producing the news as cheaply and efficiently as possible. A journalism slave to the interests of a narrow class of corporate owners can be every bit as endangered as journalism captive to the whims of a totalitarian government.

The concept of news as product began, as the scholar Stuart Allan noted most precisely in *News Culture*, as a reflection of the economic interests of publishers intent on capturing an emerging working-class readership in Industrial Revolution America, and in Allan's United Kingdom. To capture that mass market, both the "penny press" of America and the "pauper press" in Britain worked to reach the maximum number of readers. This led to the evolution of a press dedicated to notions of objectivity, which we'll turn to in greater detail later.

Many of the ways in which the American media landscape formed are in tension with each other. Capitalism has played a role in American journalism since its founding days, and much of what is laudable about capitalism supports democratic values: Democracies tend to value openness, transparency of information and unrestrained discussion. On the other hand, when markets become an end in themselves, the technologies we hail as revolutionary can just as easily serve to monopolize information. In this revolutionary period, just like the others preceding it, decisions made about news systems will have much to say about journalism's future.

All this focus on the distribution model clouds the focus on what's really at the heart of this discussion. As we have discussed, journalism's core mission is informing the citizens in a democracy.

3.3 THE VIEW FROM THE PROS: THE GAME HAS CHANGED

It's game day. Fans have been waiting restlessly for this day to come, while you have worked tirelessly on preparations to bring them what they seek. And they are seeking a lot.

In today's world of sports media, those fans are your livelihood. The driving monetary value when delivering information regarding sports no longer lies within the newspaper subscribers, but instead with how many people read online articles in order to drive advertising value. And to become valuable to a publication, aspiring journalists must establish an audience of loyal readers early on in their career.

Twitter is by far the leading social media tool for today's journalists. This holds especially true with sports, as Twitter users tend to follow and "tweet" along with events as they unfold. By creating a substantial following, you, the journalist, are making yourself valuable. When producing and tweeting content for your publication, putting a link in front of as many potential readers as possible is crucial. But how does one produce a following?

Transitioning from personal to professional in all social media, not only Twitter, is key early in one's career. This is not to say you cannot share a Facebook picture of you and your best friend on vacation, or tweet your personal take on any event—sports or not—from your personal accounts. But harnessing and becoming a media provider as opposed to a media consumer as early as possible will establish credibility that can carry on with you throughout your career.

Engage with your audience. If somebody asks you a question, answer it. Do not be shy about following some readers back. Retweet or share other's content even if it is not from your publication. The more you use social media professionally, as a tool of engagement and a digital microphone for your content, the more you'll see an audience grow, making you a valuable commodity to anybody you wind up working for.

Today's sports media also require the young journalist to be multi-lingual across many platforms. Long gone are the days when a sports journalist showed up to a sporting event just before the start, wrote a game story and could casually stroll into a locker room to gather and plug in quotes before sending it off to their editor to work into tomorrow's newspaper. Today a sports journalist shows up hours before a sporting event, works social media prior to start time, provides instant analysis through Twitter, puts together their own photography packages, posts game stories online the second the event ends, updates with quotes as quickly as

possible, provides video interviews to accompany online articles and writes a second day article full of analysis and analytics to go online to feed the need for instant media.

Did you have to catch your breath after reading that last sentence? Good. You're getting the feel for what it's like in the sports media industry.

Going into sports journalism almost always includes the unofficial prerequisite of being a sports fan. Those days of being a fan, however, are put on hold the minute you acquire a job title that includes covering any particular team or sport. Possessing the ability to work in an unbiased atmosphere requires the ability to understand that the work you are doing is just that: work. If this notion is ever doubted, try cheering in the press box, then watch how fast you are escorted out without holding onto that coveted credential around your neck.

Doing this type of work, navigating the seemingly endless platforms has to come as naturally as riding a bicycle. Knowledge of all aspects of social media is crucial. Your employer may ask you one day to ramp up the publication's Instagram account, then the next day ask you to schedule multiple Facebook posts to promote content at specific times to maximize the algorithm that may develop the most viewership. The next day you may be asked to launch a Periscope stream of pre-game warm-ups or post-game interviews, or to answer fans' questions on Twitter during a game.

But when there is no immediate direction, which is usually the case, what do the readers and viewers want to see from you? When is the appropriate time to post something?

An important and helpful rule to consider when keeping an audience engaged while covering an event is to take them behind the scenes with you. The access a credential allows a sports journalist is the same that fans pay or bid large amounts of money to experience. Tweeting out an image or short video of your entrance into the exclusive media gates, or taking your seat in the press box most have never stepped foot into can instantly create the connection between journalist and reader. Images from the field prior to an event are golden, and will not only establish credibility and comfort in the reader knowing you are there, but will keep them wanting to see more. And when they want to see more, they will also click on your content you promote at a later time.

Through today's technology and platforms, the readers are now in the press box seat with you. They will further rely on you to bring them more images and descriptions that they cannot see from the comforts of home or even in their seat at the same event you are covering. Embrace this, and understand that being one with them is far from a bad thing. So many members of the media grow into their jobs thinking they have become above the everyday fan, when the truth is they rely so heavily upon connecting with the everyday fan in order to keep their publications afloat.

Sports media are unique in that deadlines are pushed usually four to five times a day. If your aspirations are to work in journalism only for long form narratives that can stretch from weeks to months for production, cross off sports media from your list immediately. The demands of covering a team, player or event are high and very strenuous. With athletes now controlling their own social media and other platforms, stories can change or develop leading up to a previous deadline. Fans and readers are more engaged than ever, and can often become the story themselves.

As a young sports journalist, however, never lose sight of what brought you there in the first place. The sights, the smells and the prestige of the industry that likely roped you in as a child should never be lost. Sure, you may be writing on a strict deadline while producing a wide range of multimedia during an event as opposed to relaxing in the stands, but these were once your dreams as you gazed into the press box as a kid. Don't ever forget that. And be prepared for rapid changes in the industry day by day, as the next big thing is likely already in the works.

THINK ABOUT IT: Review the Twitter feeds of your favorite sports reporters. How do they interact with their followers? Do you think it makes them better sports journalists? How?

Logan Booker is a graduate of the Grady College of Journalism and Mass Communication at the University of Georgia, where he majored in magazine journalism. He also earned a certificate in the Grady Sports Media program and began his career working with Cox Media Group.

That has not changed, and will not change, no matter how quickly the wheels of modern technology spin. And it is easy to lose sight of that, with so much change afoot. That change, however wrenching and disruptive, is still external, process-oriented change—change to the way in which journalism is made in terms of the parts, the process even, but not the fundamentals. Let us ponder the scope and breadth of the changes transforming journalism, then return to these fundamentals.

Until the turn of the century, news companies found the Internet a sci-fi novelty, a hobby for geeks but hardly worthy of serious journalistic attention. News executives felt that online content cannibalized the print editions of their newspapers and magazines, and television saw no potential for the new medium.

That attitude changed over time, and most news companies began posting content, first in an experimental, on-again, off-again way, then quite seriously, building online news staffs and launching standalone websites. The content began to flow online, and it was all-free, all-the-time—an oft-regretted decision by the industry, as we'll discuss in a following chapter.

As audiences moved to the Internet for their news consumption, the industries that produce news—newspapers, magazines, radio and TV stations and a small band of newly emergent online-only properties—moved with them, although much more slowly and clumsily than the average teenager with a laptop.

Today we see a wild mix of models as news companies begin to revisit the decision to give away all their content, even as a seemingly endless stream of entrants start producing news online. Even though the Web contributes but a fraction of total newspaper advertising, and even less of consumer magazine revenue, the argument over its centrality to journalism's future has concluded: get online or get lost.

Want a sign of just how fast things are changing? In a 2011 column on *New York Times* journalists' use of Twitter, public editor Arthur Brisbane recounted this exchange with the great Nicholas Kristof, one of the world's finest reporters:

> Nicholas Kristof, the Op-Ed columnist (4,242 tweets, 1,036,906 followers), tweeted, blogged and wrote columns inexhaustibly from various hot spots in the Middle East after the revolutions there began. Now, he said, he is planning a possible trip to Mauritania and has used Twitter to query his million-man [sic] follower group in search of expertise on the country—with good results.

Kristof has used it also for something that blogs and columns just aren't appropriate for, he said: publishing a hunch.

"On Twitter in Libya, I tweeted something to the effect that I think people are a little too optimistic," he said. "That proved to be a useful caution. I didn't put it in my column. It didn't fit; I didn't have any evidence for it."

Is Twitter appropriate for "publishing a hunch?" Is any medium? Why is the relevance, the verification of information posted on a medium like Twitter somehow subject to a lower standard of proof, and should it be?

A return to Kovach and Rosenstiel seems a fitting way to conclude this chapter, for a reading of *The Elements of Journalism* certainly lends clarity to all this focus on technology.

Journalism that begins with an obligation to truth seeking, and whose first loyalty is to citizens, they write, depends on an environment in which verification is "the essence" of journalism. Think about that a moment: If we start with the proposition that journalism begins at the moment of verification, what does that tell us about Twitter? Well, that's a tool for disseminating information once it's verified, and not some high-tech shortcut for throwing stuff at the wall to see if it sticks.

And yet we see journalists trying to walk back information they've reported all the time. Instantaneous outlets demand greater emphasis on verification than ever before, not less. With information so free, it's never been more important for journalists to stake out the factual ground, to add meaning and context through their work, and to call attention to the best work of others. Today's journalist plays many roles—part reporter, editor or designer, part curator, part social networker, part thought leader. All of those roles can get confusing, but in the midst of all of these, two simple rules from Kovach and Rosenstiel must remain inviolable:

1. Journalists always verify everything before reporting.

2. Journalists must remain fiercely independent.

To which we add:

3. Journalists must demonstrate their loyalty to citizens by (a) remaining committed to truth-telling and (b) exhibiting a commitment to elevating the discourse.

Much, much more about this as we progress, but for now, it's enough to note that if journalists fulfilled those missions, journalism would come much closer to serving its democratic mission.

Each remains central to journalism connected to democracy building. Each is core to the mission of helping a society govern itself. Each is being buffeted by changes to the form and function of newsgathering.

Chapter Three Review

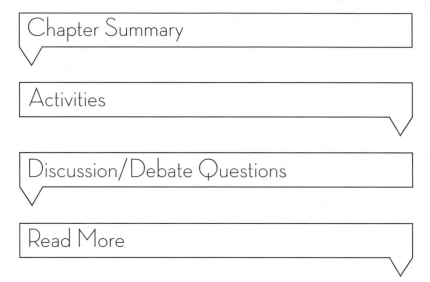

Chapter Summary

Activities

Discussion/Debate Questions

Read More

▶ **CHAPTER SUMMARY**

The best journalists have always kept an open mind and embraced the newest techniques for gathering and presenting information. Today's journalist has more tools at her disposal than ever before. The gatekeeper model of journalism—that once-proud notion of the editor as arbiter of what's news—is long gone. The gatekeeper has yielded to the engagement editor, the digital curator, and the future of journalism looks a lot more conversational these days.

▶ ACTIVITIES

1. When the Pulitzer committee awarded the *Tuscaloosa News* the 2012 prize for breaking news coverage of a devastating local tornado, it cited the paper's social media efforts as a factor in its decision. Read the Twitter feed submitted as part of the entry (www.pulitzer.org/files/2012/breaking_news_reporting/08tuscaloosa.pdf; note: you must read from the bottom up to get the story in correct chronological order). Discuss: How does this type of reporting differ from more traditional reporting? How is it the same? Are the news values similar in this environment? Does this type of reporting enhance or limit our emotional connection to the news? Are the journalists more part of the story than they are in traditional print coverage?

2. Pick a news story that interests you and either bring it to class, or keep it for homework if this activity is an at-home assignment. Analyze the story for the presence of the seven news values (timeliness, impact, currency, conflict, novelty/emotion, prominence and proximity). Instruct them to mark the words or phrases that suggest that these news values are at play in the story. Next, identify the dominant news value in the story (the main reason why the story is news). You can share your results with the class (in-class option) or bring a brief writing summary of your analysis to class (homework option).

3. Invite a local journalist to class (or Skype with a journalist from another community) to talk about how they live-tweet a breaking news event. What information should be included? What writing style is used? What consideration is given to the audience in writing these updates? How do they do the traditional parts of the job (interviewing and taking notes) while still having time to tweet? If a journalist is not available, you likely can find a journalist on Twitter at virtually any point of the day live-tweeting from an event. Follow that feed for a few minutes. Then discuss with the rest of your class the information included, the writing style and whether the journalist is considering his or her followers while posting.

4. Watch how *The Daily Show* critiqued CNN's error in reporting the June 2012 Supreme Court decision on the Obama health care plan (www.hollywoodreporter.com/live-feed/jon-stewart-daily-show-cnn-supreme-court-343537). Discuss: How might the rush to be first have played a part in this error? Why did it take CNN so long to correct the information (compared with Fox)? What are the implications for the credibility of the network? CNN issued an apology, saying: "CNN regrets that it didn't wait to report out the full and complete opinion regarding the mandate. We made a correction within a few minutes and apologize for the error." But that apology didn't stop the harsh criticism leveled by Jon Stewart, other media outlets and the general public. Some asserted that this error would become as well known as the "Dewey Beats Truman" headline. A few years down the road, is that what happened?

5. Replicate the "Cover It Live" real-time reporting experience by covering a television event live on Twitter. Watch a television program (a football game, a speech, even a guest on a late-night talk show) and begin "covering" the event. Create a hashtag and post at least three tweets during the event. What news values did you emphasize in your reporting? What writing style did you use? What thought was given to the audience? Reflect on your experience in a 400-word discussion post on what works well and what doesn't when covering an event with Twitter.

▶ DISCUSSION/DEBATE QUESTIONS

1. Do you think it's challenging for journalists to attune to all aspects their jobs while mastering new reporting and delivery tools? Is it easier or harder for journalists who have been out of school for several decades to adapt to this change? Is this a function of age or personality?

2. Information, news and journalism are not synonyms. But how do they differ? Do audiences understand this distinction?

3. Are certain media better at conveying stories with certain types of news values? For example, is emotion easier to convey through words or moving images? Is timeliness best suited for online? As media organizations converge, how might delivery format affect the types of information conveyed through each format?

4. Similarly, how is medium related to the newsgathering process? Do broadcast journalists gather information differently than print reporters or online journalists? If audiences rely more heavily on print than broadcast for information, how might the news they see differ?

5. What pressures might journalists be under to use Twitter and other media platforms in the same way the general public does? If many people are reporting a rumor, what's wrong with retweeting it? Why should journalists be held to a higher standard?

▶ READ MORE

Stuart Allan, *News Culture*, Berkshire, England: Open University Press, 2010.

Daniel J. Boorstin, *The Image: A Guide to Pseudo-Events in America*, New York: Vintage Books, 1987.

Arthur Brisbane, "A Cocktail Party With Readers," *New York Times*, March 12, 2011. www.nytimes.com/2011/03/13/opinion/13pubed.html?_r=1.

"Car Bombings and Suicide Attacks Kill Dozens in Iraq," Al-Jazeera, July 22, 2015. www.aljazeera.com/news/2015/07/deadly-double-suicide-attacks-rock-iraq-fallujah-150722083024575.html.

"The Changing Newsroom: What Is Being Gained and What Is Being Lost in America's Daily Newspapers?" www.journalism.org/files/PEJ-The%20Changing%20Newspaper%20Newsroom%20FINAL%20DRAFT-NOEMBARGO-PDF.pdf.

Michael Massing, "Digital Journalism: How Good Is It?" *New York Review of Books*, June 5, 2015. www.nybooks.com/articles/archives/2015/jun/04/digital-journalism-how-good-is-it/.

Michael Massing, "Digital Journalism: The Next Generation," *New York Review of Books*, June 25, 2015. www.nybooks.com/articles/archives/2015/jun/25/digital-journalism-next-generation/.

Derek Thompson, "ESPN's Plan to Dominate the Post-TV World", *The Atlantic*, July 9, 2015. www.theatlantic.com/business/archive/2015/07/espn-strategy-mobile-after-tv/397928/?fb_ref=Default.

4

Who Pays for Journalism?

Way back in 2008, the *Orlando Sentinel*'s new owner, Sam Zell, paid a visit to the newspaper. Zell had made his billions in real estate and decided to enter the world of media by acquiring the Tribune Company—publisher of the *Chicago Tribune* and *Los Angeles Times* newspapers, in addition to the *Sentinel* and other media properties—in a deal that saddled the company with a ton of debt and eventually forced it into bankruptcy. Getting into the newspaper business in 2008, just as an historic recession and wave of technological change were creating havoc with newspapers' viability as a business, took some serious guts and/or a healthy ego. Zell had both, along with a very particular vision about how journalism and business mix.

In his remarks to the *Sentinel* staff assembled in the newsroom, Zell talked about innovation and giving readers what they want, which all seemed fine until one of the journalists in the room, photographer Sara Fajardo, asked about how, you know, *journalism* might fit into this plan.

LEARNING OBJECTIVES

▼

See how larger economic forces and structures play out in the news media system;

▼

Explore what it means for the press in the U.S. to be "commercial" and what the implications of a commercial structure are for good journalism practice;

▼

Understand the fundamental tension between profit-making and public service in journalism;

▼

Consider ways in which the Internet is changing and challenging journalism's traditional economic model.

Things got a bit awkward.

Zell's response: "I want to make enough money so that I can afford you. You need to in effect help me by being a journalist that focuses on what our readers want that generates more revenue."

When Fajardo dared to point out that what people want and what they need might be pretty different—people might like stories about puppies more than, say, the Iraq war—Zell called that suggestion "journalistic arrogance" and finished off the cringe-worthy encounter by uttering an obscenity at Fajardo, who shook her head and walked away.

Just another day at the office, right? Thankfully, no. While Zell's obscenity made this incident a minor YouTube sensation, it's the back and forth between Zell and Fajardo that is of key interest to us. Their exchange is an excellent illustration of a fundamental tension in American journalism: the pull of profit in one direction and of public service in the other. In a commercial media system, those interests compete more often than they complement each other, so finding the balance between them (if there is one) is pretty tricky. Look at Zell's quote again: "You need to in effect help me by being a journalist that focuses on what our readers want that generates more revenue."

He is putting profit-making ahead of public service, operating on the logical premise that without money, a news organization wouldn't have the means to perform public service anyway. Fajardo, meanwhile, is rightly concerned that the profit-making motive will take precedence over and even get in the way of the public service mission of journalism. What Zell saw as arrogance, Fajardo saw as duty.

Who's right? Both are, to some extent. That's what we're going to explore in this chapter: Who pays for journalism and what are the implications of paying for it that way? The tension between profit and public service isn't new, but the amount of tension on the rope has perhaps never been greater than it is now. The Zell incident illustrates that and also offers a great example of how a media that enjoys so much freedom from government intrusion is not all that free when one considers the demands that profit-making imposes on it.

FIGURE 4.1 The scope of massive media corporations like Comcast Corp., the largest U.S. cable-television operator, raises a multitude of issues regarding the nature of competition in media markets.
Source: Jerome Kundrotas/Shutterstock.

▶ "THIS NEWS IS BROUGHT TO YOU BY": THE COMMERCIAL MEDIA

So, let's begin at the beginning. The American media system is a commercial one, which means that mass communication is conducted by and through businesses that are owned by individuals, families, or groups of people, perhaps even millions of them (through stocks and mutual funds). Maybe it seems a little simplistic to you to begin at such a basic level. The media are businesses—big surprise. What else would they be? Well, look around the world, and you'll get all kinds of answers. The point is that a commercial media is neither natural nor inevitable. It's also worth noting that there are different types of businesses.

Newspapers got their start as businesses mostly because they were one of many products or services that someone running a printing business offered. This was before the development of reporting and journalism as we know it today. As for broadcasting, consider our friends and former colonial rulers in Great Britain. In both the U.S. and Britain, the invention of radio was hailed as a great step forward in communication, but one that very quickly demonstrated the need for some sort of regulation to deal with all the battles over who got to use which frequency, etc. So the question was how to treat this new invention. Was it like the telegraph or telephone? How should frequencies be doled out? What sort of expectations could the government place on the folks who got a frequency? They were, after all, going to be using something everyone considered to be a public resource: the airwaves.

Almost immediately, the U.S. and British paths diverged. Both were (and are) democracies with capitalist economic systems. Both were considering what to do with radio at pretty much the same time. Debates in both countries centered on which structure—private or public control of media—would best serve the public interest. But in the U.S., those favoring a market-based approach prevailed over those who wanted to keep this public resource public, that is, more under government control. And in Great Britain, just the opposite happened: public (government) ownership and control of media won out over the private ownership, market approach.

**TABLE 4.1
Summary of
Media Models**

	Market Model	*Public Sphere Model*
How are media conceptualized?	Private companies selling products	Public resources serving the public
What is the primary purpose of the media?	Generate profits for owners and stockholders	Promote active citizenship via information, education, and social integration
How are audiences addressed?	As consumers	As citizens
What are the media encouraging people to do?	Enjoy themselves, view ads, and buy products	Learn about their world and be active citizens
What is in the public interest?	Whatever is popular	Diverse, substantive, and innovative content, even if not always popular

	Market Model	*Public Sphere Model*
What is the role of diversity and innovation?	Innovation can be a threat to profit-able, standard-ized formulas. Diversity can be a strategy for reach-ing new niche markets.	Innovation is central to en-gaging citizens. Diversity is central to media's mission of representing the range of the public's views and tastes.
How is regulation perceived?	Mostly seen as interfering with market processes	Useful tool in protecting the public interest
To whom are media ultimately accountable?	Owners and shareholders	The public and government representatives
How is success measured?	Profits	Serving the public interest

Source: *The Business of Media: Corporate Media and the Public Interest* by David Croteau and William Hoynes. Published by Pine Forge Press, 2001. Page 37.

Those approaches formulated in the early part of the 20th Century contin-ued through the invention of television. The dawn of the Internet sparked another "What is it?" debate, with some people arguing that it makes the most sense to treat the Internet, regulation-wise, like the telephone, and others arguing it bears more resemblance to broadcasting or cable televi-sion, and still others saying it's a whole new thing and ought to be treated as such. But let's not get bogged down in that, at least not yet. We first need to think about the advantages and disadvantages of each approach. Is more government involvement better or worse than more market control? Well, that's going to depend on some things, like how you view government and what it is you expect media to do.

In Chapter 1, you read about journalism's unique and important role in de-mocracy and the ways in which that special role is thought to place certain responsibilities for public service on the press. You might also remember that one of the things journalism needs in order to do what democracy requires of it is independence. The First Amendment to the U.S. Constitution guarantees press freedom from government intrusion. (You'll learn more about that in Chapter 6.) There's no guarantee in the Constitution or elsewhere, however, that other things won't inhibit press freedom. Does the need to make a profit sound like something that might constrain freedom? To be sure, any arrangement involves some sort of constraint. The question is what's the source of the constraint and what does it force or prevent journalism from doing?

In the U.S., what we might call the "market" group was able to successfully argue that having the government in control of the media could threaten independence and that the government had no business interfering with or depriving individual entrepreneurs from creating a vibrant broadcasting industry. So unlike nations with significantly less press freedom, say North Korea, the government can't control the information people get. That's a big advantage however you slice it.

In Britain what we might call the "public sphere" group successfully argued that leaving mass communication (at least broadcasting) to market forces would not serve the public interest at all. The media would be so busy meeting the demands of business that it would be unable to focus on public service goals. In owning the media, the government could assure that it lived up to its public interest obligations. That's a huge advantage too.

And where does all of this leave us? Right back at the doorstep of the fundamental tension—the Zell/Fajardo exchange—again.

What's interesting to note here is that, in some sense, both "sides" in the radio debates ended up being right *and* wrong about the best structure for a media system in a democracy. The press in the U.S. media system manages to fulfill its public service mission at least some of the time, in spite of market demands to do otherwise. Meanwhile, the press in the British system likewise manages to fulfill its public service mission without a load of government interference. In saying that both were right and wrong, though, we risk over-simplifying the outcome. There is growing and sustained dissatisfaction with press performance in the United States, which is largely absent in Britain. And the dissatisfaction stems almost entirely from by-products of a private ownership, market-oriented system: news that is focused on trivial matters that are entertaining and cheap to cover but do not provide

On the BBC Trust's website, you'll find the six "public purposes" the BBC defined in its Royal Charter. They are:

1. Sustaining citizenship and civil society;

2. Promoting education and learning;

3. Stimulating creativity and cultural excellence;

4. Representing the UK, its nations, regions and communities;

5. Bringing the UK to the world and the world to the UK;

6. In promoting its other purposes, helping to deliver to the public the benefit of emerging communications technologies and services and, in addition, taking the leading role in the switchover to digital television.

Check out more information here: www.bbc.co.uk/bbctrust/governance/tools_we_use/public_purposes.html

citizens with needed information, and under- and misrepresentation of certain groups in society. The journalism produced by the British Broadcasting Corporation (BBC), which now operates as a quasi-government trust, is of very high quality and exhibits fewer of these problems.

Let's examine the market approach more closely to see why it sometimes produces such undesirable results.

▶ WHO OWNS THE MEDIA?

Here's one thing you know from this chapter so far: In the United States, the media are (almost entirely) privately owned. In other countries around the world, the ownership picture is more mixed, involving government and private actors.

But let's take a step back briefly. People tend to talk about "the media" as though it's a single, monolithic thing. Every now and then, you might see a "don't trust the media" bumper sticker on a car; far more often, you hear people complaining about "the media" being biased or sensationalistic or immoral or whatever. But are all these people complaining about the same thing? Or are some referring to *60 Minutes*, while others are thinking about

▶ **MEDIA OWNERSHIP:** Who owns the media—whether an individual, a corporation that issues stock, or the government—has a big impact on how the media operate, particularly the kind of content an outlet produces as well as expectations about how much profit (if any) the outlet is expected to make. The vast majority of media in the United States is commercially owned, meaning they are for-profit businesses owned by individuals or, more typically, corporations.

The Big Bang Theory or something else? It's hard to say. The lines between news and entertainment aren't exactly neon yellow and blinking. But that's a problem for another day and another chapter.

For now, let's define "the media" as all the entities sending and receiving messages on a mass scale—the mass media. That includes television, radio, magazines and newspapers (the printed and online kind), websites, individual blogs, movies, books, etc. Even with just this list, you begin to see how complaining about "the media" doesn't make much sense, unless one really wants to argue that all media—whether books or blogs—are producing biased, sensationalistic and/or immoral garbage.

More useful for us is to define "*news* media," which may be what people who complain about "the media" have in mind anyway. "News media" would include any of those entities listed above that, on a mass scale, send and receive a particular kind of message: news. That definition helps narrow things down a bit, though you might still think that it doesn't make much sense to criticize a television newscast in the same way you would a magazine profile of a politician or commentary about the local school system on a blog. Point taken. And we'll get to that.

People who have complaints about products—the shirt shrank the first time you washed it, the package arrived damaged—might reasonably seek out the owner of the store or company to register their displeasure. So following that logic, where would people with complaints about the news media go? If I don't like something that appeared in my local newspaper, I can call the publisher, though he or she might not be the ultimate owner. What if I don't like what a correspondent on *20/20* had to say? It would be a little more difficult, but I could eventually track down the names and contact information for that correspondent's boss and maybe even the head of the news division at ABC, which broadcasts *20/20*. But if I wanted to talk to the owner? I'd need to track down the number for the Walt Disney Company, which owns ABC, ESPN, and a bunch of radio stations and book publishers, along with its film and theme park businesses. And if I really wanted to split hairs, I'd need to contact all the people—millions, maybe—who own stock in Disney.

In fact, just a handful of corporations—six at the time this book was published—own the vast majority of broadcasting, cable and book publishing companies in the U.S., and a few newspaper chains, including the Tribune

Company Sam Zell led into bankruptcy (which has since spun off its newspapers into a separate company called Tribune Publishing) own a good chunk of the nation's 1,400 newspapers. (See *Columbia Journalism Review*'s "Who Owns What" for details.) This situation when ownership rests in only a few hands is called concentration of ownership. Over the past few decades, ownership of mass media in the U.S. has become increasingly concentrated.

▶ CONCENTRATION OF OWNERSHIP

From the owners' perspective, one of the main advantages of concentration of ownership is dealing with a relatively small number of competitors. Fewer competitors means it's easier to get a bigger piece of the pie. From the consumers' perspective, such reduced competition is one of the chief *dis*advantages of ownership concentration. Fewer competitors means there's little reason for companies to be innovative or keep prices low.

Concentration of ownership in the media industry also offers opportunities for horizontal and vertical integration—again, things that look good from the owners' perspective, but may have less than good outcomes from the consumer perspective. Horizontal integration describes the situation when a single large media corporation owns a number of different kinds of media products or outlets. Vertical integration describes the situation when a media corporation owns companies involved in different phases of the media production process—creating media products, distributing them, showing them, etc. A media corporation can be both horizontally and vertically integrated.

The Hearst Corporation, which owns newspapers, magazines, television and radio stations, cable channels, a book publisher and a number of websites, is a good example of horizontal integration. The arrangement allows Hearst to cross-promote its media products by, for example, using its A&E cable network to promote books published by Hearst, or to take content from *Cosmopolitan* magazine and turn it into a book. To remember that this is the *horizontal* kind of integration, just think of all the media products as different boxes of cereal lined up on the same grocery store shelf. They are all cereal, but differ greatly in terms of who mostly eats them—say, All Bran for older people, Lucky Charms for kids. If the same company owned both All Bran and Lucky Charms, it might offer a coupon for Lucky Charms

▶ **INTEGRATION:**
How the many businesses within a media conglomerate work together to create advantages within a market segment. Horizontal integration refers to a conglomerate owning a number of media outlets across the marketplace. Vertical integration refers to a conglomerate owning companies up and down the chain of production and distribution of media products. A media company can be horizontally integrated, vertically integrated, or both.

on the All Bran box so that grandparents can stock up on the good stuff for when their grandkids visit. That would be a kind of cross-promotion (and a reason for grandkids everywhere to rejoice!).

Comcast Corporation's 2011 purchase of NBC Universal from General Electric, offers a good example of how a corporation can increase its vertical integration. Comcast had been primarily in the distribution business, with its group of cable companies. Buying NBC means that Comcast is now in the creation/production and exhibition business too. It has all the steps on the ladder covered (a ladder is vertical, get it?), from creating a media product to selling it, which helps Comcast manage costs and compete. It also provides what economists call "economies of scale"—the cost advantages that a business obtains due to expansion. The bigger the potential market, the lower a producer's average cost per unit, so for media owners, bigger is better.

So what's the big deal about whether and which way a corporation is integrated? It's all about risk and responsiveness. Heavily integrated corporations have, in a very real sense, integrated themselves out of risk. Let's take an example from the world of entertainment. The Walt Disney Company, which is both horizontally and vertically integrated, is known for animated films. But for every *Toy Story 3* or *Frozen* that breaks box office records, there's at least one *Mars Needs Moms* or *Treasure Planet*—movies that just plain bomb. Now, of course Disney would prefer that every Disney film perform at the level of *Toy Story 3*. But even when they don't, Disney still makes some money. How? Thanks to integration, Disney can run *Mars Needs Moms* on its cable channel and sell commercials to run during the show. It can distribute the film on DVD and reach an audience that maybe couldn't be bothered to go out to the movies. It can sell the soundtrack through its record company. Maybe it can even turn the story into a children's book published by Disney Publishing. Spreading the same content across a variety of Disney's media products and distribution channels means the risk of taking a loss on a bad movie is pretty small.

Not bad. Not bad at all. At least if you're Disney. There's a potential downside to consider, though. That's where the responsiveness part comes in. If there's little to no risk involved in producing certain kinds of movies, then chances are you'll want to make lots and lots of those kinds of movies, right? What happens, though, when someone comes to you with an idea for a movie that hasn't really been done before or might appeal to a smaller audience only? Your incentive to take the risk of trying something new and untested (people might hate it) or responding to the needs or desires of a less mass-sized audience (you might not be able to spread the content across all your different platforms and properties) would be pretty low indeed. That's one reason why, for all the volume of content pouring forth from the mass media faucet, there isn't as much variety as there could be. Not everyone gets what they want; not everyone's voice gets heard. That's a bit of a wrinkle in the law of supply and demand.

Now let's take this out of the entertainment context and back into journalism again. The same economic forces that encourage, if not compel, corporations to create certain kinds of entertainment fare also encourage, if not compel, those same corporations to focus on certain types of news content. What is tried and true? What is cheap to produce? What appeals to the widest possible audience, even if a somewhat smaller audience could benefit greatly from something else? Even if you are not particularly concerned about how those economic forces shape the variety of movies available at your local theater, you would be rightly concerned about the limitations they pose on your ability to get quality journalism from your local newspaper or television station.

To summarize, mass media owners are most responsive to the needs of the bottom line. They have to be. After all, they've got lots of shareholders who expect—demand—a return on their investment. This is one reason why we said at the beginning of this chapter that the government isn't the only, or even the most important, entity that can get in the way of journalism doing what it's supposed to do in a democracy. The commercial nature of the mass media industry can also get in the way.

4.2 THE VIEW FROM THE PROS: NEW PATHWAYS

At 24, I was a newspaper grad. At 27, I was a newspaper layoff victim.

A week after graduation, I moved to Cambodia to become a reporter. Eighteen months later, I joined the foreign desk at France's largest daily. I was paying my dues, working the night shift for two years on a succession of temp contracts, but I was on track.

At least I was until there were no more temp contracts. The newspaper was bleeding money. First were the early retirements; then the easily broken ties—I was one of those. Later, dozens of experienced journalists would take buyouts and walk away, not just from the paper, but from their life's work.

When, after a few months of unemployment disguised as freelancing, I happened upon a job opening for an editor at LinkedIn, I hesitated: Was I giving up on my vocation? What could a journalist possibly do in a tech company? It took me weeks to even apply. I wish I could say it was a decision borne out of foresight and a keen sense of the media landscape, but I really stumbled into the best move of my career. I hope you won't.

LinkedIn editors spend their day creating and encouraging the creation of stories that help professionals be better informed and inspired. We write, we edit and we constantly seek new voices with knowledge to share. It's not a typical newsroom: a small band of editors serves a community of 364 million members, of whom more than one million have already written on our platform. We work side-by-side with engineers and shape technology as much as story. But it certainly is a newsroom: there's a wall of TVs set to every news channel out there, daily budget meetings to plan our coverage, a noticeable buzz whenever news breaks, and debates on the Oxford comma. Here, I came to understand that mission, not medium, makes a journalist.

That mission—and stop me when I get grandiose—is to shine a little bit of light on the corner of the world you're assigned to, whether White House corridors, middle school recitals or, in our case, the working lives of people and businesses. You keep truth as your true north and you make humble steps in its direction every day. That mission comes with two mandates: non-negotiable independence from the people you cover and those who pay the bills, and a genuine love for the community you serve. This makes a journalist. All else is technology and business model, and that will change twelve times over before you or I retire.

There were 54,100 full-time newsroom jobs in America when I entered the Missouri School of Journalism in 2005, near enough all-time highs, according to the American Society of Newspaper Editors. Ten years later, there are 36,700. These numbers have been discussed to death. But there's another side to that story. Dozens of tech companies now employ journalists or are about to: to name only the big ones, Facebook, Twitter, Snapchat, Apple and of course, LinkedIn. Other journalists lead the way in creating their own jobs and revenue models: look at Alex Blumberg, founder of Gimlet Media, or Walt Mossberg and Kara Swisher of re/code.

Far from me to make light of the upheaval in journalism—what we do in no way can replace the hard investigative work and community coverage that is lost when newspapers die. It's just one piece of a puzzle we are all still putting together. While media companies seemingly can't wait to get out of the business, everyone else wants to be one. Note that I've used the word journalist throughout: you don't have to become a PR manager, social media expert or "branded content strategist," unless that's your thing of course. More and more companies—and my hunch is this is only going to grow—see the value in having an independent editorial voice people can trust. They hire them and get out of their way.

There used to be a straightforward career path that went something like this: join a small daily after graduation, move on to the state capital after a couple years, then a metro daily on a minor beat, then a major beat, make the move to editor maybe, and eventually land in the national press at the *Big City Times*, *Post* or *Tribune*. If really you were inclined to diversify, you'd write a couple books. I never knew that path; you won't either.

You'll write many places at once and build an audience who follows you there. You'll join a company that's never done media and show everyone in and outside of it how it's done. You'll start your own company too, teach and speak at conferences. You'll have twelve careers when others had one. Above all, you'll have to allow yourself to change. Your life, professional and otherwise, may not look like you had pictured it. You won't be any less yourself in it. And you are a journalist.

THINK ABOUT IT: Beyond the predictable outlets for journalism, new forms of digital media are emerging that offer new promise for journalists, much like LinkedIn. Can you name some other "new" homes for journalists? And what other career paths might journalism training prepare you for?

Isabelle Roughol is international editor at LinkedIn and a class of 2008 graduate from the University of Missouri School of Journalism.

This is not to say that profit and public service are mutually exclusive. Indeed, research shows that quality journalism sells just as well if not better than junky journalism. It's just that the pressure to do more with less, to cut corners to make shareholders happy, to focus on cheaper and lighter news rather than expensive and serious reporting, is always there. It's worth noting that in the early days of television in the U.S., the news was something networks offered to meet their public interest obligations. It wasn't expected to make a profit. When the news magazine program *60 Minutes* came along and demonstrated that news *could* make money, well, then, the news was *expected* to make money. It had to stand on its own without whatever cash the commercials from the entertainment shows might bring in. Once that happened, entertainment values began seeping more and more into the news, not just in television, but in print media too. Trouble is, it's often hard (or even just wrong) to make serious news, like war in Syria or a drought in California, entertaining.

There is yet another twist to this story of how the commercial media system encourages certain kinds of responsiveness—to shareholders, to the mass audience—over others. So far we've been talking about media "products"

FIGURE 4.2 Business concerns—from how much news gathering equipment costs to how much money is in the travel budget—can have an impact on the practice of journalism.

Source: Picsfive/Shutterstock.

being sold to media "consumers." It turns out that even those terms take on different shapes and meanings in a commercial media system, with more implications for how journalism is practiced.

▶ THE DUAL-PRODUCT MODEL

Imagine you own a restaurant; let's say a seafood place. To operate such a restaurant, you need to develop a menu, design a nice dining room, equip a kitchen, purchase lots of fish and ingredients for tartar sauce, and hire chefs, servers, busboys and maybe a bartender or hostess. People come to your restaurant, order something delicious off your menu, receive excellent service, pay the bill—maybe even leave a hefty tip!—and go on their way. Who is who in this scenario is pretty clear: You are the merchant selling seafood and the experience of eating a nice meal in a restaurant. Your customers are the people who bought and ate the food and enjoyed that experience. With any luck, what the customers pay covers your costs to provide all that tartar sauce and service, plus leave a bit of profit for you.

Now think about the news business. If you own a cable channel, let's say CNN, you also have some designing and planning to do, equipment to buy and people to hire. You need people who can create video packages from anywhere in the world, who can do research, interview guests and deliver the news on the air clearly, and handle all the behind-the-scenes technology of sending content to and from satellites. You need cameras and computers—lots of them. You might even need body armor for the journalists reporting from war zones. At first glance, you might think that who is who in this scenario is just as clear as it was with the seafood restaurant. You are, in some sense, a merchant who sells the news and other interesting content via your channel. Your customers are the people who watch that programming. But where's the transaction, the exchange of money between merchant and customer? The person who orders a lobster dinner at your restaurant pays for the lobster dinner, right? But the people who watch your shows on CNN pay only indirectly, if at all—and what they pay doesn't begin to cover the costs for all that body armor, set design and editing software CNN needs to produce those shows.

So who pays? Well, advertisers do. Toyota and Walmart and Applebee's. Geico and Gatorade. They and a host of other companies pay loads of money to CNN to run commercials during all that programming. In the days when

FIGURE 4.3 Times Square is an icon of New York City and of bold and flashy advertising. Photo taken in January, 2011.
Source: Andrey Bayda/Shutterstock.

people watched only over-the-air broadcasting, commercial advertising made TV essentially "free" to viewers. All you needed was a television set (and an antenna!). With cable and satellite, people do pay for television—they pay for access to certain channels or packages of channels. Depending on the channel, those payments mostly go to the cable and satellite companies, not the networks or channels producing the programs. So advertisers are still paying your television bill for you. Isn't that nice? Well, sure. We like free stuff as much as the next guy. But this model of media funding—the advertiser-supported model—has some trade-offs and downsides too.

4.1 THE VIEW FROM THE PROS: PUBLIC SERVICE NEWS

As traditional newsrooms have shrunk in recent years, nonprofit news organizations have grown. Most are founded by journalists dedicated to public service over profit. In St. Louis, for example, the nonprofit online news site St. Louis Beacon, which I founded and edited, merged with St. Louis Public Radio to bring more journalists and more resources to bear on public service journalism. But, as the saying goes: No margin, no mission. High quality reporting costs money. Creating sound business models and healthy revenue streams are among our most urgent challenges.

While building the financial engine to sustain our work, we must build in ethical principles to sustain its quality and credibility. Protecting the integrity of the reporting is paramount. "Always be drastically independent," Joseph Pulitzer said years ago, and he's still right.

But the bright lines that used to demarcate acceptable practices must be redrawn to fit new circumstances. Nonprofit news organizations have different sources of funding than traditional media, different ways of engaging readers and different attitudes about partnering with outside organizations.

Take funding. Nonprofits typically get most of it from individual donors, sponsors and foundations rather than advertisers. An ad rep's conversation with a prospect focuses on capacity to deliver eyeballs. Our conversations with funders focus on capacity to report news that matters and on why this is essential for creating a better St. Louis. Funders give because they support that mission. But most of them also have other personal, professional, financial or civic interests—interests that could raise questions about undue influence on the news coverage.

In our ethics policy and in conversations with funders, we emphasize that our most precious asset is the integrity of our reporting. It's the foundation that supports public trust. Our news coverage is not for sale, and that's what makes it valuable to support. To further allay suspicion, we disclose donors' names on our website, identify them in stories where they play a major role and take other steps to limit the potential for problems.

Take engagement. In the digital world, it's important to listen as well as talk. We welcome discussion of our news coverage and solicit advice about how to make it more compelling. We converse with readers not only on the air and through our website, but also on social media, through the Public Insight Network, podcasts and in person at events.

But we draw a line between acceptable advice and unacceptable interference. Clearly, it would be unethical to promise favorable coverage—or any coverage, for that matter—to individuals or organizations that do not otherwise merit attention. Taking money to fund such coverage would be even worse, as would special attention to donors, board members and others with close ties. While welcoming discussion, we need to make news judgments independently.

Take partnerships. Competition still has its place, but in the new media ecosystem, collaboration with other organizations is often the best way to increase the reach and impact of our work. We welcome the opportunity to learn from and work with others, but always maintain control over our work.

Based on experience with funders, engagement and partnerships, we've begun to redraw the bright lines that clarify ethical practices for a new era. Here are some key points:

- News judgments should be based on merit, not connections or finances.
- Funding should be transparent.
- Multiple revenue streams enhance independence.
- A broad spectrum of donors protects against undue influence by any particular interest.
- Funding for general operations and broad coverage topics raises fewer conflicts than funding for specific articles or projects.

Guidelines like these help journalists know what's right in a new age. Doing what's right still requires what it always did—fortitude and courage.

LEARN MORE: Visit the St. Louis Public Radio website and explore all the information related to ways the audience can engage, connect with and donate to the news organization. How is this different from what you might find on a commercial news site? (You can compare the site with www.stltoday.com, the website of the *St. Louis Post Dispatch*).

—————————

Margaret Wolf Freivogel is the editor of St. Louis Public Radio.

Why does a company like McDonald's advertise? Lots of reasons. To tell customers and potential customers about new or seasonal menu items—is it McRib time yet?—and special promotions. To tell you why it thinks its combo meal is superior to a competitor's combo meal. To plant a seed in your mind about McDonald's so that the next time you're looking for a quick, hot breakfast on the road, you think of them first.

The bottom line, so to speak, is that McDonald's (and every other company that advertises) wants your attention. And they're willing to pay big money to try to get it. Did you catch that? Advertisers are paying for your attention. That means you—your eyeballs watching CNN—are a product too. That is the essence of the dual-product model. Media companies, like CNN, are really selling two products. The first is the programming, which is sold to viewers. The second is the viewers' attention, which is sold to advertisers. But in that model, only the advertisers really pay the bills.

This model doesn't apply just to television. Consider the newspaper (the printed kind). Newspaper owners spend money to gather and distribute news, paying for reporters, computers, wire services, paper, delivery drivers, etc. But the amount of money people pay in subscriptions or at the newsstand doesn't even come close to covering all those production costs. Advertisers pay the lion's share. And they do it because they need to get their message out to customers. They need your attention.

Indeed, pretty much every kind of media in the United States follows this model. Sure, there are a few magazines, such as *Consumer Reports* and *Cook's Illustrated*, and a few public radio and television stations that don't run commercial advertising. But on the whole, the dual-product model reigns supreme.

Welcome to your life as a product. (And here you thought you were just a mere consumer and citizen . . .)

So, are both products in the dual-product model created equal? Not really. Given that viewers don't really pay CNN every time they tune in to watch, which product do you think is most important? The one that really pays the bills. This brings us back to the responsiveness issue we mentioned earlier. Because owners are inclined to be most responsive to the demands of shareholders, they also are inclined to be most responsive to the advertisers who help them meet those demands. That means the advertisers have quite a lot of say in the kinds of eyeballs they want to buy which, in turn, influences the content produced to attract those eyeballs. This all sounds disgusting. How about a non-eyeball-related story?

This might just be urban legend, but the CEO of Bloomingdale's department store was once rumored to have told Rupert Murdoch, owner of the *New York Post*, a tabloid newspaper: "Your readers are our shoplifters."

◀ **DUAL-PRODUCT MODEL:** Media companies sell two products, not just one. The first product is the content, whether it's news, entertainment or whatever. It is sold to consumers. The second product is the attention of the audience reading, viewing or otherwise interacting with that content. This is the product sold to advertisers. Given that most of the money is made off the second product, the needs of advertisers can sometimes override the needs of consumers.

Yes, that was intended as an insult. It was the CEO's way of saying that Bloomingdale's had no interest in advertising in the *Post* because no one Bloomingdale's wanted to reach was a reader of the *Post*. Those readers were, instead, the kind of people Bloomingdale's would be happy to keep far, far away from their stores.

Even if untrue, it's kind of a fun story and a useful way of explaining how the dual-product model might encourage news media organizations to cover certain kinds of news over others. Want to get the Bloomingdale's account? How about some nice stories on luxury vacations and the stock market? The Bloomingdale's demographic might not be as interested in a story about public housing. If that kind of thinking really takes hold—and we're exaggerating a little here to make the point—then some of the basic functions and obligations of journalism begin to erode. If there are problems in public housing, then the public probably needs to know about them, even if they'd rather read about Acapulco and the increase in Google's stock price.

▶ CONCLUSION

So now you know where Sam Zell was coming from when he made the claim that giving people what they want comes first and giving them what they need comes second. He was speaking as a businessman, not a public servant. He was taking the market approach to media. And you also know why at least one journalist, Sara Fajardo, was a little concerned to hear him say so. She was thinking about the content people need as more important than the entertaining stuff they often want. That's the public sphere approach.

When we talked about the debate over regulating radio earlier in this chapter, we also used those labels—"market" and "public sphere"—to refer to the different perspectives about whether the radio industry should be under private or public ownership. Indeed, those labels are a convenient way to compare and contrast two ways of thinking about media's purpose and the implications of taking one perspective or the other. (See Table 4.1 for points of comparison.)

A similar debate arose in 2011, as one of the worst recessions in U.S. history and growing concerns about the budget deficit led to a number of proposals for spending cuts. Even though it represents just a tiny fraction of the federal budget, funding for public broadcasting (the Corporation for Public Broadcasting and National Public Radio) was at the top of some people's lists to be cut. Why? Because some people believe the government has no business paying for something that, they argue, the market can provide more efficiently. Those defending public media from cuts, though, argued that leaving all media to the whim of the market virtually ensures that certain kinds of important programming will disappear. Profits, they argue, aren't the only or best way to measure the success of media. The quality of the content and how well it serves the overall public interest is. In the end, no funding cuts were made. But this is exactly the kind of battle that will arise again and again, as the U.S. continually tries to square its democratic needs with its commercial media system.

Chapter Four Review

Chapter Summary

Activities

Discussion/Debate Questions

Read More

▶ CHAPTER SUMMARY

The economic structure of mass media can and does shape how journalism is practiced. While a commercial media, such as that in the U.S., enjoys freedom from government control, it faces other pressures on its performance from the requirement to make profits and satisfy (sometimes numerous and fickle) owners. How the Internet is presenting some challenges to traditional economic formulas but also might make worse some of the constraints on media's ability to produce quality news, is the subject of the next chapter.

▶ ACTIVITIES

1. Pick two or three local news outlets in your region (a newspaper, a television station, a radio outlet). Find information about the ownership.

Are the outlets owned by families, chains, a non-profit group? What other entities does the company own? How easy is it for students (and the public) to find this information? How transparent is ownership? Can you find evidence of cross-promotion and content sharing across entities? The findings can be shared through a class discussion or written up by students in a short report.

2. Read Ken Doctor's 2011 Neiman Journalism Lab blog post about media concentration (www.niemanlab.org/2011/07/the-newsonomics-of-u-s-media-concentration/). After reading this chapter, find out if these trends have continued in recent years. Are we seeing "smart, digital-first roll-ups align with massive consolidation?" What evidence can you find as to whether Doctor's 2011 prediction was right or wrong? Share your findings in a class discussion or brief paper.

3. Invite the publisher of your local newspaper or the general manager of a local broadcast outlet to class to discuss issues raised in this chapter. What pressures does he or she feel from above to maximize profits? How do you balance that with the need to do quality journalism? Are there parts of the newsroom that are more profitable than others (for example, sports)? What are the implications in a digital delivery era when we can easily track which stories attract audiences? How do you balance what people need vs. what people want?

4. An alternative if you cannot connect with a local media executive is a video on the same issues. In 2015, some former members of the Federal Communications Commission were part of a panel discussion on "Regulation of Digital Media and Communications." Watch this short clip— www.c-span.org/video/?c4532616/media-ownership—and consider how the commissioners' views complement the material in the chapter.

5. Visit an interactive Stanford University history project on the spread of American Newspapers throughout the United States (www.stanford. edu/group/ruralwest/cgi-bin/drupal/visualizations/us_newspapers). The site is fun to play with and to visualize the spread of newspapers west as the country grew. Most pertinent to the issues in this chapter, however, are the changes documented in the past 75 years. Start on the timeline in 1945 and then hit the next entry to read about these developments. Pay close attention to the visuals. What can you learn? What

will the visual look like in 10 years? 20 years? Write a 350–500 word post on the class discussion board on this topic.

▶ DISCUSSION/DEBATE QUESTIONS

1. Some say that profits and good journalism are constantly in conflict. Do you agree? Can they co-exist in the U.S. market-driven journalism structure?

2. Are media businesses owned by families more immune to market pressures than publicly owned companies? How might their pressures be different compared to those companies who answer to shareholders?

3. How do you react to advertising on websites you visit? Do you find it an annoyance? Would you rather pay directly for the content or endure increasingly intrusive online advertising? Will the advertising model work to support media companies as they scale back their legacy products (newsprint, broadcasting)?

4. In a digital delivery environment, executives can easily track where audiences go for information and how long they stay there. Is this good or bad for the media business? For journalism? Can it be good for both?

▶ READ MORE

Suzanne Kirchhoff, "The Newspaper Industry in Transition," Congressional Research Service, September 9, 2010, accessed July 14, 2015. www.fas.org/sgp/crs/misc/R40700.pdf.

"Members Only: Two Cheers for High-cost Subscription Journalism," *Columbia Journalism Review*, March/April 2011, accessed July 14, 2015. www.cjr.org/editorial/members_only_marchapril11.php.

Steve Waldman, "Information Needs of Communities: The Changing Media Landscape in a Broadband Age," Federal Communications Commission, July 2011, accessed July 14, 2015. www.fcc.gov/info-needs-communities#read.

"Who Owns What," *Columbia Journalism Review*, accessed July 14, 2015. www.cjr.org/resources/

5

New Voices, New Models

Brent Gardner-Smith never meant to be a media owner. It's just worked out that way.

Gardner-Smith runs a five-year-old organization, Aspen Journalism, whose mission "is to produce investigative, in-depth and insightful journalism."

Sounds like journalistic nirvana, doesn't it?

Gardner-Smith says it certainly can be, especially as it was just a pipe dream back when the real estate recession teamed up with the lingering newspaper depression.

"I can humbly say that I'm the executive director, editor, reporter, photographer, and digital manager at Aspen Journalism," Gardner-Smith said. "But when I tell people tell that, I still marvel that it is true."

LEARNING OBJECTIVES

Think about the changes transforming journalism, and what they mean for the future of news;

Understand the economic backdrop creating the changes in journalism;

Understand the emerging models reshaping the field;

Learn how these changes should influence the career paths of future journalists.

Back when Lehman Brothers fell and the luxury real estate market froze in Aspen, local real estate firms stopped advertising. The *Aspen Daily News* and *Aspen Times*, both heavily dependent on real estate ads, cut salaries and staff.

It appeared the dominant trend in the newspaper industry had reached even the lofty heights of Aspen, which still had two competing free daily newspapers.

Long-time locals started asking questions. What if one paper closed? Or both thinned their ranks so hard they lost their ability to produce investigative reporting?

And when Gardner-Smith got the news from his boss at the *Daily News* about his own salary reduction and mandatory six-week furlough, he was already in the process of getting his master's in journalism through the Missouri School of Journalism's online program—already obsessing about the potential viability of a "local, online, nonprofit, investigative" news organization.

In 2010, after writing a paper about how the Voice of San Diego and Pro-Publica were getting the word out about their reporting, Gardner-Smith was invited to apply for an internship in the communications department at ProPublica—the gold standard of non-profit journalism.

ProPublica had captured headlines when it was established in 2007 with a $30 million initial commitment primarily from billionaire banker Herb Sandler and his wife, Marion.

The ProPublica budget was structured at about $10 million a year over three years. Their goal: fill in some of the gaps left by the erosion of investigative journalism in daily newspapers by creating an institution freed from the profit pressures of corporate ownership.

At ProPublica, Gardner-Smith was wisely advised that it would take $1 million a year—ten people at $100,000-a-head—to emulate ProPublica's quality of reporting on the local level. He was already talking with the board of a local community foundation, whose members agreed that an independent source of watchdog reporting needed to remain to serve Pitkin County, the communities of Aspen and Snowmass Village, and the Roaring Fork River watershed.

But would local philanthropists give $3 million to hire ten journalists for three years, even in a town like Aspen, which Aspen Journalism has documented is the home to 50 billionaires?

To date, no.

But Aspen Journalism has raised over $500,000 from local donors since launching in January 2011 and spent over $400,000 producing in-depth, investigative and insightful journalism.

How?

Upon returning from his stint at ProPublica, Gardner-Smith secured a one-year grant for $50,000 from the Manaus Fund, gave four months' notice at the *Daily News*, formed a nonprofit corporation, populated an engaged board, secured nonprofit status, opened a bank account, rented a small office, bought libel insurance, set up a website, joined what is now the Institute for Nonprofit News, started collaborating on in-depth stories with both the *Daily News* and the *Aspen Times*, began paying local freelance reporters, photographers and editors to do quality reporting, and kept talking to local major donors who value journalism.

"We've proven the nonprofit investigative model can work locally, and we've produced some good work," Gardner-Smith said. "And an increasing number of donors recognize that our approach—local, nonprofit, collaborative, and investigative—makes sense. So, thankfully, we can keep pursuing our journalistic vision."

Similar stories are unfolding across the country, as journalists determined to keep telling stories create new platforms for distributing news and experiment with new ways to get paid for doing journalism. Some follow the non-profit model, others are based on what is being called "hyperlocal" and still others are straight-ahead for-profit plays. The economic struggles of the traditional press are engendering more experimentation and innovation than ever before. The pace of innovation in the field is dizzying, but a look at all that's happening reveals an interesting glimpse at the future of digital media.

Out of the seeming chaos, we can say with some confidence that a few trends in developing the "new news" seem to be gaining attention:

▶ The market still has not found an efficient way to encourage payment for digital access to news.

▶ New funding models for journalism keep evolving, with no "silver bullet" in sight.

▶ Responding to search trends to develop news content and shape the presentation and selection of news grows in importance as the tools get better and better.

▶ New approaches to local news development continue but have not solved the economic woes of the business.

▶ Engagement, through stories or through other interactive features, grows in importance daily.

From startups such as Voice of San Diego and MinnPost and the nationally ambitious rollout of ProPublica with a $10 million annual pledge from its creator, to more recent additions such as California Watch, the Texas Tribune and the St. Louis Beacon, these new models are fostering a rebirth in local news coverage with an emphasis on engagement through the online channel.

It's been a bumpy ride for the digital-first startups. For every ProPublica, there is a GigaOm, the respected tech-news site started by the writer Om Malik, which folded its tent in 2015 after nine years, or The Dish, the famed blogger Andrew Sullivan's project, shut down this year after Sullivan confessed that the one-man shop approach was working him into the ground. Circa, a truly revolutionary mobile news application much praised for its ease of use and seamless design, opened with $5.7 million in venture capital funding but shut down in June 2015 after failing to figure out a workable business model.

The first edition of this text focused this chapter on Digital First Media, a pioneering company at the time making headlines for its digital-first strategy. Today that company is shedding news assets, having failed to find sufficient profits in the news business to satisfy its equity firm owners.

Even lavishly funded startups can struggle to gain their footing in the digital landscape. First Look Media—bankrolled by eBay co-founder and billionaire Pierre Omidyar—does not hurt for funding. Yet the company's plans—a general news site and a series of digital magazines—has in two years yielded but a single niche site, The Intercept, which focuses on government surveillance and privacy and is led by Glenn Greenwald of Edward Snowden/National Security Agency fame. It's an excellent site, full of rich content, but it's far from a general-interest news product. Reportedly, its newest offering which launched in 2015, is a bold experiment in social media publishing: Rather than publishing on its own site, the First Look experiment aims to curate eyewitness and expert perspectives, filter them in real time and allow people to provide perspectives from social media sites they already are visiting.

If it all sounds like a grand experiment, well, that's because it is just that. It's not just the so-called "legacy media" which are struggling to re-engineer themselves in the digital age. Still, these disparate models are worth examining. It's also worth taking a close look at one old-school company, Gannett, a media giant that has staked a great deal of its future on embracing the digital transition.

Best known as the creators of *USA Today*, Gannett's strategy can teach us a great deal about the forces transforming journalism, and how one media company charts a course for the future can tell us a lot about the broader market.

To set the tone, look at what online journalism sage Clay Shirky wrote way back in 2009 in an essay entitled "Newspapers and Thinking the Unthinkable":

> So who covers all that news if some significant fraction of the currently employed newspaper people lose their jobs?
>
> I don't know. Nobody knows. We're collectively living through 1500 [a reference to the revolutionary period following Gutenberg's printing press], when it's easier to see what's broken than what will replace it. The Internet turns forty this fall. Access by the general public is less than half that age. Web use, as a normal part of life for a majority of the developed world, is less than half *that* age. We just got here. Even the revolutionaries can't predict what will happen.

◀ **LEGACY MEDIA:** Media products predating the Internet, typified by a dependence upon heterogeneous audiences, advertising income and one-way communication from sender to receiver.

Right. Exactly right. But we can glean a bit of insight from looking at what's working, or even at what's not. In an age of total upheaval, everything is a lesson, a step forward.

Experimentation yields failure more often than success, of course, but that's not the lesson here. The lesson is that not trying is a sure ticket to obsolescence.

A VIEW FROM THE PROS: SOCIAL MEDIA HAVE CHANGED THE GAME

The last five years have seen an enormous shift in not just the way the news is presented, but how it gets to the viewer in the first place. Crews get to a story and instead of grabbing a camera to shoot video, they grab a smartphone, and either post it to social media directly, or e-mail it back to the newsroom to post on social media or the web. It's presumably hours before the newscast starts and the viewer is already able to consume what's happening.

Facebook, Twitter and Skype have been game-changers when it comes to the news gathering and news distributing processes. When news breaks, viewers will send you pictures of what's happening. Need some feedback? Post on Facebook and your customers will tell you (in a brutally honest way) what they think. It's like you have tens of thousands of citizen journalists all around the city. Use it responsibly to your advantage. I've found if you ask the viewers for help, they'll help.

At WABC-TV in 2014, a gas leak caused a massive explosion in East Harlem. We were on the air within a few minutes with aerial footage and minutes later with a reporter at the scene. But that wasn't before we tweeted, posted on Facebook, the website, and sent out an e-mail alert about what was going on. The live television coverage, which went on for hours, happened last, after the news broke on social and digital platforms. Social media was a major component of our coverage. Hundreds of pictures flew in to our Twitter and Facebook accounts to complement the coverage. It helped tell the story with other angles and images we had never seen and from an execution standpoint, it allowed our reporters to take a breather while they had to gather information and facts. In addition, one of the Web producers was live tweeting the coverage so people who weren't in front of a television set could follow what was happening on Twitter, in addition to live streaming the broadcast on mobile devices.

While I was producing the 10:00 p.m. news at Houston's KTRK-TV in 2010, a major earthquake struck Haiti. As our crews rushed (or more precisely waited at the airport) to get to the island, we gathered pictures on Twitter to complement our coverage. We asked on Facebook if Houstonians had made contact with their loved ones and were able to tell some emotional stories of heartache, compassion and eventually, elation.

Even though Twitter is seen by far fewer pairs of eyes than Facebook, it is still a valuable tool in the news gathering process. It is a way to get quick information out instantly. It is often incredible to see all of the news coming in from around the world second by second. It is often a play-by-play situation or breaking news event, and with various hashtags and retweeting, you can turn that into a good way to get the news from the field to the viewer.

As an Executive Producer at Charlotte's WCNC-TV, I dealt with many different severe weather issues—tornadoes, heavy rain, ice, heat, you name it. With a big Twitter push, we were able to add tens of thousands of followers when the bad weather rolled in. This helped us with our newscasts and from a strategic standpoint, as we could look at the damage, which would help us deploy and change locations if needed.

Skype can get you interviews from around the world and get you to places where you don't need a massive live truck. In this "right now" culture of information facts and pictures, the consumer will forgive you if the picture isn't crystal clear—they've shot video with their smartphone too—just like you. Most television viewers just want the news, and if your sleeves are rolled up and you get a little dirty in the process, that's fine.

Some television news stories you learn about on Facebook, tweet about it while you're headed there and then Skype at the scene. Call that the social media trifecta! Just be sure to break it online and don't wait for the late newscast.

The reality of television today is that you have to be quick. But you have to be right. You have to doublecheck all of the facts and information you receive from viewers, just like you would a source. Receiving news and tips immediately isn't a substitute for being accurate, complete and correct. If your viewer is helping you out, you owe that to them.

THINK ABOUT IT: How has the rise of social media changed the way you can consume news? What about your parents? Your grandparents? See any trends there?

Adam Darsky is an award-winning journalist who currently serves as assistant news director at WTNH-TV in the Hartford, Conn. television market. It's the most recent stop in his television career of more than 17 years. Previously, Adam was executive producer of the most-watched local morning newscast in the nation at New York City's WABC-TV. Adam's television career has taken him from Sherman, Tex., to Savannah, Ga., to Tucson, Ariz., Houston, Charlotte and New York. Adam received a First Place National Headliner Award in 2011 for best newscast. In 2009 he was awarded with an Emmy for News Producer of the Year in Texas.

Let's take a look at just a fraction of what's going on out there in the world of new models and new voices for journalism.

▶ NEW FUNDING MODELS: NON-PROFIT JOURNALISM?

Gardner-Smith's Aspen Journalism finds itself one of many non-profit journalism shops that emerged in the aftermath of years of shrinking newsroom budgets, staff layoffs and outright closures.

Literally dozens of non-profit or break-even propositions have been launched in recent years, recession or not. They range from ProPublica to the *New Haven Independent*, a scrappy non-profit startup launched by a 30-year news veteran with an annual budget of $575,000, an editorial staff of nine and a keen eye on local news.

Across the country, the realization that many traditional news organizations today view investigative journalism as a luxury that can be put aside in tough economic times, and the vacuum created in communities large and small as newsrooms shrink, has ushered in a wave of news startups. In some markets, the newcomers are filling a critical gap in investigative reporting, which has grown even more intense since a 2005 survey by Arizona State University of the 100 largest U.S. daily newspapers showed that 37 percent had no full-time investigative reporters, a majority had two or fewer such reporters, and only 10 percent had four or more. Television networks and national magazines have similarly been shedding or shrinking investigative units. Moreover, at many media institutions, time and budget constraints are curbing the once significant ability of journalists not specifically

FIGURE 5.1 Media startups offer tremendous promise—and sometimes overwhelming risk—as new forms of journalism enter the marketplace daily.

Source: Adapted from a photo by Mike (dierken) on Flickr. Reprinted via Creative Commons license (CC BY 2.0).

designated "investigative" to do this kind of reporting in addition to handling their regular beats.

These startups have for the most part featured news being ignored by struggling metro media outlets. At the *New Haven Independent*, the journalism is intensely local. A typical day's coverage is the stuff of local journalism: local political races, crime coverage much more granular than its mainstream competition, and a host of interactive features aimed at engaging a lively, well-educated community.

ProPublica's the exception to the rule, really: an incredibly deep-pocketed organization with ample reporting staff and a national footprint.

ProPublica is also an exception to the startup rule—a well-funded, organic media organization formed in the digital age. So-called legacy media companies have had to do a lot more work to transform their operations—some have tried and failed, others moved too slowly and succumbed to economic reality. Others have found their footing, and not a moment too soon.

▶ GANNETT: A MEDIA TITAN PIVOTS

Go big or go home.

That's a popular saying likely tossed around Gannett these days, after the company's buying spree made it abundantly clear that it was anything but pessimistic about the future of the news business. In 2013, Gannett paid $2.2 billion for Belo Corp., nearly doubling its TV stations in the process. The company is now the largest independent station group of major network affiliates in the top 25 markets, with 21 stations in those regions.

Gannett is a diversified media company that owns television stations, newspapers, magazines and digital media including websites such as Career Builder.com and Cars.com. The company owns or services 46 TV stations. It owns non-daily newspapers, *USA Today* and 81 community newspapers including the *Arizona Republic*, the *Indianapolis Star* and the *Detroit Free Press.*

In 2015, Gannett announced plans to spin off its TV stations and digital media into a separate company. Gannett then will return to its publishing-oriented roots, as the newspapers and publishing businesses remain, but little will stay the same. In June 2015, the spinoff became official, meaning that 19,600 employees of Gannett newspapers work for a new company now, one with an ambitious digital-first strategy. Gannett's 43 local television stations remain the core of the remaining company, renamed TEGNA, an acronym for Gannett without the double letters. The local television business remains healthy with TEGNA looking at continued growth and a bonanza in political advertising in 2016.

The challenges on the Gannett side continue, with sluggish earnings in print requiring new approaches. In 2014, the company announced an ambitious restructuring aimed at creating what it described as "the newsrooms of the future": A total of 16 new job descriptions laid the foundation for an innovative reconstruction of newsrooms in five Gannett newsrooms. Staff at the *Tennessean* in Nashville, the *Asbury Park Press* in New Jersey, the *Greenville News* in South Carolina, the *Pensacola News Journal* in Florida and the *Asheville Citizen-Times* in North Carolina "reapplied" for jobs as content coaches, community engagement editors, and producers, among other newly constructed jobs.

Here is the job description for Gannett's audience engagement positions:

> Plans and executes engagement opportunities to maximize community impact and story resonance in print, digital, community event and social media settings. Oversees content that highlights discussions and debates on important community issues. Should possess expertise in social media, marketing and events planning. Connects content with creative ways to generate community interaction both virtually and through events. May directly supervise the work of producers.

◄ **DIGITAL FIRST:** An editorial strategy of serving their audience as quickly and as locally as possible, meaning that legacy media organizations reorder their publishing priorities to break news over digital media first.

Engagement drives much of Gannett's newsroom strategy. It's even leapt the bounds of the newsroom, as its properties have invested time and resources in what the company calls In Real Life (IRL) engagement. In coffee houses and movie theaters and bookstores, Gannett papers have reached out in new ways to the communities they serve.

In 2015, Gannett's publishing division launched a training program called Picasso aimed at strengthening ties with the readership. Then the company rolled out new newsroom roles reflecting the elevated role that community engagement plays in the company's journalism. Don't want to interact, many times daily, with your audience? Then this may very well not be the career for you.

Liz Kelly Nelson, director of Events and Strategic Consumer Engagement for News at Gannett, described Gannett's strategy in a recent blogpost as equal parts experimentation and old-fashioned community journalism.

> We taught journalists in every single one of our newsrooms that connecting with community is a key to our future success and we put the onus on our local staffers—who best know their communities—to develop engagement opportunities, Nelson wrote. Then, when we rolled out our reimagined newsroom roles, many of the job descriptions included language that stresses the importance of engagement across the board: digitally, in the very tone of our writing and, yes, in real life.

Engagement now fuels Gannett's publishing strategy. The company is betting that by creating digital platforms that give users a whole lot more of what they want when they want it, they can convert free-riding Web and smartphone news consumers into subscribers. At the same time, the company wants to use all of its best content to strengthen the print versions of its 81 community dailies in the U.S. and 17 in the U.K.—which, after all, still have 3.1 million subscribers daily and 4.7 million on Sunday.

As the president and publisher of Gannett's Nashville *Tennesseean*, Laura Hollingsworth, said in a 2014 speech:

> The only choice that is left for my business is that WE must change and we must change dramatically and urgently to meet the new demands of consumers if we are to survive and thrive. We are going to have to

figure out a new business model and how to scale and structure our businesses for a new era.

Gannett is far from alone in this: Media companies including the *Guardian*, the *New York Times* and the *Texas Tribune*—and many others—are experimenting with events as a revenue source as well as an engagement device.

Note that all of these efforts seem to be changing what's valuable, and thus valued, in terms of media performance. In yesterday's world, news audiences were aggregated and sold to advertisers—we were essentially selling attention—literally, numbers of eyeballs on a single title—to advertisers.

Early online business models were all about "traffic"—clicks were the coin of the realm. Impressions are just another way of counting those eyeballs, though; the goal still was to create the largest, heterogeneous audience you could build for your site.

The fragmentation of the Internet, and the rise of social networks, gives the news media a new metric: engagement. As Alan D. Mutter said in a blogpost on the wildly entertaining Reflections of a Newsosaur: "large and undifferentiated audiences don't matter in the digital realm as much as ones that are homogeneous, engaged and readily targetable for advertisers."

So we've moved from a goal of a mass audience to a goal of a carefully selected, highly engaged audience. No longer can we sell a huge market we know little about to advertisers merely craving eyeballs. That fundamental difference in terms of the goal of online journalism—from audience attraction to audience engagement—is more than just economic, however. It promises to reinvigorate the relationship between journalists and audience, a relationship that grew far too distant in the era of mass audience.

In *The Story So Far: What We Know About the Business of Digital Journalism*, the Tow Center for Digital Journalism at Columbia University offers a rich look at why big audiences are no longer the ultimate goal of journalism.

▶ **ENGAGEMENT:**
The depth of the
involvement that
a news customer
has with a media
product. Engage-
ment can be mea-
sured empirically
or through anec-
dotal evidence.

In a chapter entitled "The Trouble With Traffic: Why Big Audiences Aren't Always Profitable," the researchers break down the problem:

> At its most basic level, advertising is a numbers game. A news organization needs a certain number of readers or viewers, and the more it gets, the more ads it can sell and the more it can charge those advertisers. Users also spend varying amounts of time with the magazine, newspaper or broadcast, and the more time they spend, the more an advertiser values the audience.

So we can boil it all down to numbers: (1) numbers in terms of eyeballs and (2) numbers in terms of engagement, or time spent with the media product.

Digital platforms are great at the first part of the numbers game. News sites pull in millions of online readers, every day. The problem is, chasing eyeballs is an outdated way of thinking about audience.

Where we once thought of the product itself as the basis of revenue—that big stack of magazines waiting to be mailed, or that truckload of newspapers—in the digital world, consumption of media is the basis for revenue. Engagement itself has become the measuring stick for assigning value to content, modifying the dual-product model you learned about in Chapter 4.

By chasing large audiences rather than deeply engaged ones, news organizations are sacrificing advertising revenue in the short term for what they hope is a more lucrative relationship with the reader in the long term. Publishers who have a "direct relationship with fans can push better contextual advertising"—that is, ads that relate directly to a user's habits and interests. In the meantime, how to pay for all of that journalism?

5.1 THE VIEW FROM THE PROS: HOW THE JOB HAS CHANGED

When I first started at the *New York Times* in 2003, the newspaper was located on Times Square and the building had a library. Several weeks after being hired, I remember visiting that library—a stodgy, whispering place manned by a dapper gentleman who only ever wore bow ties. I had been sent to the library by a Metro desk editor and told to consult some obscure electoral and city maps that apparently were only to be found in hard copy. Even then that dusty room felt like a throwback. It also carried a gravitas I expected from the paper of record. Now, neither the headquarters in New York nor the newspaper's D.C. bureau has a library. Those maps—and virtually everything else—are online.

The Internet has radically expanded journalism's horizons. I've used Skype to interview factory workers in remote areas of Bangladesh. I have sent blast e-mails to nearly a thousand human rights lawyers globally to query them all at once on a story that had to be filed the same day. I tried a fun reporting experiment recently with a magazine piece I wrote about the stories hidden within people's personal passwords. The topic was one that seemed to have the potential to resonate with readers globally since virtually everyone has to deal with technology and passwords in daily life. I hoped to collect as many of these buried anecdotes as possible that are hidden in passwords. Who better to ask for help than young, tech-savvy students? So, I reached out to the editors of campus newspapers in English-speaking countries abroad.

Many of these newspapers had student bodies larger than 20,000 people. They were perfect platforms for reporting in bulk. I asked the student editors if they might post the *Times*' password story and solicit their readers for more stories. Dozens of editors in many countries agreed. Of the 500,000 page views that the *Times* story got within the first week after publication, half of them came from abroad, most likely due to this digital collaboration.

The Internet has undoubtedly made the world a smaller place, which means you can reach people that you previously could not. But it also means they can now reach you—and there are lots of them. In a typical day I get thirty to sixty e-mails from readers, advocates, press agents and others following up on past stories or pitching new ones. The public has come to expect direct access to reporters. That's a good thing, though it's also immensely time consuming. Social media has also created growing pressure for reporters to have an independent "digital" presence. Tweeting is strongly encouraged and we are expected to have robust follower counts. Adding content to our Facebook page and replying to comments there is also assumed. All of this divides reporters' attention and saps their time immensely.

As the *Times*' website overtook the print edition in readership, the news cycle accelerated and became continual. I remember covering the Virginia Tech shooting in 2007, where a gunman killed 32 people. We were expected to file stories virtually every hour while also preparing to say something smart, broad and distinct for the next day's print publication.

Digital expectations mean that the launch of big projects is far more complicated than in the past. What do we plan to publish on Instagram? Do we have a Reddit strategy? Will we conduct a Facebook Q&A? Should we plan for blog posts to elaborate on the video that we will release with the story? Has the reporter created any listicles with practical solutions to the problems highlighted in the series? All questions that would have been non-sequitur only three years ago. Stories now also have new layers to them because of the digital revolution. Previously, when writing strictly for the newspaper, I imagined a piece as though it were a two-dimensional thing, a narrative that was printed on paper. Now, stories are online and they can have hyperlinks that pull the especially interested reader in deeper. Stories are three-dimensional platforms, often with original documents creating layer upon layer of additional reporting beneath key passages in a story.

For example, in 2011 we ran an investigative series called "Drilling Down" about the oil and gas industry in the U.S. One of our core ambitions was to make the series a document-driven piece of journalism, where much of our reporting was backed up with primary source materials. We wanted to show readers the sort of buried and sometimes misleading language that was embedded in leases that landowners were signing giving energy companies the right to drill on their property. We held the story for an extra two months so that we could use open records laws in 20 states to get actual leases, digitize them, make them searchable and put them online so that landowners could compare leases and see how terms varied and what certain cryptic clauses actually meant.

THINK ABOUT IT: How has the concept of audience changed for reporters like Urbina? What are the upsides of being in such close contact with readers, and what potential pitfalls might there be?

Ian Urbina is an investigative reporter for the *New York Times* and he is based in the newspaper's D.C. bureau. He was a member of the team of reporters that broke the story about then New York governor Eliot Spitzer and his use of prostitutes, a series of stories for which the *Times* won a Pulitzer in 2009.

▶ PAYWALLS: THE ANSWER? AN ANSWER?

The story is timeworn by now: Media companies came late to the Internet party, and its most enthusiastic early adopters kicked off the online journalism business model by giving away content even as Craigslist, Google and AutoTrader.com, to name but a few, cannibalized the classified business and placement ads that long had served as a financial rock for the news business. TV followed print media's lead, all with the unrealized promise that with traffic would come lucrative advertising dollars.

For a variety of reasons, that never quite worked out. The metrics for click-through ads never reached the predicted heights, and while media brands became a trusted source for online news, the market for online journalism has suffered mightily in the free content ecosystem.

▶ **PAYWALL:**
A system that prevents Internet users from accessing webpage content without a paid subscription. "Hard" paywalls allow minimal to no access to content without subscription, while "soft" paywalls allow more flexibility in what users can view without subscribing. "Metered" paywalls allow users a set number of page views, then charge for further access.

Enter the paywall, or "metered content"—the attempt by news businesses to charge readers and viewers for online content. Some of the earliest paywalls in the business offer a predictable tale: steep drops in traffic but unforeseen benefits, as discourse improves and a smaller base of paid online circulation replaces a much larger but unprofitable readership. At *Variety*, which put up a paywall in 2009, traffic on the magazine's site fell from 3.2 million impressions in December 2009 to 1.9 million in March 2010.

When Penske Media Corporation bought *Variety* from Reed Business Information in October 2012, it almost immediately took down the paywall and moved the print publication from a daily to a weekly schedule.

"Internally, we've been referring to the paywall dropping as 'the end of an error,'" said Jay Penske in a release announcing the decision. "It was an interesting experiment that didn't work. We look forward to welcoming back longtime Variety readers when the paywall drops March 1 [2013]."

The theory of free content is yielding to the theory that a higher-quality audience will lead to higher engagement, and better response to online ads, but the paywall has proven to be far from a cure-all for the industry's ills.

And despite the general assumption that charging for digital content will inevitably result in a drop in traffic, that's not always true—at least when news outlets adopt a more measured approach to their paywalls. The earliest paywalls—like *Newsday*'s way back in 2009—resulted in dramatic drops in traffic and along with them, drops in digital advertising. *Newsday* saw traffic drop by more than half in the year after it launched its paywall.

It was more a moat than a paywall, however: For a while, the company was charging an eye-popping $260 annually for access unless you subscribed to its parent company Cablevision's high-speed Internet access, in which case you got to read *Newsday* for free (this plan has since been abandoned). The moat gave way to a more charitable approach: the metered model approach, or "freemium" strategy, in which visitors can view the majority of website content for free, while unlimited access requires a weekly or monthly subscription.

FIGURE 5.2 Paywalls represent one of the most prevalent ways media companies attempt to make money from online content.
Source: Dja65/Shutterstock.

Metered paywalls are catching on as a critical access point for news widely available on the Web while producing at least some revenue. A case in point is Cox Newspapers, which in 2015 announced plans to move its newspaper sites from hard paywalls to a metered paywall system designed to drive engagement and increase traffic on social media.

Mark Medici, SVP of audience strategy and group lead for Cox Media Group and its flagship paper, the *Atlanta Journal-Constitution*, told Net-NewsCheck the company views social as interwoven with audience development and a crucial distribution channel currently driving a whopping 32 percent of traffic to all of its sites.

The most startling statistic from Cox: Across all markets, the company sees incredible results when it can get a print subscriber to engage with one or more of its digital platforms at least once a month. When Cox can engage a subscriber more than one time in 30 days, they are 121 percent more likely to retain their print subscription than those subscribers who don't engage with the company digitally.

The *New York Times'* website—which allows visitors 20 daily free visits before asking them to obtain a digital subscription—ensures that users who don't want to pay can return the following month, or even the next day, for more stories. This is essential to growing readership, as casual users continue to come back to the site.

It's a particularly low paywall, but that's a design feature, not a flaw. In other words, the *New York Times* thinks (and there is evidence to support this) that sharing content pretty freely brings them new readers who then will pay for digital content, not so much because they are forced to, but because they are encouraged to.

The *Times* allows anybody, anywhere, to read any article they like. If you follow a link to the *Times* from a blog or an aggregator, you'll never hit the paywall. It's an open-door, grownup way of dealing with content and with payment, and it is built on the assumption that, as a *Wired* blogger so eloquently put it, "Paying for something you value, even when you don't need to, is a mark of a civilized society."

And it is working.

In the spring of 2015, four years after it imposed its "metered model" paywall, the *New York Times* had more than 900,000 digital subscribers. The *Los Angeles Times* has a paywall now. So, too, do the *Dallas Morning News*, *Newsday*, the *Houston Chronicle*, the *Orange County Register*, the *Star Tribune* of Minneapolis, the *Philadelphia Inquirer*, and hundreds more.

A 2014 study by researchers at the University of Missouri School of Journalism found that metered paywalls are now commonplace. Eighty-one percent of newspaper publishers with circulations exceeding 75,000, for instance, had a meter. Of those using a meter, 28 percent allowed five or fewer free views, 44 percent allowed 6–10 free views, and 18 percent allowed 11 or more free views.

Magazines have joined the game, too. Time Inc., the granddaddy of them all, recently announced plans to roll out metered paywalls across its magazine titles, beginning with *Entertainment Weekly*. According to the New York-based publisher, the goal is to gain greater insight into the digital preferences of its audiences and to grow another stream of revenue. Following *Entertainment Weekly*'s website, the program rolled out to other titles, including *Health*, *People*, *Money*, *Real Simple* and *Time* later in 2015.

Again, if it seems that news companies' strategy is all over the map, well, that's because it is. Still, the potential is exciting. And that's because news companies now realize that the real currency of online news is engagement and sharing—the realm where the news meets the social network. We are in an era of wildly different approaches to the same age-old problem of how to pay for journalism.

▶ HYPERLOCAL: COMING FULL CIRCLE

In the end, journalism online is witnessing a return to the small-town, local news flavor that many veterans remember as the origin of their career in the news business. Having lost the franchise on international and national news to the largest players, and having watched as news staffs shrank in the face of the economic recession and an eroding print business model, an increasing number of journalists are turning to so-called "hyperlocal" news—hyperlocal meaning it is intensely focused on a defined geographic niche, be it a neighborhood, a zip code or in some cases, a city. Hyperlocal news most often is generated by a resident of that geographic area, is often distributed through blogs, and citizen-generated content is welcome.

Some hyperlocal sites offer general interest community news; others are tightly focused on a single issue such as public schools, the environment or the police. Many are one-person operations, fueled by the passion of a single person, but a host of for-profit hyperlocal sites have emerged as well, with decidedly mixed early results.

▶ **HYPERLOCAL:** A form of journalism marked by its intense focus on locality, community news defined by geography, often with a single-issue lens.

Like paywalls, hyperlocal content has seen its fits and starts as a strategy. The 400-pound gorilla of hyperlocal—AOL's Patch.com—grew by meteoric leaps from its launch in 2007 to 900-plus sites in 2013, only to succumb to lingering losses in 2014, when the company sold the majority of its ownership to Hale Global. Patch is a fraction of its once-mighty self, but the thinking behind its rise lives on in a variety of other players large and small. Patch remains a cautionary tale about the difficulty of turning hyperlocal news into a sustainable advertising market: By getting so intensely local, it's hard to reach beyond local mom-and-pop advertisers to the larger retailers and car dealers that can pay the bills.

Building a scalable media business that generates revenue through local advertising has proven a challenge, but there are hopeful signs out there like Local News Now LLC, a company that owns ARLnow, a hyperlocal site devoted to community news in suburban Virginia. ARLnow publisher Scott Brodbeck has built a small empire of hyperlocal news sites which now includes Reston Now and Borderstan.com, as well as Hill Now.

To get a sense of just how local hyperlocal can be, Hill Now covers the Capitol Hill area of D.C., while Borderstan.com covers the Dupont Circle, Columbia Heights, Logan Circle and U Street neighborhoods. Its journalism is a rich mix of neighborhood news and good old-fashioned shoe leather reporting, and it leverages a dynamic back-and-forth with its readers to break news of importance in its own backyard.

Lest you think it's all the stuff of neighborhood associations and elementary school calendars, keep in mind that Brodbeck's sites have broken many major stories that reverberated far beyond northern Virginia.

ARLnow broke a story on a Columbia Pike bus stop, the so-called "super stop," that cost $1 million to build. That story resulted in Arlington County launching an independent review of the super stop before rolling out the model to 23 other planned super stops.

ARLnow also broke the story about Jeff Krusinski, an Air Force officer charged with sexual assault who was removed from his position as chief of the military's Sexual Assault Prevention and Response Office. This local story renewed national attention to combating sexual assaults in the military.

Best of all, Brodbeck's sites are profitable, thanks to a fast-growing mix of advertising and sponsored content—a hybrid form of content paid for by the writer. Once haughtily dismissed as "advertorial" content, sponsored content plays a major role in many hyperlocal offerings.

◀ **SPONSORED CONTENT:** A specific and distinct section of content located on a website that is often sponsored by a single advertiser. The sponsored content will often match the subject matter, as well as the targeted audience, for the advertisement on the website.

Other hyperlocal sites that have adopted a multi-site strategy include Hulafrog, a specialty site for children's events and news. Hulafrog is now in 28 communities with plans to roll out to another 100-plus markets in the next year. The operating model is a hybrid of franchising and direct sales: Local publishers run the digital community guides, do the local marketing and ad sales and get a commission on what they sell.

Home Page Media Group, which serves four suburban Nashville, Tenn., neighborhoods is another rapidly growing hyperlocal site. Its sites are drawing 176,000 unique visitors monthly and more than 589,000 page views, and again, is profitable.

Finally, there's Billy Penn, the Philadelphia-centric hyperlocal startup of digital guru Jim Brady, perhaps the most interesting of them all. Opening up the content mix to aggregation and curation of local news from a variety of sources, combined with original reporting and off-line community gatherings, Billy Penn has a distinct voice and a millennial-friendly mix of news, opinion and lifestyle. It's incredibly smart, engaging, plugged deeply into social media and built for the smartphone. In other words, it may not be *the* future of journalism, but it is a strong hint about its direction.

It's not all startups, either. The venerable *Dallas Morning News* has taken a major turn toward hyperlocal, and in doing so is reinventing itself as less a *news* company and more a *media* company. The distinction is noteworthy, and we can debate the merits of it later, but it's clearly a new direction for the company, one with repercussions industrywide.

In 2015, A. H. Belo, owner of the *Dallas Morning News*, sold the *Providence Journal* and *Riverside Press-Enterprise* to reduce its reliance on print advertising and then turned around and bought three Dallas-based marketing companies.

Grant Moise, senior vice president, business development and niche products at the *Dallas Morning News*, said that the driving force behind the changes at the company has been to find ways to maximize revenue from the news company's huge audience.

> We have transformed what was once a newspaper company into a company still squarely into journalism but also into a broader marketing and information solutions company, he said. We have a unique audience we can sell, and we are not an agency, but we now have a suite of services that performs like an agency.

So, rather than simply sell clients a print or digital ad, the *Dallas Morning News* wants to engage that client in a holistic relationship: sell it ads, sure, but also host its website, do its search engine marketing, host events for it and plan its media strategy.

The three acquisitions specialize in local marketing automation, search engine marketing, direct mail and promotional products. Add them to Speakeasy, a two-year-old social media and content marketing agency owned by the *Dallas Morning News*, and three-year-old 508 Digital, the paper's local digital Internet marketing group, and what emerges is anything but a traditional news company. Instead, the *Dallas Morning News* looks more and more like a modern digital information services company, able to lean on its newsroom to create content that's particularly suited to hyperlocal consumers and advertisers. Its arts and entertainment website, Guide Live, for example, is specifically designed as a resource for local consumers. That should hopefully lead to the site being a destination for an audience based in the Dallas area, which in turn makes it a more attractive proposition for local advertisers.

Moise said that ultimately, the question boils down to replacing all that income from print advertising with a mix of other revenue streams created from that huge audience for DMN products.

"We have more people consuming our products, every minute, than ever in our company's history," he said.

> We have almost 4,000 advertising relationships. We have the services
> these advertisers need to build their overall marketing mix, and we
> have the audience to get their products in front of—we just have to
> put it all together in a way that replicates to some degree the money
> we made from the previous generation of newspapers.

Until that day occurs, Moise said, "we're not going to sit on our hands and watch it all crumble."

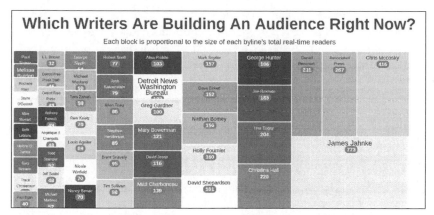

FIGURE 5.3 This dashboard uses Chartbeat to give a real time view of how reporters are performing—live at: http://onlinejournalism blog.com/2015/07/01/dashboards-and-journalism-why-we-need-to-do-better/.

In July 2015, the *Dallas Morning News* announced voluntary buyouts of 167 news employees. In his memo announcing the cuts, editor Mike Wilson signaled clearly the company's strategy:

> It is essential that we save money this time as well. But part of the reason for this voluntary program is to prepare us for a change in direction.
>
> In the weeks and months after this buyout, we will add positions back to the newsroom, with a focus on hiring outstanding digital journalists. Adding new digital skills will make us more competitive in a fast-changing journalism marketplace now and in the future.
>
> This is an important time for our Company. We know the audience for newspapers is shrinking and the digital audience is growing, especially on mobile. Other media organizations are launching new technologies and telling stories in new ways in an effort to take some of that digital audience away from us.

The next time a relative corners you at a family gathering and asks why in the world you are going into the world of journalism, counter with one of these examples—provided that you intend to become one of those "outstanding digital journalists" that Wilson alluded to. Better yet, direct them to the work of Michele McLellan, who has been keeping tabs on online news start-ups for years now. McLellan surveyed independent online news publishers in 2013, and found that 30 percent of respondents had a steady flow of revenue, and had turned a profit in 2011. By 2014, more than 60 percent of the publishers responding said they increased their revenues in 2013 over 2012.

It's no path to untold riches: only one third reported turning a profit and nearly half reported $50,000 or less in annual revenue. Still, it's encouraging, a hopeful sign of greater things to come.

Indeed, this was intended to be a hopeful look at an industry composed of a wild mix of startups and so-called legacy media, all attempting to figure out how to monetize digital content. The result of all of this activity is an emerging media ecosystem in which legacy media compete with an ever-evolving array of hybrids—some more distribution platform, others more content engine.

5.2 THE VIEW FROM THE PROS: WHO IS YOUR JOURNALISM FOR?

Let's think about that question on multiple levels. Why, and for whom, are you a journalist? To whom is your publication directed? For whom did you cover today's news event?

It's not for yourself, not for your colleagues, and not for your sources. It's for the audience. The community. The readers, viewers, listeners and users.

On the surface, that's no problem. Journalists tend to have a strong service ethic. Many would say they got into the business to make their communities, and democracies, better by providing needed information. If we're here to serve a need, it follows that we must identify a community's needs and have a sense of whether we're really meeting them. That requires the news processes and products to be audience-focused.

And today's audience is changing rapidly.

The days of news as a one-way broadcast are ending. Many people get their news not by tuning in to a specific channel, publication or website. Instead, the news comes to them, in e-mail and RSS feeds, in soundbites and channel surfing, and on social platforms such as Facebook, Twitter and YouTube. They consume snippets of information all day, in many locations and on multiple devices. In addition, they're often creating their own media, and documenting their own lives and stories. Forward-thinking journalists are finding new ways to be part of a rapidly changing, increasingly crowded media landscape.

The role of journalists is fundamentally shifting. We're not the only providers of information. Instead, we need to focus on being credible, authoritative voices in a noisy world. We need to figure out what we offer that no one else can, and make sure we're providing that service or content in a way that respects readers' habits and time. We need to harness the wisdom and power of the crowd, respecting how the community can contribute to telling its own story.

And we need to accept that, rather than deciding what information users have access to, we're instead helping them decide what to pay attention to.

One way we can do that is by amplifying other voices, not just promoting our own. Some news organizations are forming robust partnerships with local bloggers. Rather than assuming all other media are competitors, they're teaming up to cover stories. Their extensive linking back and forth leads to more audience for all involved.

Knowing that users' attention is what we (and advertisers) seek, we need to have the audience firmly in mind when we decide how, when and where to share our content. It's

no longer enough to publish a story (regardless of platform or media type) and hope the audience finds it. Journalists have an obligation to identify the people who most want and need their content and make an effort to take the content to them.

When the staff of Voice of San Diego covered the story of a refugee who was deaf and unable to speak, they were shedding light on issues and problems they felt deserved attention. Rather than simply posting the story and moving on, they actively sought out audience, taking the links to the parts of the community they thought most needed the content. For the package to do the most good, it needed to be seen by those who could effect change.

So let's ask again: Who is your journalism for?

Journalism can't be just about the product—the "what" of the five W's. Who is already talking about what you're covering? Can you take your information to that conversation, making it richer and more contextual? Can you picture where and when what you're providing will be most useful? Have you shown why and how it's relevant?

Journalists are great at the craft of storytelling and information providing. But without incorporating a focus on audience, we'll find ourselves talking to an empty room.

That's the real meaning of "social media." It's not about Twitter or Facebook. The news has always been social. Clipping out an article and mailing it to a family member is a social act. If we recognize that people create and share media all day, how are we encouraging them to make our content and products part of their naturally social lives? And how can we best invite them to share their content with us, collaborating with us to tell the stories of their communities?

Journalists have long trusted their gut feelings about what news consumers want to read, view or listen to. But in the world of online media, we can know what people are reading. Not only that, we can know how far into the video users are watching, what time of day they like what kind of content, what search terms brought them to us, what kind of technology they're using—all information that will help us provide content they're likely to respond to.

We have the opportunity, in other words, to structure our time and resources to best cover the topics and stories our news consumers have shown us they most value. We have the ability to know what information needs we're trying to serve, and how well we're doing it.

We have a chance to adapt in exciting ways—to create a journalism that is truly focused on its audience. As we do that, we're faced with some key questions:

- How do we preserve the journalism we find most fundamentally important while also responding to audience desires?
- How can our storytelling be responsive to actual, demonstrated community information needs?
- How do we make sure the work we're doing reaches the people who most want and need it?
- And if a journalism tree falls in a forest and no one consumes it, does it do any good?

Joy Mayer was an associate professor at the Missouri School of Journalism. She spent a year as a fellow at the Reynolds Journalism Institute studying audience engagement in journalism.

▶ **MONETIZATION:**
The process of converting something that once was free into a product that is sold.

For ease of thinking, let's organize that ecosystem into loose, fluid categories, subject to change daily:

1. *Aggregators and Curators (Platforms):* Think Flipboard, Instagram, or even Facebook. Then there's Storify and Summify—curated aggregation platforms that allow you to summarize the entirety of a story in the social networks.
2. *Personality-fueled Blogs/Single-Issue Deep Dives*: (DeadSpin, TechCrunch, Talking Points Memo, BusinessInsider). These are brands that began with a borderline-obsessive dive into a single topic and then morphed outward.
3. *Disruptors*: Some of these are startups that were purchased by legacy media, such as Everyblock, Zite and @BreakingNews, but each began as an organic news company bent on delivering content in news ways— ways that changed the marketplace. Disruptors go about things in completely new ways, altering the landscape.

These new types of media companies are redefining what it means to be in the journalism business. In his book *Here Comes Everybody*, Shirky offers three requirements for social action sites:

1. *Is there a plausible promise?* Why would anyone want to join? Is it a promise that will draw the crowd?
2. *Are the tools effective?* Do the site's tools facilitate collaboration and allow the community to easily come together? The tools must be easy enough for users of all technological levels to use the site in its intended purpose.
3. *Is there an acceptable bargain with the users?* What is expected of the user and are the returns to the user enough to make the user want to participate?

The emerging media platforms are working to address these three critical requirements, with varying levels of success. Some, like Spot.Us, are valuable not for what they are accomplishing immediately, but also because they generate secondary levels of innovation and collaboration.

A keen digital entrepreneur, David Cohn, put it this way in a blog post:

> What we need right now is 10,000 journalism startups. Of these 9,000 will fail, 1,000 will find ways to sustain themselves for a brief period of time, 98 will find mediocre success and financial security and two will come out as new media equivalents to the *New York Times* . . . I don't know what that organization will look like or who it will be—but that's what we need and we face some serious challenges along the way.

The wide range of experimentation in this space offers tremendous hope for journalism's future. The stakes couldn't possibly be higher.

One last word from Shirky:

> Society doesn't need newspapers. What we need is journalism. For a century, the imperatives to strengthen journalism and to strengthen newspapers have been so tightly wound as to be indistinguishable. That's been a fine accident to have, but when that accident stops, as it is stopping before our eyes, we're going to need lots of other ways to strengthen journalism instead.

> When we shift our attention from "save newspapers" to "save society," the imperative changes from "preserve the current institutions" to "do whatever works." And what works today isn't the same as what used to work . . . Any experiment, though, designed to provide new models for journalism is going to be an improvement over hiding from the real, especially in a year when, for many papers, the unthinkable future is already in the past.

It's that critical.

Chapter Five Review

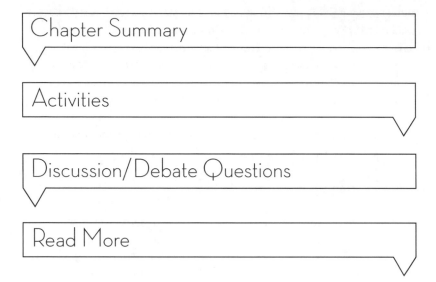

Chapter Summary

Activities

Discussion/Debate Questions

Read More

▶ CHAPTER SUMMARY

The field of journalism is experiencing transformative change ushered in by the digital age—change that offers both promise and peril for news organizations. The Internet has been an incredibly disruptive technology, but has also yielded an incredible array of innovative new models for doing journalism. Everything we thought we knew about the way journalism is created, distributed and paid for is being challenged, if not replaced, by other technologies that shrink time, space and speed to market. While the legacy media continue to struggle with the pace of change, hopeful signs emerge daily. It's an exciting if terrifying time to enter the business.

▶ ACTIVITIES

1. If there is one thing the modern media economy has given us, it's a never-ending supply of brand-new media companies. Research and find a list of interesting media startups. Use the list to contact someone—an entrepreneur at the heart of one of the startups—and arrange an online chat or e-mail Q&A. Basic questions might include: What sparked the entrepreneur's idea? What have been the biggest challenges in getting that idea off the ground? What's the company's business model?

2. Spend about 10 minutes in class looking at job listings for journalists (a good site is www.journalismjobs.com). What jobs can you find that might not have existed 10 years ago? Are jobs out there that could have been filled by someone graduating in 1990? Discuss your findings with the class. What do the job listings tell us about changes in the industry?

3. Watch this clip from *The Colbert Report* about CNN's layoff of editors and photojournalists: www.colbertnation.com/the-colbert-report-videos/403149/november-28–2011/stephen-colbert-s-me-reporters. Lead a discussion on the points Colbert was trying to make by poking fun at CNN's "iReport" social network news gathering concept. What are the risks of relying too heavily on the public to produce content?

4. Go take a look at one of Gannett's many news organizations, at www.gannett.com/brands/ and pick one of interest. Look at the features not common in other community newspapers. Next, review the features that are similar to those in other papers. In what ways is this company promoting innovation? In what ways could it go further?

5. Spend one week reading ProPublica (www.propublica.org/; or if you have a local non-profit news site, use that). Keep a diary of each day's experience. Was there new content daily on the site? What sorts of stories were broken? Did the stories appear to be written by journalists or citizens? Was there a mix of news and entertainment features? Write a brief summary of what you saw and reflect about how what you read differed from a traditional news site (for example the site of their local newspaper). Post a 500-word entry to the class discussion thread set up for this topic.

▶ DISCUSSION/DEBATE QUESTIONS

1. In recent years, we've been exposed to news reports of publications cutting back circulation and production days, journalists being laid off and sharp cuts in media operations. Why might news about shifts in the news industry be covered differently than these same shifts in other industries? Can journalists be objective in reporting this news? Do these stories take on more importance because journalists are covering their own industry?

2. What are the risks to the role journalism plays in democracy when news organizations eliminate reporters devoted to investigative journalism? Can this role truly be filled by other journalists as they cover their beats or by non-profits working with the outlets to fill the gaps? Do shrinking numbers of investigative journalists make the press more susceptible to well-funded advocacy groups providing their own data as they make claims? Are media owners making a mistake when they choose to cut these jobs?

3. What do you do when you encounter a paywall (or even a registration requirement) when you click into a site you've been referred to on Facebook, Twitter, Pintrest or e-mail to read a story? Will you register? Will you pay? Think about the types of content you would consider paying for online (typically entertainment content like music, movies, games and books). What would digital news have to offer you for you to make that leap to beyond the paywall?

4. Go to http://features.journalism.org/nonprofit-news-outlets/ and find the community nearest to you with a site—or just one that interests you. What content is covered? What is the quality of the writing and reporting on the site? How does this compare with local newspaper coverage of the same community?

5. In what ways might general news organizations, which have been aiming to serve large audiences for many years, work to build smaller but more deeply engaged audiences? Should core products be divided and given their own identity?

▶ READ MORE

Mark Briggs, *Journalism Next: A Practical Guide to Digital Reporting and Publishing*, Washington, D.C.: CQ Press, 2010.

Dan Gillmor, *We the Media: Grassroots Journalism by the People, for the People, North Sebastapol*, Calif.: O'Reilly Books, 2006.

Jeff Kaye and Stephen Quinn, *Funding Journalism in the Digital Age*, New York: Peter Lang Publishing, 2010.

Alan Mutter, "Reflections of a Newsosaur," at newsosaur.blogspot.com/

Clay Shirky, "The Story So Far: What We Know About the Business of Digital Journalism, Tow Center for Digital Journalism." www.cjr.org/the_business_of_digital_journalism/.

Chris Sutcliffe, "How the Dallas Morning News Is Tackling the Challenges of Hyperlocal Content," March 3, 2015. www.themediabriefing.com/article/how-the-dallas-morning-news-is-tackling-the-challenges-of-hyperlocal-content.

6

What Do Journalists Owe Us?

"I said things that weren't true."

Let's hope the only time you ever utter that sentence is when you admit to lying about your best friend's terrible new haircut. Let's hope, in other words, that you never find yourself sitting across from Matt Lauer on the *Today* show, as former NBC News anchor Brian Williams did, telling the world you violated the central element of journalism, truth-telling, out of nothing more than self interest.

The scandal took off in 2015, when Iraq war veterans disputed Williams' account of having been in a helicopter hit by ground fire during the 2003 invasion of Iraq. In fact, Williams had never been fired upon. Rather, he was a passenger in another helicopter that met up with the crew of that first helicopter and took pictures of the damage later. Williams first told his tall tale as a correspondent on NBC's *Nightly News*, then later repeated it, notably, during a 2013 appearance on *Late Night* with David Letterman and in other stories after he had moved up to the anchor chair at NBC.

LEARNING OBJECTIVES

Discover how journalism's broader principles translate into specific guidelines for ethical performance;

Become acquainted with codes of ethics in journalism;

Begin developing skills in ethical decision-making, using a philosophically grounded framework.

With each retelling, the story and Williams' role in it seemed to get more dramatic.

Here's Williams attempting to explain himself to Lauer, after NBC announced it was demoting Williams (sort of) to MSNBC:

> Lauer: Did you know when you went on *Nightly News* that you were telling a story that was not true?
>
> Williams: No. It came from a bad place. It came from a sloppy choice of words. I told stories that were not true, over the years, looking back. It is very clear. I never intended to. It got mixed up. It got turned around in my mind.
>
> Lauer: I worry as you say this, Brian, that people who are going to have listened to your apology on air [. . .] who heard you use words like "conflated aircraft" or "made mistakes with my memory" on certain things are now going to hear what you're saying [. . .] and they're going to say, "He's still saying he didn't intend to mislead people, and yet he didn't tell the truth, and he had to know as the guy who lived through those experiences that it wasn't the truth."
>
> Williams: I see why people would say that. I understand it. This came from clearly a bad place, a bad urge inside me. It was clearly ego driven, the desire to better my role in a story I was already in. That's what I've been tearing apart and unpacking and analyzing.

In the annals of terrible apologies, Williams' interview with Lauer has to rank pretty highly. Williams says he didn't mean to mislead, didn't realize he wasn't telling the truth, but also that he was sloppy and egotistical. (Here's a pro tip: When you need to apologize, actually apologize. Don't get all wrapped up in excuses and rationalizations.) And the Iraq story was not an isolated incident, as it turns out. NBC found problems with several other stories, including coverage of Hurricane Katrina in which Williams claimed to have seen dead bodies in the streets when that could not, in fact, have happened as he described.

So, Williams' ego and his impulse to entertain—this is a person popular for slow jamming the news on the *Tonight Show* after all—got the best of him, squandering his credibility, not to mention NBC's. It is a little amazing that he wasn't fired outright. Indeed, that's what happened to former *New York Times* reporter Jayson Blair. In his case, the news organization's handling of his dismissal was at least as dramatic as his ethical offenses.

FIGURE 6.1 Brian Williams' suspension tells a cautionary tale about the blurred lines between journalism and entertainment.

Source: Everett Collection/ Shutterstock.

Here's the beginning of a story occupying coveted front-page space on May 11, 2003:

> A staff reporter for The New York Times committed frequent acts of journalistic fraud while covering significant news events in recent months, an investigation by Times journalists has found. The widespread fabrication and plagiarism represent a profound betrayal of trust and a low point in the 152-year history of the newspaper.
>
> The reporter, Jayson Blair, 27, misled readers and Times colleagues with dispatches that purported to be from Maryland, Texas and other states, when often he was far away, in New York. He fabricated comments. He concocted scenes. He lifted material from other newspapers and wire services. He selected details from photographs to create the impression he had been somewhere or seen someone, when he had not.
>
> And he used these techniques to write falsely about emotionally charged moments in recent history, from the deadly sniper attacks in suburban Washington to the anguish of families grieving for loved ones killed in Iraq.

Wow, talk about harsh! The message here is: Plagiarists, liars and other assorted cheaters, beware! You won't get away with it forever, and when you're caught . . . well, let's just say it won't be pretty.

Indeed the *Times* devoted a lot of resources to investigating and exposing all of Blair's misdeeds. The story, which five reporters and three editors spent a week reporting and writing, catalogued Blair's journalistic crimes and the multiple failures at many levels of the *Times'* management to notice and stop him sooner. The tale took 150 interviews to uncover and 14,000 words and more than four newspaper pages to tell. Why all this effort? Think back to your earlier reading about the kind of verification that's so central to journalism. That's true even if the story is, uncomfortably, at your own doorstep. In the end, "disgraced reporter" became Jayson Blair's unofficial title.

There's a chance—a chance that causes us pain, but a chance nevertheless—that some of you reading this might be wondering just what the big deal is. So Blair copied some things here and there and wasn't always where he said he was.

That has to be pretty common, right? And who does it really hurt, anyway? Why all the drama? Well, the answers are "no," "lots of people" and "because the *Times* takes its responsibilities seriously."

But wait—the *Times* story says it better:

> Every newspaper, like every bank and every police department, trusts its employees to uphold central principles, and the inquiry found that Mr. Blair repeatedly violated the cardinal tenet of journalism, which is simply truth.

The *Times* is saying that, in toying with the truth, Blair undermined the integrity of the paper, potentially damaging its relationship with the readers who depend on it and with the news sources and subjects it covers. To call the truth the "cardinal tenet" of journalism is to say that the truth is the key standard by which it is judged. Without truth, journalism isn't really journalism.

But of course you know that already from Chapter 2, where you discovered that journalism, even though it resists easy definition, is *aimed at gathering, verifying and reporting truthful information of consequence to citizens in a democracy*. Furthermore, you learned that to "do" journalism—to meet the requirements of the definition—is to think about the audience as citizens first, to practice a rigorous verification process and to act independently. One way to think about journalism ethics—the subject of this chapter—is that it involves the kinds of situations in which something or someone gets in the way of a journalist being able to meet the letter and the spirit of that definition.

▶ **BLACK, WHITE AND GRAY**

For all the handwringing in the journalistic community over the lack of ethics Williams and Blair demonstrated—and trust us, there was a lot of handwringing—the episodes actually aren't very interesting as ethics case studies. Williams' saga *is* a very interesting example of the problems with blurring news and entertainment, and Blair's story *is* a fascinating case study in newsroom (mis)management. But all the things Williams and Blair did wrong are *obviously* wrong, and they knew it. They violated the truth,

◀ **PLAGIARISM:** A kind of intellectual theft, in which one passes off someone else's work and ideas as one's own.

FIGURE 6.2 Wall-to-wall coverage of sensational crime risks public backlash and weakens ties between journalists and the public.

Source: Photo courtesy of Paul Wellman/Santa Barbara Independent.

the "cardinal tenet of journalism." There's no gray area when it comes to the kind of outright fiction Williams and Blair were producing. If you say you were on a helicopter that came under fire, then you better have been on that helicopter. If a story indicates you interviewed someone, then you better have interviewed that person. To do otherwise is to lie to readers and viewers, to trivialize the experiences of others, and, in Blair's case, to steal from the other journalists whose work you copied. Really. It's just that simple. Williams and Blair didn't face any tricky ethical dilemmas. Williams made stuff up because he wanted to be more important and entertaining. Blair made stuff up because he wanted to look like a better journalist than he was. That huge front-page investigation into the mess made it crystal clear that Blair's actions were completely contrary to the *Times'* understanding of its ethical obligations. That Williams didn't lose his job is a lingering point of controversy and a hint about the very different pressures and expectations at play in network news.

As you've seen throughout this book so far, the press is powerful. It ought to exercise its power responsibly. (Spiderman fans will recognize these as Uncle Ben's wise words to Peter Parker: "With great power comes great responsibility." The philosopher Voltaire, though, probably gets first credit for it.) To act responsibly often means going beyond what the law requires. Neither Williams nor Blair did anything illegal. But they were entirely contrary to their obligations as journalists. Being a journalist is voluntary. So is being a doctor or a lawyer—you decide that's what you want to do, and you go do it. Doctors and lawyers get licenses and take oaths. Journalists in the United States don't do either of those things because, as we have seen, they are considered contrary to free press principles. Nevertheless, in taking on the role of journalist, you are—voluntarily—taking on a set of responsibilities related to that role. Doctors and lawyers make commitments to serve their patients' and clients' interests. Journalists make commitments to the public. The voluntary nature of all this means that journalists are self-policing. One of the things this chapter addresses is how to think about what the rules are and how to "police" them, even if only for yourself.

Neither of these scandals, thankfully, represents a common ethical issue in journalism. They are dramatic, interesting cases that have received tons of attention, and rightly so. But the vast majority of ethical questions journalists face aren't about whether or not it's OK to make stuff up. Let's look at a couple other examples to get a sense of the kinds of ethical situations journalists face more routinely.

In the spring of 2014, Isla Vista, California—home to the University of California–Santa Barbara—joined the already-too-long list of communities victimized by a mass shooting. In a spree that targeted women and minorities, Elliot Rodger killed 6 people and injured 14 others before turning a gun on himself, ending the rampage. While covering a killing spree isn't a part of a journalist's typical day (thank goodness), covering tragic events of all kinds is indeed something journalists do a lot. Reporters come to the scene to interview eyewitnesses, survivors, family and friends. They show us the bullet holes and the blood and the makeshift memorials marking the sites where victims died. They attend press conferences and pester officials for answers. It's what reporters do. And it's what they *should* do, isn't it? So what, if anything, raises an ethical caution flag here?

In the aftermath of the tragedy, as the days and the news coverage wore on, many community members began to see the news as adding to their grief rather than providing helpful information. And they let their feelings be known by holding protest signs behind television journalists doing live reports from the scene:

OUR TRAGEDY IS NOT YOUR COMMODITY

Remembrance NOT ratings

Stop filming our tears

Let us heal

NEWS CREWS GO HOME!

It is a problem of scale. Journalists working on high-profile stories like the Isla Vista rampage, especially when those stories attract international attention and scores of journalists come to the scene, are caught between informing the public about an event and potentially harming those involved in the event. Now *that* is much closer to a true ethical dilemma—a conflict between two legitimate interests—than anything in the Williams or Blair cases. How can a journalist do her job without causing undue harm? What's the ethical path to take?

In the Isla Vista case, the rampage was over by the time the journalists arrived. But what about those situations when journalists can offer a picture of what happened, as it was happening? Any ethical flags you can think of? Let's turn our attention to North Charleston, South Carolina, and the case of Walter Scott.

Scott was pulled over by police for a broken brake light. He ran away, was tasered when Patrolman Michael Slager caught up to him, then managed to run away again. And then Slager shot him. In the back. Eight times. The police report said Slager had fired out of fear because Scott had taken his taser.

Scott's death might have been just another sad statistic were it not for Feiden Santana and his cellphone camera.

Turns out Santana had captured the entire incident—and the video did not match the police report. The video shows Scott running away and Slager shooting him, then picking up an object from the site of their earlier scuffle, walking back to where Scott lay dying, and dropping the object next to Scott's body. The speculation is that that object was the Taser.

The video changed everything.What had been a terrible fatal police shooting became an even more terrible potential murder of an unarmed black man by a white police officer. And in the wake of deadly force incidents in Ferguson, Baltimore, Staten Island and elsewhere, Scott's death sparked protests. As we write this, Slager is awaiting trial on a murder charge.

But about that video . . . remember, you're supposed to be thinking about ethical red flags. What comes to mind here? How about the fact that the video shows a person being killed? Journalists in this case had to weigh the value of showing the video as a piece of evidence in the verification process against its graphic and disturbing content that might be seen as exploitative or even add to the Scott family's grief. While the circumstances of Scott's death were extraordinary, dealing with graphic materials is pretty ordinary for journalists. Still, there is no magic or one-size-fits-all answer to how to do it. And, as in the Isla Vista case, journalists faced a situation in which doing their jobs—informing the public—could create harm.

You're probably beginning to realize this ethics business might look easy on the surface but can get pretty complicated, pretty quickly. What does it mean to say that an action is "unethical"? What kinds of difficult choices do journalists routinely face, and how do they decide what to do? To answer those questions, we'll first need to lay some groundwork in ethics and then build from that groundwork to the specific case of journalism, using some of the insights you gained about the norms and expectations of journalism in previous chapters. By now you have a pretty good idea of what journalism is supposed to do in a democracy and all of the factors (economic, technological, etc.) that can help or hinder journalism's ability to do its job. With ethics, we enter murkier territory, where doing one's job as a journalist has the potential to cause harm to others, where journalists are often required to balance the interests of the public against other equally important interests. Murky indeed. Let's get started.

FIGURE 6.3 Public dialogue over media coverage remains an essential component of the relationship between journalists and the communities they cover.

Source: Meet the Press.

6.1 THE VIEW FROM THE PROS: HOW GOOD JOURNALISM CAN HARM

Five years later, I still wonder what happened to the four Ethiopian farmers whose names I used. In the months leading up to Ethiopia's May 2010 elections, reports emerged that the ruling party's campaign message in some parts of the East African country were as simple as this: vote for us or starve. Poor families in the Ethiopian countryside who did not support the ruling party were being denied access to the food aid supplied by the U.S. and other Western countries that supported more than 6 million people in the country.

Reporting this story as a foreign correspondent was not easy. Then prime minister Meles Zenawi's government had been intolerant of critical reporting since taking power in 1991. Foreign correspondents were sometimes detained or expelled for reporting on human rights abuses or on issues such as malnutrition that portrayed the country as impoverished and ineptly governed. Local journalists were, and are, regularly jailed on trumped up charges or flee into exile.

In addition, those affected by the politicization of food aid were mainly in the countryside—often hundreds of miles from the capital. In December of 2009, seven farmers from northern Ethiopia traveled to the capital, Addis Ababa, to meet with rights groups and foreign diplomats to talk about the problem. They were arrested, jailed and interrogated by security personnel. After the farmers were escorted back to their villages, a British researcher for Human Rights Watch who had planned to meet with them was expelled from the country. A week later, when a translator and I traveled to the north to try to track the men down and interview them, we were captured by the intelligence service. We were held for two days and taken back to the capital, where I was threatened with expulsion.

I spent weeks cooling my heels in Addis Ababa trying to figure out how to report the story without getting ejected from the country where I'd lived for three years. The foreign aid agencies were of little help—while many aid workers privately acknowledged the problem, the agencies themselves did not want to risk having their programs shut down by facilitating such a story. And as I had learned, a foreigner traveling in the affected areas asking questions drew near-instant attention from plain-clothes security personnel.

Eventually I decided to send a brave Ethiopian journalist named Eskinder Nega to the countryside by himself to try to quietly meet with farmers willing to talk to a foreign reporter. Eskinder, who had already been jailed six times by the government, would then send the men to the capital one by one by bus so as not to attract attention, and I would interview them individually there.

As my plan moved forward, my ethical dilemma was this: Should I use the names of the farmers? Each of those interviewed had given permission for their names and hometowns to be used in any story. But was it the right thing to do?

On the one hand, planning and enacting the scheme was a big task. It involved multiple two- and three-day trips to the countryside by Eskinder, paying for the farmers to travel up to two days to Addis Ababa and arranging for them to be discreetly housed and fed without attracting the attention of watchful eyes.

As such, I wanted a story that would be bulletproof when I presented it to my editors. I thought strong evidence would be needed to publish such articles because the situation implied complicity by U.S. and other Western aid agencies in the abuses. Naming those making the accusations only added to the credibility of the story.

On the other hand I knew the government could be ruthless with those who criticized it or made it look bad, no matter how vulnerable they were. Most memorably, in 2008 the government had closed two feeding centers for severely malnourished children in the midst of a drought, sending all the patients home to their drought-stricken villages to fend for themselves. The reason? The foreign nuns who ran the feeding centers had allowed television crews from the BBC and Al-Jazeera to film on their grounds and conduct interviews. Further, the only other organization that had done research on food aid politicization—Human Rights Watch—had published a lengthy report but withheld the names of the farmers it interviewed.

In the end I decided that for the credibility of the story, I would use the real names of the farmers, though I described only the general part of the country where they came from in the hope that this would provide them with some measure of protection.

The stories they told me had been universally sad: One man reported losing a three-year-old daughter after his family had been kicked out of an aid program because of his support for a small opposition party. A second opposition supporter reported that his wife had divorced him so that she would be allowed back in to the food aid program in their district. A third was beaten so badly by ruling party officials that his finger had to be amputated.

After they went back to their villages, the *New York Times*, *Newsweek* and IRIN, a humanitarian news service operated by the United Nations, carried some of what they had told me. I left Ethiopia soon afterwards, and the ruling party won 99.6 percent of the seats in parliament that year. To this day I don't know what became of any of the farmers.

Shortly after the reports were published and amid continuing pressure from human rights groups, Western donor agencies announced they would investigate allegations that aid was being politicized. But the investigation was quietly dropped under pressure from the Ethiopian government.

Eskinder, the local journalist who did much of the legwork, was put back in jail in September 2011 on trumped-up terrorism charges after criticizing government corruption and the torture of prisoners. As of July 2015, he's still in prison serving an 18-year sentence. Zenawi died in 2012, but his ruling party has continued to guide Ethiopia as an authoritarian one-party state with strong support from the U.S. and its allies. Given how little impact any of the articles had in affecting the policies of the Ethiopian government or Western aid donors, I worry the decision I made to name the Ethiopian farmers—poor people caught in a repressive system—may have been the wrong one.

THINK ABOUT IT: Would you have used the farmers' names? Would the credibility of the story have been harmed with partial names or pseudonyms? If the farmers willingly gave permission to use their names, was the journalist right to respect these wishes? Is it the duty of the journalist to protect sources who speak openly and know the risks they are taking?

Jason McLure was an Africa correspondent for *Bloomberg News* from 2007 to 2011. He now teaches international journalism at the University of Missouri and is managing editor of the *Global Journalist* radio program and website.

▶ ETHICS IS . . . NOT WHAT YOU THINK

Our first task is to define "ethics" so we can go about our business of apply-ing ethics to journalism. Scholars at the Markkula Center for Applied Ethics say people often (mistakenly) equate ethics with their personal feelings, reli-gion, the law, or societal standards. While ethics might be connected to each of these, none defines ethics on its own. After all, one's personal feelings, a society's standards and even the law can often deviate sharply from what is right. As the Markkula Center scholars note, Nazi Germany was morally corrupt, and laws permitting slavery violated fundamental notions of eth-ics. And even though most religions have high ethical standards, to equate ethics with religion would mean that ethics would apply only to religious people. Certainly an ethics that applies to everyone would be preferred.

▶ **MORALITY:**
A code of conduct. As the *Stanford Encyclopedia of Philosophy* notes, this term can refer either to a descrip-tion of how a group or society actu-ally behaves (what norms and stan-dards it follows), or to a more universal code of conduct that everyone should endorse.

If ethics isn't the same thing as personal feelings, religion, law or societal standards, what is it?

> Ethics is two things. First, ethics refers to well-founded standards of right and wrong that prescribe what humans ought to do, usually in terms of rights, obligations, benefits to society, fairness, or specific virtues. [. . .] Secondly, ethics refers to the study and development of one's ethical standards. As mentioned above, feelings, laws, and social norms can deviate from what is ethical. So it is necessary to constantly examine one's standards to ensure that they are reasonable and well-founded.
>
> (Markkula Center)

We will spend most of our time dissecting the first "thing" in that definition, though in doing so we are suggesting just how important the second "thing" is too. The more you learn about and develop your own ethical standards, the more you can contribute to the maintenance of high ethical standards in journalism overall.

So, first things first. What are those standards, rights, obligations, and so forth mentioned in the first part of that definition, and where do they come from? Thousands of years of philosophy have offered many different answers. Because we are not philosophers and, more important, because knowing the source of those obligations is less important for our purposes here than simply learning what the obligations are and how to act on them, we will not attempt to recap all of moral philosophy. (We strongly encourage you to take an actual philosophy course to explore this incredibly interesting stuff in depth.) Rather, we are going to present just one approach, an approach that has the benefit of being pretty straightforward and practical as well as including insights from major strands of philosophical thought.

▶ MEET W. D. ROSS, INTUITIONIST

Ethics helps us figure out what we, as moral beings in the world, ought to do. As the definition suggests, knowing what we ought to do involves knowing what our duties are. W. D. Ross, an influential British philosopher of the 20th Century, developed a moral framework based on the idea that our intuition can tell us what those duties—what he called *prima facie* duties—are. Some journalism ethics scholars, notably Thomas Bivins and Christopher Meyers, have discussed ways to incorporate Ross' insights into journalistic practice. We will use Meyers' recent work to help us understand where Ross is coming from. To say these duties are *prima facie* is to say they are self-evident, obvious, universal, intuitively knowable. If that sounds a little magical or weird, Meyers says, consider that recent advances in biology, neurology and psychology suggest human beings might be "hard wired" for ethics. But even without that scientific support, Ross' argument makes some, well, intuitive sense. For example, think about the duties you have just by being a person in the world. What do you owe other people? It's hard to disagree with the idea that if you make a promise, you should keep it—that you have an obligation to the person to whom you made the promise. Likewise, it's tough to argue against the notion that avoiding harm to others is an obligation everyone has. These ideas seem obvious and universal, don't they? Of course you ought to keep promises and avoid causing harm; to act otherwise is to call into question your ability to live in society with others. There's a word for that: psychopath.

So the basic idea in Ross' theory is this: There are several *prima facie*, or common sense, duties that—all other things being equal—you are obligated to act on. The "all other things being equal" part is important, as you'll see when we apply Ross' theory to actual decision-making. But let's have a look at all the duties first, again with Meyers' help. The following list divides the duties into "perfect" and "imperfect" ones and includes very brief descriptions of what the duties mean. Perfect duties are those that are strictly binding—you *must* do them—while the imperfect ones are strongly encouraged—you really, really should do them if you can. This distinction, too, will be important when it comes to decision-making.

Perfect Duties

1. Fidelity (Keep your promises.)

2. Nonmaleficence (Avoid causing harm. An easier way to say it: Noninjury.)

3. Reparation (Make up for harm you've caused others. Meyers notes this is a perfect duty only if the harm was intentional or the result of gross negligence; otherwise it's an imperfect duty.)

4. Respect for persons, including oneself (Treat every person as a being whose autonomy—for example, their ability to make choices—must be honored.)

5. Formal justice (Give people what they've legitimately earned and treat people equally.)

Imperfect Duties

1. Beneficence (Do what you can to improve the lives of others.)

2. Gratitude (Show appreciation for what others have done for you.)

3. Distributive justice (Distribute social goods in a way that benefits the least advantaged people and protects liberty.)

4. Honesty (Avoid misleading people into believing what is false. Note that Meyers includes this as an imperfect duty, not because truth isn't important—it's essential!—but because some forms of deception are meant to actually help prevent harm.)

5. Self-improvement (Work to develop your moral, intellectual and physical qualities.)

Being able to recognize which obligations are most at stake in any given situation and to weigh them against one another is the essence of ethical decision-making based on Ross' framework. Even though these duties aren't really ranked, nonmaleficence usually overrides all the other duties, and perfect duties generally come before the imperfect ones. The imperfect duties are "imperfect" because you won't always be in a position to act on them.

It wouldn't be fair to hold you strictly accountable for beneficence—improving others' lives—for example, if the choice you are facing involves picking the lesser of two evils and not choosing between something that will improve others' lives and something that won't. On the other hand, the "perfect" duty of nonmaleficence—to avoid causing harm—always holds. You can be held accountable if you don't choose the least harmful course of action.

How would this work in real life? Let's take the Walter Scott video example from a few pages ago. Which of these duties were most relevant for the news organizations trying to decide how to use the video of the shooting? Certainly avoiding harm was important, as pictures of the dead and dying might be traumatizing to people, including Scott's family. What about formal justice? Respect for persons? In this particular case, justice and respect could refer both to the power of the video to give a voice to Scott, who cannot speak for himself, and to inappropriately sensationalize his death. The autonomy of the public also could be enhanced by having access to the kind of information about public events the video provides. Avoiding harm, formal justice and respect for persons are all perfect duties, so news organizations faced a difficult decision. Were any imperfect duties relevant here? Maybe honesty, if you wanted to argue that not showing the video would be misleading to the wider audience. After considering these duties, you might decide that formal justice for Walter Scott and the autonomy of the audience outweighed whatever obligations the journalists had to avoid harm to Scott's family that publicizing the video might cause. And having reached that conclusion, you would be on your way to making ethical decisions about how to use the video in coverage of Scott's shooting. Notice we said "on your way" to making ethical decisions. Thinking about the duties is a big part of the decision-making strategy, but it's not everything, as you'll see later.

One last general note about Ross before we turn our attention entirely to journalism. In focusing on duties, what is Ross *not* focusing on? Consequences. Two of the main categories of ethical theory are consequentialism and deontology. In very rough terms, consequentialism, as the word implies, argues that one may judge the rightness or wrongness of an action according to the consequences it produces. If the action produces a good outcome, then the action is itself a good one. Utilitarianism, which you may have heard of, is a consequentialist theory. A criticism of consequentialism is that it requires one to be able to accurately predict outcomes and who will benefit the most from them. Deontological theories do not judge an action by its consequences, but by . . . well, what? Whether and how well the action conforms to the rules—or, as we have been discussing in this chapter, duties. Philosopher Immanuel Kant was a strict deontologist. W.D. Ross, not so strict. Perhaps too simply put, Ross offers rules, or duties, but also flexibility in applying them according to the needs of a specific set of circumstances. And while he does not ignore consequences—indeed, carefully considering how acting on any of the duties might affect the people involved is key to this framework—outcomes alone cannot determine what's right. Philosopher Anthony Skelton says Ross "outlines a view that attempts to avoid the alleged deficiencies of utilitarianism without embracing the alleged excesses of Kantianism." There's also a bit of Aristotelian virtue theory, another category of ethical theory, in Ross' approach, most obviously in his identification of self-improvement as a *prima facie* duty. Virtue ethics doesn't contradict consequentialism or deontology, but is more concerned with the development of moral character. Pursuing virtue is what makes one a moral person.

▶ **ETHICAL THEORY:** Generally speaking, there are three categories or approaches to ethics: Deontology focuses on duties or rules; teleology focuses on consequences; and virtue ethics focuses on development of moral character.

Enough philosophical background, at least for now. The bottom line is this: Ross' common sense, practical view incorporating insights from these three different strands of philosophical thinking offers a useful way to approach ethical issues in journalism. The question is how do we move from these general, common sense duties to understanding what our actual duties in a specific situation might be? How do these duties help us decide what to do?

▶ HOW JOURNALISTS SEE THEIR DUTIES

In thinking about ethics, what we are attempting to do is translate the broader principles of journalism into specific actions by real people. It's one thing to say that journalists ought to treat people as citizens first and act independently, but quite another to say exactly how that plays out as a journalist covers a story. Journalists have responded to this need for more specific guidelines for ethical behavior by creating what are called codes of ethics. One of the oldest codes is the Journalist's Creed, written around 1906 by Walter Williams, the founding dean of the University of Missouri School of Journalism (see box on p. 159). It says, in part, that "the supreme test of good journalism is the measure of its public service" and cites accuracy, truthfulness, fairness and independence among the key attributes of good journalism. But you knew that already, right? Even though it offers a few specifics—about avoiding all kinds of bribery, for example—the Journalist's

Creed is more of a mission statement for journalism than a decision-making strategy for the working journalist.

THE JOURNALIST'S CREED

The Journalist's Creed was written by the first dean of the Missouri School of Journalism, Walter Williams. A century later, his declaration remains one of the clearest statements of the principles, values and standards of journalists throughout the world. The plaque bearing the creed is located on the main stairway to the second floor of Neff Hall.

I believe in the profession of journalism.

I believe that the public journal is a public trust; that all connected with it are, to the full measure of their responsibility, trustees for the public; that acceptance of a lesser service than the public service is betrayal of this trust.

I believe that clear thinking and clear statement, accuracy and fairness are fundamental to good journalism.

I believe that a journalist should write only what he [sic] holds in his heart to be true.

I believe that suppression of the news, for any consideration other than the welfare of society, is indefensible.

I believe that no one should write as a journalist what he would not say as a gentleman; that bribery by one's own pocketbook is as much to be avoided as bribery by the pocketbook of another; that individual responsibility may not be escaped by pleading another's instructions or another's dividends.

I believe that advertising, news and editorial columns should alike serve the best interests of readers; that a single standard of helpful truth and cleanness should prevail for all; that the supreme test of good journalism is the measure of its public service.

I believe that the journalism which succeeds best—and best deserves success—fears God and honors Man; is stoutly independent, unmoved by pride of opinion or greed of power, constructive, tolerant but never careless, self-controlled, patient, always respectful of its readers but always unafraid, is quickly indignant at injustice; is unswayed by the appeal of privilege or the clamor of the mob; seeks to give every man [sic] a chance and, as far as law and honest wage and recognition of human brotherhood can make it so, an equal chance; is profoundly patriotic while sincerely promoting international good will and cementing world-comradeship; is a journalism of humanity, of and for today's world.

(http://journalism.missouri.edu/jschool/#creed)

Professional organizations such as the Radio Television Digital News Association, Society of Professional Journalists, and National Press Photographers Association have developed codes for their members that get a bit closer to how-to-make-an-ethical-decision territory. Let's see how they do that.

The RTDNA code states, "Professional electronic journalists should operate as trustees of the public, seek the truth, report it fairly and with integrity and independence, and stand accountable for their actions." Sounds like the Journalist's Creed. But for each element of that general statement—public trustee, truth, fairness, integrity, independence and accountability—the code offers much more specific instructions. For example, under the heading "Integrity," the code says journalists should:

- ▶ Identify sources whenever possible. Confidential sources should be used only when it is clearly in the public interest to gather or convey important information or when a person providing information might be harmed. Journalists should keep all commitments to protect a confidential source.

- ▶ Clearly label opinion and commentary.

- ▶ Guard against extended coverage of events or individuals that fails to significantly advance a story, place the event in context, or add to the public knowledge.

- ▶ Refrain from contacting participants in violent situations while the situation is in progress.

- ▶ Use technological tools with skill and thoughtfulness, avoiding techniques that skew facts, distort reality, or sensationalize events.

- ▶ Use surreptitious newsgathering techniques, including hidden cameras or microphones, only if there is no other way to obtain stories of significant public importance and only if the technique is explained to the audience.

- ▶ Disseminate the private transmissions of other news organizations only with permission.

Now that's a pretty detailed list! And notice how many of the instructions on that list fit with Ross' common sense duties. For example, "clearly label opinion and commentary" sounds an awful lot like something related to the duty of respect for persons as well as the duty of honesty. And "refrain from contacting participants in violent situations while the situation is in progress" would appear to relate to the duty to avoid causing harm, wouldn't it? How about the rule that begins, "Guard against extended coverage . . . "? What duty might that speak to? The RTNDA is essentially admonishing journalists to avoid sensationalizing a story or giving an event too much coverage. If you were thinking that sounds connected to some kind of justice—formal or distributive—you'd be on the right track. The duty to avoid causing harm is connected as well.

The main sections in the Society of Professional Journalists code are "seek truth and report it," "minimize harm," "act independently," and "be accountable and transparent." Like the RTDNA code, more specific guidelines are offered for each section. Notice, too, how similar the SPJ code and Kovach and Rosenstiel's elements of journalism from Chapter 2 are. (It's worth noting that the SPJ code was revised in 2014 to highlight transparency as well as be more inclusive about new platforms and technologies. See Sidebar 6.2 for more about this process.)

The "seek truth and report it" section has the longest list—17 items—including the following related to duties of respect for persons, justice, beneficence and self-improvement. Journalists should:

- ▶ Diligently seek out subjects of news stories to give them the opportunity to respond to allegations of wrongdoing.

- ▶ Tell the story of the diversity and magnitude of the human experience boldly, even when it is unpopular to do so.

- ▶ Examine their own cultural values and avoid imposing those values on others.

- ▶ Avoid stereotyping by race, gender, age, religion, ethnicity, geography, sexual orientation, disability, physical appearance or social status.

> ► Support the open exchange of views, even views they find
> repugnant.

> ► Give voice to the voiceless; official and unofficial sources of
> information can be equally valid.

These codes of ethics show how the journalism profession has translated general ethical duties into the sphere of journalism practice. So far, so good. But even specifics like these can only get you so far. Where in the code does it say what to do if you uncover evidence that a candidate for public office cheated on his fiancée (now wife) 20 years ago? You could think back to what you've learned about perfect duties and remember you're supposed to avoid harm. OK, you might think, "I'll drop the story because it will harm the candidate." But if you also consulted, say, the RTDNA code to get a better idea of how duties play out in the professional arena, you would discover you're supposed to "provide a full range of information to enable the public to make enlightened decisions." Hmm. There's so much more you need to know and so much more to think about, you realize. Is a candidate's personal life important for citizens to know about? Has the candidate stressed his character as an important reason to vote for him? Does it matter how long ago the cheating happened? Does his wife know about the cheating, or will your story be the first time she's heard about it? Does that matter?

So many questions. And it almost seems like the more you ponder the duties and whatever a code of ethics has to say, the more questions you have. Congratulations! You have officially entered the murky world of ethics. Trust us—that's a good thing. Understanding your duties and how the profession puts them into practice can help you recognize an ethically problematic situation when it arises and sensitize you to the issues and factors you'll need to consider in making a decision—a good decision—about what to do. But there's always the chance, indeed the near certainty, that the situation will involve two or more potentially conflicting duties or that the code of ethics will be silent on the specific situation you are facing. The world rarely offers up problems with simple, black or white solutions, so you need to be able to navigate the gray area a little bit. You just need a way to bring order to your thinking.

6.2 THE VIEW FROM THE PROS: ETHICS IN A DIGITAL AGE

One would imagine that writing an ethics code for a professional group would be a relatively simple task.

In theory, you gather people of like minds who hold common moral beliefs, and rationalize what to put in the code. If everyone can agree that lying in a story is a bad practice, you say that. Next step.

But what seems simple in theory can be an entirely different matter in execution. And ethics can be complicated. Is it immoral to not provide links in a news story? Should you always honor promises for anonymity? How do you define sensitivity when dealing with minors?

I understand why the Ten Commandments are a divine edict and not the work of a committee. After chairing the Society of Professional Journalists' national ethics committee through ethics code revisions in 1994 and 2014, it's safe to say no sentence in the code is without justification.

How's this for a code workout? During the revision process between October 2013 and July 2014, the 16-member ethics committee generated 532 unique code discussions on its intranet site. Additionally, it's estimated that more than 1,000 people offered comments through regional conferences, online surveys, e-mails, phone calls and letters sent to headquarters. Every one was reviewed and considered.

This differed greatly in terms of outreach from SPJ's code revisions in 1994–96.

Times have changed for journalism. We have different types of people in journalism, different platforms and business models. In the mid-1990s we could, with a fair degree of success, identify the people and the media for which the code was intended. No one held that thinking this last go-around.

We discovered the best way to write an ethics code in today's media environment is to challenge beliefs and assumptions and include as many people as possible in the process. In a word: inclusiveness. While we did that to some extent in 1994–96, it wasn't the focal point of our work.

To understand the process in both decades more thoroughly, one needs to look at the underlying circumstances for both revisions, what really drove the rewrites.

In 1994, SPJ was coming off its first successful ethics textbook, *Doing Ethics in Journalism*, and the code, last touched in 1987, was lacking the heft needed to support the new book and its call for ethical journalism education. So, the decision by the committee and supported by SPJ's

officers, was to not just edit the code, but to blow it up and completely rewrite it. Since the code was adopted in 1926 that had never been done.

With a committee of 23 people our work started with a goal of having a revised code to the national convention in 1995 for SPJ delegate approval. In order for the code to be accepted, bylaws say the delegates, representing the membership, must approve it.

At that national convention in Minneapolis, two chapters opposed the revisions. A floor debate lasted for hours. Weary of rewrites from the floor and getting nowhere, the decision was made to table the discussion, invite the principal authors of the two other codes onto the committee and spend another year revising.

The 1996 completed version borrowed from the 1975 code but adopted wording from the committee's 1994 revision and the other two. The end result was a code that made an immediate impact in the profession. It was translated into 14 different languages and used in newsrooms around the globe. It was recognized as the benchmark for journalism standards. It spurred two more ethics books and appeared in countless more.

But it wasn't meant to remain untouched for 18 years.

Enter the new millennium.

After years of failed coaxing to revisit the code, even for minor changes, the decision to move forward in grand fashion with a revision was made in 2013 by then SPJ president Dave Cuillier.

But, three years before him, the groundwork had been laid, in part to navigate the political scene, but more so to tap into ideas of those who have a strong understanding of journalism ethics. Presidents before Cuillier were supportive of the code revision process and helped champion support for it within SPJ in the three years leading up to the rewriting.

And so it was that the real revision of SPJ's code of ethics began in 2011 with conversations about how journalism had changed, what the predominant ethical concerns of the times were, and what were the developing concerns.

College professors accepted the challenge of letting their classes evaluate the code in modern day terms. Working journalists were informally surveyed and offered their views. We asked journalists from legacy media and new age ventures. Digital operators and media entrepreneurs all talked about ethical standards from classrooms to newsrooms and shared advice. We even talked to other journalism organizations contemplating revisions of their codes.

By the time the SPJ 2013 convention came around we were ready to offer a town hall meeting to engage members in a full-throated debate on revisions. It was not unanimous, but the majority within SPJ agreed 18 years of upheaving change should prompt a rework.

The committee makeup was intentionally structured to include representation from legacy and new age media. Gender, age, sexual orientation, professional platforms and experience were all used in fashioning the committee of 16 people. There were six college professors, all of whom had taught ethics courses in college. Three had doctorates and were experts in media ethics. There were representatives from two of the world's largest wire services, digital media professionals, retired professionals, broadcasters, print and freelance representatives.

A question that we asked and answered early on was "Who is this code for?" That's a fair question since SPJ is a membership organization of about 8,000 people, certainly not all working journalists. But, because SPJ's code had earned such remarkable success over the years outside the organization, we took the view that it should be representative of all people working in journalism. In a time when almost anyone can call themselves a journalist, it was important to make the distinction early on and stand firm that we think these standards apply to any and all who are conducting journalistic activities—pros, students, citizens.

The second important decision was to make sure we stipulate in the code that while we recognize the different methods of executing journalistic duties we don't differentiate the ethical principles between, say, reporting for a newspaper or reporting on social media. Medium isn't an excuse for unethical conduct.

By December 2013 we had divided the committee into subgroups, each tasked with revising one of the code's four guiding principles—Seek the Truth, Minimize Harm, Act Independently and Be Accountable. From those hundreds of online discussions we produced the first draft in March. It was shared with the board and membership. We solicited suggestions and we received quite a few. We went back to work in subgroups, switched the members to gain fresh perspective and started revising again. By May we had a second draft and asked for more commentary.

In July of 2014 the committee came together in person and spent more than 10 hours in painstaking editing and discussions over what we had created. By the weekend's end we had a third code revision we felt confident to present to the convention.

At convention, once again, two separate parties made efforts to make wholesale amendments to the code, but through diplomacy and negotiations we agreed to accept a few changes before handing the document to delegates. With overwhelming support the code was approved.

The key to its passage rests with two key elements, the first being the inclusion of many voices. Anyone who wanted a say in the code's revision had plenty of opportunities to share thoughts.

The second, which we believe will give this code staying power, is the idea that we will build behind it a repository of documents and materials that will remain active in their use for solving ethical dilemmas. That has already been created and is expected to grow in the coming years.

Writing codes is challenging but necessary if we hope to uphold the principles of responsible and ethical journalism.

THINK ABOUT IT: Review the SPJ Code at www.spj.org/ethicscode.asp. Which points of the code are most difficult to resolve, in your opinion? Which would you label as bright-line rules? Which would you debate?

Kevin Z. Smith was a 22-year member of SPJ's national ethics committee and six years its chairman. He was SPJ president from 2009 to 2010.

▶ A PROCESS FOR ETHICAL DECISION-MAKING

Chances are you consider yourself to be a pretty good person, capable of making sound ethical decisions. We're not disputing that. By offering up a process for making decisions, we are simply trying to engage your ethical reasoning abilities in an organized way. And we are trying to help you avoid an all-too-common trap: going on gut instinct alone. What your gut tells you is important "data"—it's especially good at alerting you to situations that involve a potential ethical issue—but ethical decisions need to involve your mind too. Even if you reach the same conclusion at the end of the ethical decision-making process that your gut told you was the right decision upfront, philosopher Deni Elliott points out that going through the process offers important benefits. First, you will know you considered all the important factors surrounding the situation that needed to be considered, which means that, second, you will be better able to defend your decision to people who might disagree with you.

Yes, people will probably disagree with you. That's the nature of the beast when you're dealing with potential harms, conflicting duties and the like. But we're willing to bet that if you go through this process and can communicate about what you weighed and considered at each step, even those who disagree with your conclusion will agree that your process was sound. That's more than half the battle. Also, keep in mind that journalism is a distinctly public enterprise—you provide information about the public, to the public. Of course your ethical reasoning should be open to public view as well.

Meyers proposed a framework based on Ross that we have adapted for your use. There are nine steps:

1. Start with an open mind.
2. Get all the facts you can.
3. Listen to what your gut is saying.
4. Identify which duties are at stake.
5. Figure out what kind of conflict you're facing.
6. Brainstorm and analyze.
7. Reach a conclusion—and try to reach consensus with co-workers too.
8. Try to minimize whatever harm your decision might cause.
9. Look toward the future.

Now let's go step by step, using the cheating candidate example from a couple of pages ago. As you will recall, our hypothetical candidate for public office—let's say he's running for governor of your state—cheated on his fiancée 20 years ago. That former fiancée is now his wife. You are wondering whether you ought to report this information about him. You are hesitating, because your gut tells you this kind of information could cause harm to the candidate, to his wife, or someone else, but that it might also be the kind of information that it is your job, as a journalist, to report.

Step One   You might have opinions about adultery or politics or this candidate or his wife that could blind you to important details or otherwise skew your decision-making process. Try to clean the slate. One way to do that is to engage in ethical decision-making with others, so you'll have multiple perspectives on the issue. If you work in a traditional newsroom, you'll have an editor or producer or news director with whom to talk things over. If you're working more independently, perhaps blogging for your own site, you'll want to find a trusted friend to fill this role.

Step Two   Time to do some reporting! All those questions we raised about this case earlier—for example, has the candidate used his personal character as a campaign issue, does his wife already know—are essentially factual questions. Here are some different kinds of facts that might be relevant to the case at hand:

> ▶ **Journalistic facts** These are the kinds of things you would need to do a real story, but with a particular focus: figuring out who has the most at stake—who will be most affected—in this situation. Let's say you learned about the affair from the woman with whom the candidate cheated, who said, "People ought to know what a terrible person Mr. X is." Let's also say the candidate has not made personal character an important part of his campaign, his wife (as far as you know) is unaware of the cheating, the election is just two weeks away, and the candidate's opponent trails the candidate by just 3 points in the latest opinion poll. All of these facts suggest that the revelation of the cheating could affect the outcome of the election and harm the candidate and his wife personally. As you think about who would be affected by this story and how, you might uncover even more questions that require more fact-finding. Keep going until you think you've got everything relevant to the situation.

▶ **Professional facts** This is where you get to put those fundamental principles of journalism into action and make use of a code of ethics and any kind of policy your workplace might have. In this case, we know that the basic job of journalism is to gather, verify and report *truthful information of consequence to citizens in a democracy*. Most codes of ethics include similar language about journalism's purpose. So you're right to be thinking that this affair might be something you should report, as it provides voters with additional information about the candidate. But it also means that, even if you decide to report it, you might still have some work to do to get the information up to the standard of "verified." What do professional codes or norms tell you about basing a story entirely on one person's statement, especially if that person seems to have some sort of grudge?

▶ **Legal facts** Are there any laws or rules that might affect what you would cover in your story or how? This case doesn't seem to offer any particular legal issues, but consider how important these kinds of facts might be if the candidate were accused of cheating on his taxes, not his fiancée, or if the information about the candidate came to you via illegal means, perhaps sealed court documents.

▶ **Social/political facts** What political party does the candidate belong to? Is your state socially conservative or socially liberal? These are facts about the context in which you would be reporting this information. You might also include under this heading any background about the woman who tipped you off. She says she wants people to know the candidate is a terrible person—is that a personal motive, or does she have a particular political agenda? Why are you learning this information now, just two weeks before election day? Can you verify the information?

▶ **Big picture facts** These facts are sort of like social and political facts, but on a much bigger scale. Sure your story is just one story, but it is happening in the larger context of an increasing polarization in American politics. Partisanship is stronger than it has been in decades. That's one "big picture" factor that influences how people would understand your story. Another factor might be changing norms and expectations about personal relationships. Is cheating on a fiancée as big a deal as cheating on a spouse? If you decide to do the story, would you characterize what the candidate did as "cheating"?

Just two steps into this process, and you already have gathered tons of information. Time to pause and reflect on whether you still have an ethical conflict on your hands. Yep—You might be done! Listen to what Meyers says:

> More often than not, when step two has been properly completed, the conflict disappears. That is, the clear majority of ethics conflicts are really about confused facts . . . or about different stakeholders believing different facts. When these are corrected, agreement routinely follows over the value questions, and the problem resolves.
>
> (Meyers, 2011, p. 326)

Starting with an open mind and getting lots of facts will let you know pretty darn quickly whether the problem is one of conflicting facts or conflicting duties. If the woman's claim about the cheating turns out to be false—well, that's easy. No story. Or if we uncover the additional fact that the woman was paid by the opponent to tell her story, that's easy too—but a very different story. Nothing we've uncovered so far, however, suggests that this is a simple case of confused facts. So let's proceed with the rest of the steps. The next one makes a lot more sense now that we've taken this pause.

Step Three   Gut check. We weren't kidding when we said your gut can provide valuable information in ethical decision-making. Here's where that happens, but with a bunch more facts on the table, your gut can make a more informed choice. Also, this is a good opportunity to compare what your gut is telling you with what other folks' guts—your editor, best pal or whoever—are telling them. Does everyone seem to be leaning toward doing the cheating story? Why? Perhaps you all agree that this is exactly the kind of story journalism is supposed to do—inform the public so it can make good choices—and that nothing you've been able to find suggests that the story is untrue. Maybe you're heading toward a consensus that the question isn't so much whether to do the story, but how best to do it. That's fine, but you've got to keep going.

Step Four   Go back to the list of perfect and imperfect duties and think about which ones are particularly relevant to this case and how. You'll want to go beyond just listing the duties to thinking about which ones are most strongly at issue and to whom you owe the duty. For example, you might think differently about a perfect duty owed to the person likely to suffer the most harm and an imperfect duty owed to the person likely to be harmed least. At least two perfect duties—nonmaleficence and respect for persons—seem to be involved in our candidate cheating case. Both are owed to the candidate, his wife, and the woman who brought the information to you. A duty to avoid causing harm is also owed to the public. What about the duty of fidelity? The relationship between journalism and the public implies a certain kind of promise about telling the truth. As the SPJ code of ethics says, truth-telling isn't just about not lying, it's about being forthcoming with information too. Perhaps that applies here.

Are there any imperfect duties that seem especially relevant? Could you make an argument for the duty of beneficence? Do you believe that giving voters information about the candidates constitutes a way of helping them improve their lives or at least avoid some kind of future harm? It's something to consider, but also something difficult to pin down.

Step Five   So, what type of conflict is this? By "type," we mean is this really an ethical dilemma or, rather, something that causes ethical distress but is not, technically, a dilemma? A dilemma, Meyers tells us, exists when two legitimate, but competing duties are at stake so that any decision you make will produce a moral harm of some kind. Ethical distress occurs when even though you might agree on what the ethically best course of action is, something prevents you from acting on it. That something might be institutional pressures or legal constraints. Why is this distinction important? Because it can have a bearing on how you decide to try to resolve the issue. A dilemma means that whatever you choose, harm is likely to occur. So you'll want to figure out how to minimize it. If there's distress but no dilemma, you might focus your efforts on overcoming whatever barrier to ethical action you face.

As we determined in Step Four, we have at least two perfect duties at stake in our candidate scenario. That sounds like an ethical dilemma. Whatever we decide to do about the story, then, we will also have to come up with ways to minimize the harm we cause. More on that in Step Eight.

Step Six   Think. And think some more. You've come into this process with an open mind, assembled lots of facts, checked your gut, determined which duties are most at stake, and figured out you're facing an ethical dilemma. Now is the time to mull all of that over. Think through several different scenarios. As Meyers points out, this is the easiest step to describe, but probably the most difficult one to do. One trap to avoid: framing your decision as either/or. Whichever route you choose, there are more and less ethically defensible ways to travel it.

Step Seven   With any luck, you've been conducting all or part of this decision-making process in the company of others who share your desire to make an ethically sound choice. Step Seven is when you try to reach agreement with one another about that choice. Consensus isn't always possible, but try to come to agreement on as many things as you can. Then, well, someone has to make a decision.

Step Eight   Try to minimize the harm that will accompany your decision. In Step Five, you identified which people have the most at stake and are, therefore, the most likely to suffer harm. Knowing what kind of duty you owe them might help you figure out how to minimize that harm. The various scenarios you considered in Step Six will be helpful here as well.

Let's say you decide to produce some kind of story about the 20-year-old cheating incident. Often, as is arguably the case here, providing as much context as possible will be important, including the fact that this happened a long time ago when the candidate was not yet married. You'll want to offer the candidate and his wife the opportunity to respond to the cheating claims. You'll want to be as clear as you can about the woman's motives for bringing the information forward so close to election day. This is just for starters. Also think about things like how big a headline the story should get or whether it would appear at the beginning of the newscast too.

Step Nine   Looking toward the future means considering ways you can avoid facing this kind of ethical dilemma again. Would it be helpful to develop some new policies or offer additional interpretation of the ethics code? It's entirely possible that this is the kind of ethical dilemma that is almost unavoidable in journalism. If so, your focus would be on developing policies to minimize harm, not avoiding the dilemma altogether.

▶ WANT TO KNOW WHAT *WE* WOULD DO?

So would we! Seriously, there are too many unknowns in this hypothetical to render a verdict now. But we *are* pretty suspicious about the timing of this revelation, so close to election day. Our decision would focus on what we could determine about the source's motives. Sketchy motives and this "story" might not be a story at all, or a very different kind of story about campaign politics. Our gut feeling—and that's all we've got now, with all those unanswered questions—is that there's a story of some kind here, but maybe not the story the source is trying to tell.

If making your way through the case of the cheating candidate made your brain hurt a little, take comfort in knowing that going through the steps of this process gets easier the more you do it. With practice and experience, you will get better at thinking about duties and what is at stake for the people involved. Use the resources listed to find other cases to practice on.

Chapter Six Review

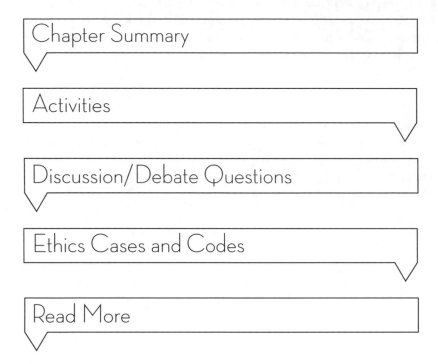

Chapter Summary

Activities

Discussion/Debate Questions

Ethics Cases and Codes

Read More

▶ **CHAPTER SUMMARY**

Journalism ethics involves figuring out how to align our job duties with the duties we have to people. There's no getting around the fact that harm to someone is a frequent byproduct of journalism—even, and sometimes especially, the journalism most closely aimed at helping citizens be self-governing. Good journalism involves uncovering things people would prefer remain hidden or pointing a finger at a problem for which no one seems to want to take responsibility. Ethical journalists try to fulfill their duties to citizens and the subjects of news, while also trying to avoid or minimize harm to them and even, where possible, working to prevent it. Philosopher W. D. Ross helps us understand the nature of our "common sense" duties, perfect and imperfect, so we can weigh them in all kinds of situations. But harm is likely to be a routine part of your life as a journalist. Being able to thoughtfully consider and defend your actions using the kind of ethical decision-making framework we introduce in this chapter will help ease that burden.

▶ ACTIVITIES

1. Meeting your ethical responsibilities as a journalist involves having a good sense of what your general responsibilities are. Think about the type of job you'd like to have after graduation (TV producer, sports editor, multimedia reporter or even a job outside of journalism). Next, break into small groups (find one or two students who have similar aspirations to yours) to make a list of what job responsibilities you would have ("interview people," "create slideshows," etc.). Then, in a second column next to that list, write down how those tasks relate to an ethical obligation discussed in this chapter. The idea is to connect job duties with ethical duties.

2. Discuss with your classmates how you use journalism in your daily life. Should standards be different for journalists? Read this post from Poynter.org on how to use Facebook ethically: www.poynter.org/how-tos/digital-strategies/176649/7-ways-journalists-can-make-better-ethical-decisions-when-using-facebook/. Write down how you might change your Facebook profile or alter your activities after reading this (and after the class discussion).

3. Watch the last 10 minutes of Jayson Blair's address to students at Washington and Lee University, found online at www.youtube.com/watch?v=kFePfsBlocA&feature=related. (The best information starts at about 14 minutes into the clip). Should a journalism program have invited Blair to give lessons on ethics? Can we learn the most from the worst practices? How do you feel about Blair after watching this presentation?

4. Watch some excerpts from recent movies or television shows about journalists. (One good one is *State of Play*, starring Russell Crowe. Or see other suggestions at: http://teachj.wordpress.com/2007/05/28/10-great-journalism-movies-for-summer/). Where do the Hollywood version of journalistic ethics and what this book tells us about ethics diverge? What rings true for how ethical journalists behave? What impact do movies like this have on public perceptions of the profession?

5. Select a case from the Indiana University page listing a variety of journalistic ethical scenarios (found at http://journalism.indiana.edu/resources/ethics/). Each member of your class should choose a different case. On a discussion thread set up for the class post brief details about your case, and then work through the ethical decision-making process outlined in this chapter. Post a 300-word reaction to the board to go with your summary. Which steps were most difficult to address? What decision did they reach? Did their conclusion surprise them? Comment on at least one other post on the board.

▶ DISCUSSION/DEBATE QUESTIONS

1. Why did the *New York Times* take such effort, give so much space in its paper and give so much attention to unraveling the lies and plagiarism committed by Jayson Blair? How and why was the approach NBC News took in handling the Brian Williams scandal so different? Does the medium—newspaper versus television—matter?

2. Tragic, dramatic events like the Isla Vista mass shooting attract reporters from across the nation, sometimes even the world. What do the protests in Isla Vista tell us about the kind of ethical issues that can arise when so many journalists are on the scene? What gets overlooked when discussions of ethical decision-making focus on individual journalist behavior and not the performance of the news media more broadly?

3. How are ethical challenges journalists face in their daily work similar to those faced by average citizens in daily life? How are they different? Couldn't journalists use their innate sense of right and wrong to guide them through most challenges they will face on the job? Why do we need special codes?

4. Doing good journalistic work often means that a journalist contributes to causing some sort of harm. Many cases involve weighing competing harms. Does that mean journalism is an inherently unethical profession? Why or why not?

5. How much of a role should potential consequences play in your final decision-making? Immanuel Kant would argue they should play no role at all. Utilitarian thinking would suggest they should be at the center of all action. In what cases can journalists truly see the consequences of their actions before they formally act?

6. Ethical decision-making is—or ought to be—a collaborative process involving discussion with colleagues and stakeholders so that many voices and perspectives can be considered. What, if any, potential disadvantages are there to a collaborative decision-making process? Should the final decisions rest with one person at the top of the organization?

▶ ETHICS CASES AND CODES

Ethics Cases

http://ethics.unl.edu/ethics_resources/online/journalism.shtml.

http://journalism.indiana.edu/resources/ethics/.

www.scu.edu/ethics/practicing/focusareas/cases.cfm?fam=MEDIA.

www.poynter.org/how-tos/10532/tip-sheets-ethics-1994–2010/#Studies.

www.spj.org/ethicscasestudies.asp.

Codes of Ethics

Radio Television Digital News Association

www.rtdna.org/content/rtdna_code_of_ethics.

Society of Professional Journalists

http://spj.org/ethicscode.asp.

National Press Photographers Association

https://nppa.org/code_of_ethics.

Online News Association

http://journalists.org/resources/build-your-own-ethics-code/.

NPR Ethics Handbook

http://ethics.npr.org/.

The New York Times

www.nytco.com/who-we-are/culture/standards-and-ethics/.

American Society of Magazine Editors

www.magazine.org/asme/editorial-guidelines.

▶ **READ MORE**

Dan Barry, David Barstow, Jonathan D. Glater, Adam Liptak and Jacques Steinberg, with research support provided by Alain Delaquérière and Carolyn Wilder, "Correcting the Record: Times Reporter Who Resigned Leaves Long Trail of Deception," *New York Times*, May 11, 2003. www.nytimes.com/2003/05/11/us/correcting-the-record-times-reporter-who-resigned-leaves-long-trail-of-deception.html?pagewanted=all&src=pm.

Thomas H. Bivins, *Mixed Media: Moral Distinctions in Advertising, Public Relations, and Journalism*, New York: Routledge, 2009.

Ben Bycel, "Ethics and the Breaking Story," *Santa Barbara Independent*, June 8, 2014. www.independent.com/news/2014/jun/08/ethics-and-breaking-story/.

Kate Mather, "Isla Vista Slayings: Community Growing Weary of News Media," *Los Angeles Times*, May 26, 2014. www.latimes.com/local/lanow/la-me-ln-isla-vista-shootings-community-growing-wary-of-news-media-20140526-story.html.

Christopher Meyers, "Appreciating W. D. Ross: On Duties and Consequences," *Journal of Mass Media Ethics* 18 (2003): 81–97.

Christopher Meyers, "Reappreciating W. D. Ross: Naturalizing Prima Facie Duties and a Proposed Method," *Journal of Mass Media Ethics* 26 (2011): 316–331.

Jay Rosen, "NBC Would Be Insane to Let Brian Williams Return," Pressthink. org, March 14, 2015. http://pressthink.org/2015/03/nbc-would-be-insane-to-let-brian-williams-return/.

Anthony Skelton, "William David Ross", *The Stanford Encyclopedia of Philosophy* (Fall 2010 Edition), Edward N. Zalta (ed.). http://plato.stanford.edu/archives/fall2010/entries/william-david-ross/.

Scott Stump, "Brian Williams Sits Down with Matt Lauer in First Interview Since Suspension," *NBC Today*, June 19, 2015. www.today.com/news/brian-williams-opens-first-interview-suspension-t27276.

Margaret Sullivan, "Graphic South Carolina Video and Details from a Rap Sheet Distress some Times Readers," *New York Times*, April 9, 2015. http://publiceditor.blogs.nytimes.com/2015/04/09/graphic-south-carolina-video-walter-scott/.

Al Tompkins, "Graphic New York Times Video Seems Justified," Poynter.org, April 7, 2015. www.poynter.org/how-tos/visuals/333613/graphic-new-york-times-video-seems-justified/.

"What Is Ethics?" Developed by Manuel Velasquez, Claire Andre, Thomas Shanks, S.J., and Michael J. Meyer, Markkula Center for Applied Ethics. www.scu.edu/ethics/practicing/decision/whatisethics.html.

7

The Foundations of Free Expression

June 27, 2011 was a banner day for fans of *Grand Theft Auto, Mortal Kombat, Postal 2* and any number of other violent video games played by millions of hardcore gamers.

On that day, the United States Supreme Court handed down its ruling in *Brown v. Entertainment Merchants Association,* striking down as unconstitutional a California law banning the sale of such games to minors.

Concerned with the level of graphic violence in video games, California had enacted a law prohibiting the sale or rental of violent video games to minors. The law addressed video games that allow the player to "kill, maim, dismember or sexually assault an image of a human being."

Writing for a 7–2 majority, Justice Antonin Scalia said the country has no tradition of restricting depictions of violence for children. He said California's law did not meet the high legal bar set by prior First Amendment cases to infringe on the First Amendment or the rights of parents to determine what's best for their children.

"No doubt a state possesses legitimate power to protect children from harm," Scalia wrote in the majority opinion. "But that does not include a free-floating power to restrict the ideas to which children may be exposed."

Although regulating children's access to depictions of sex has long been established, Scalia said there was no such tradition in the United States in relation to violence. He pointed to violence in the original depiction of many popular children's fairy tales like Hansel and Gretel, Cinderella and Snow White.

"Certainly the books we give children to read—or read to them when they are younger—contain no shortage of gore," Scalia added.

No matter that video games don't fit anyone's standard definition of free speech, like books, plays and movies, video games communicate ideas, and that was good enough for the Court to protect them. It's one case in a long line of decisions empowering speakers and stymying attempts by governments large and small to restrict disfavored forms of expression.

FIGURE 7.1 The government generally cannot punish what you say, but can often regulate where and when you can say it.

Source: Laurin Rinder/Shutterstock.

▶ THE POWER OF FREE EXPRESSION

The freedoms afforded speech, and yes, even violent video games, in America truly are breathtaking. The First Amendment, enshrined in the Bill of Rights, remains deceptively straightforward:

> Congress shall make no law respecting an establishment of religion, or prohibiting the free exercise thereof; or abridging the freedom of speech, or of the press; or the right of the people peaceably to assemble, and to petition the Government for a redress of grievances.

Have any 45 words generated more controversy, engendered greater debate and resulted in more titanic legal clashes in our nation's history?

Think, for a moment, about those words, and their central meaning. We can see, in these 45 words, the intent of the Founding Fathers to create an institution—the press—free to say what it wants, freed from government efforts to censor or punish that viewpoint.

It's also quite clear that the First Amendment is about telling the government what it *can not* do—"Congress shall make no law . . ."—rather than telling people what they *can* do. That's an important distinction, known as the difference between "positive liberty," in which governments grant rights to people, and "negative liberty," in which the people tell their government what it can and cannot do.

We could also logically conclude that should government seek to punish the press after the fact, for what it has said, it will face an uphill fight: the First Amendment, if it means anything, means that you should be free to say or publish what you like. The colonists suffered under the British system of prior restraint, meaning that the Crown could stop a publication before it even hit the presses. Stopping speech before it happens is the ultimate form of repression, and became a major point of contention in pre-revolutionary America.

It's easy to assume that the American patriots, who used the colonial press to foment popular discontent into full-blown revolution, wished to completely reject the British system of media controls. The reality is much more complex.

◀ **PRIOR RESTRAINT:** Government prohibition of speech in advance of publication.

That's not to say that the colonists appreciated the British law of the press. The British recognized the disruptive power of the press in the early 16th Century and began devising numerous schemes to restrict publication. The Crown for many years used an elaborate system of patents and monopolies to control printing in England. Licensing or prior censorship was also common. Criticism of the government, called seditious libel, was outlawed. Not only was truth not a defense against government punishment for seditious libel; the maxim of the day was "the greater the truth, the greater the libel."

Freedom of the press today is recognized as a uniquely robust element of the American legal tradition, but it is important to note that it is a right that has been won only through many hard-fought battles.

7.1 THE VIEW FROM THE PROS: A FREE PRESS FOR STUDENT JOURNALISTS?

If you think press freedom is all a big history lesson, take a second to reflect on what happened to journalist Chase Snider.

The setting was Springfield, Mo., in the fall of 2010, and a public gathering was quickly getting out of hand.

A young woman was trampled and had to be taken away by ambulance. Another suffered an allergic reaction as partiers began flinging food at each other, prompting a second emergency response.

Snider was there covering the event as editor of a local news website, taking photos and working with his staff to write a story about what happened.

None of that coverage, however, would ever see the light of day.

Officials ordered Snider to turn over copies of his photographs and then delete them. The story was not to run. As far as the readers were concerned, it never happened.

While it all sounds like something from a third-world dictatorship, it's just one of the many blatant acts of censorship that happen every year in this country.

Snider was a high school senior covering that campus event as editor of the student newspaper. That fact forces him and thousands of his colleagues across the country to live in a different First Amendment universe.

Since the Supreme Court's 1988 *Hazelwood* decision, school officials have had vast (though not unlimited) power to control the content of student publications. The theory among the justices back then was that schools should have reasonable control over what happens in the classroom—a fine idea, assuming you trust administrators to act reasonably.

The reality in many schools has been a concerted effort to squelch anything that might create controversy, embarrass the school, or cause discomfort. For journalism—a discipline that prides itself on holding the powerful accountable and creating dialogue—that environment is intolerable.

Since we opened our doors more than 35 years ago, we staff of the Student Press Law Center—a D.C.-area nonprofit that provides free legal support to student journalists—have had our work cut out for us. Each year we take about 2,500 calls from high school and college students, along with their advisers, with questions about the law. That number doesn't include the countless schools where censorship has become so routine that no one thinks to question it.

Unfortunately, it's no longer a safe assumption that you're free and clear when you get to college, either. While it was unthinkable at one time, some courts have begun applying the *Hazelwood* standard to public colleges and universities. And dozens of schools have tried doing an end-run around the First Amendment by firing journalism advisers or pulling funding when the coverage gets too hot.

Fortunately, there's reason for optimism. Seven states have passed laws nullifying *Hazelwood* for high school students. An eighth, Illinois, has done so only for college students. Some school districts and colleges have declared their student publications to be "public forums," and recognized the importance of uncensored journalism. Volunteer attorneys like those from the SPLC are standing up for students in court.

A free press is a fragile concept. That's why the founders protected it in the Constitution, so it wouldn't be up for repeal with every new controversy. America's students, however, don't have the luxury of taking the First Amendment for granted.

The good news is that where student press freedom does exist, students are empowered to tackle the important issues we expect of journalists. They have a voice and a means to use it responsibly. They learn by doing.

As for Chase Snider, he and censorship would go on a second date. A few weeks after the "mosh" event, he tried to cover a minor car accident in the school's parking lot. Officials threatened to suspend him if he didn't stop taking photos. And after he posted a written account to the newspaper's website, the story was quickly pulled offline. Snider was suspended as editor.

He didn't learn about the promise of a free press from a history book. He learned about it through the reality of a tumultuous and intimidating senior year. He learned that, at least within the schoolhouse gates, the promise can ring pretty hollow.

Brian Schraum is an instructor in the Edward R. Murrow College of Communication at Washington State University. He received his master's degree from the Missouri School of Journalism in 2010.

▶ NO LAW?

And as for that clear-as-a-bell "Congress shall make no law . . ."? Well, that lasted for less than a decade after the nation was founded.

In 1798, Congress enacted the Alien and Sedition Acts, as repressive an assault on free speech as we've ever seen. Dozens of political editors and politicians were prosecuted under the laws, which made it a crime to criticize both the president and the national government. Several justices of the Supreme Court presided at sedition act trials and refused to sustain a constitutional objection to the laws.

When John Adams was voted out of office in 1800, his political rival, Thomas Jefferson, brought this embarrassing chapter to a close—for 117 years, anyway.

In World War I and again in the 1940s, Congress enacted new sedition laws aimed at a wide variety of opposition speakers, as war protesters, socialists, anarchists and other political dissidents became the target of government repression.

Even as the legislative branch was largely ignoring the First Amendment, something remarkable was taking place in the judicial branch. The United

◀ **SEDITION:**
Sedition is the crime of revolting or inciting revolt against government. Under First Amendment doctrine it is quite rare, but sedition remains in the United States Criminal Code.

States Supreme Court, in a series of decisions ranging from 1919 to 1957, slowly but steadily began to raise the bar when it came to punishing so-called "dangerous speech."

What changed? Well, a lot of things. In a series of rulings stemming from the World War I sedition cases, the Supreme Court created the "clear and present danger test."

Justice Oliver Wendell Holmes put it this way:

> The question in every case is whether the words used are used in such circumstances and are of such a nature as to create a clear and present danger that they will bring about the substantive evils that the United States Congress has a right to prevent . . . When a nation is at war, many things that might be said in time of peace are such a hindrance to its effort that their utterance will not be endured so long as men fight, and that no Court could regard them as protected by any constitutional right.

It's a paranoid test reflective of a paranoid era, a period in which a fragile federal government embroiled in an unpopular foreign war saw threats, some real, some imagined, and responded by stifling speech. The problem with the "clear and present danger" test, as Holmes began to realize almost immediately, is that it equates speech with action—a huge logical leap, and one that placed the Court in the unenviable position of determining the tendency of speech.

Then in *Gitlow v. New York* in 1925, the Court ruled that the guarantees of freedom of speech apply to actions taken by all governments. Free speech became a fundamental liberty, opening the door to a much broader protection of freedom of expression in the nation.

Meanwhile, the American mass media was taking shape, and along with it, new First Amendment challenges. The Red Scare of the 1940s and 1950s ushered in a new round of sedition laws aimed at suppressing suspected communist sympathizers—but by then, the courts had grown more resistant to government punishment of mere speech, absent any sort of action.

Finally, in 1957, the Supreme Court ruled in *Yates v. U.S.* that to sustain a conviction, the government would have to be able to prove that the defendants advocated specific violent or forcible action toward the overthrow of the government.

It was a signal moment: from that day forward, the government found it impossible to prove such intent, and the laws that made the Red Scare possible crumbled.

In 1969, the Supreme Court raised the bar even higher, ruling in *Brandenburg v. Ohio* that advocacy of unlawful conduct is protected by the Constitution unless it is directed toward inciting or producing "imminent lawless action and is likely to incite or produce such action."

In the course of 50 years, the Supreme Court had moved from the near-total deference of the "clear and present danger" test to requiring the government to demonstrate that speech is so closely tied to action that the danger is imminent. It's a remarkable journey, one that reflects a nation increasingly confident in letting its speakers speak freely.

▶ THE LIMITS OF FREEDOM

The same process of judicial expansion of protection for speech has taken place in the law of defamation.

Libel occurs when a false and defamatory statement about an identifiable person is published to a third party, causing injury to the subject's reputation. A libelous statement can be the basis of a civil lawsuit brought by the person or group allegedly defamed or, in rare cases, a criminal prosecution.

There is no uniform law for libel. Each state decides what the plaintiff in a civil libel suit must prove and what defenses are available for the media. Prior to 1964, libel law in America represented a modest improvement over the British law of colonial times, but truth as a defense still barely registered in state libel laws. Then a case emerged that gave the Supreme Court an ideal vehicle for bringing libel law under the protections of the First Amendment.

◀ **DEFAMATION:** Any intentional false communication, either written or spoken, that harms a person's reputation; decreases the respect, regard, or confidence in which a person is held; or induces disparaging, hostile, or disagreeable opinions or feelings against a person.

▶ **LIBEL:** Written or broadcast defamation. A false statement that damages a person's reputation.

New York Times v. Sullivan remains one of the Court's most majestic opinions, a watershed moment for free speech. It was as much a civil rights case as a libel case.

In *Sullivan*, the Court again demonstrated its growing commitment to free speech—and its clear relationship to democracy—by striking down Alabama's libel law.

The case arose from an ad that appeared in the *New York Times*—a newspaper reviled by segregationists in the South for what they saw as its meddling coverage of the Civil Rights Movement. The ad was placed by the Committee to Defend Martin Luther King and the Struggle for Freedom in the South, and called attention to what the committee described as a system of repression:

> In Montgomery, Alabama, after students sang "My Country, Tis of Thee" on the State Capitol steps, their leaders were expelled from school, and truckloads of police armed with shotguns and tear-gas ringed the Alabama State College Campus. When the entire student body protested to state authorities by refusing to register, their dining hall was padlocked in an attempt to starve them into submission.

L. B. Sullivan, a commissioner of public affairs for Montgomery, sued the New York Times Co. for libel. His argument was that the assertions in many places were factually incorrect. And he was quite right: In several places, errors of fact were made. The students sang "The Star Spangled Banner." The police didn't exactly make a ring around the campus; they merely inundated the campus. Though unmentioned in the advertisement, Sullivan nonetheless claimed that the charges of police mistreatment implied his involvement.

On the basis of such minor, and arguably unimportant, errors, Alabama juries handed down $3 million in damages. The first case, a $500,000 judgment, was upheld on appeal by the Alabama Supreme Court. The Alabama court's opinion consisted of a single sentence: "The First Amendment of the U.S. Constitution does not protect libelous publications."

And so far as any court up to that moment had ruled, they were quite right. The U.S. Supreme Court was about to change all of that.

In a ringing endorsement of the importance of free speech in a democracy, the Court struck down the Alabama verdict and rewrote the law of libel in a single day.

Justice William Brennan Jr. wrote for a unanimous Court, with Justices Hugo Black and Arthur Goldberg writing concurring opinions.

This was the first time that the Court invoked the First Amendment to prevent libel actions. Such actions, wrote Brennan, could no longer claim "talismanic immunity from constitutional limitations." The Court also likened the Alabama libel law to the old threat of seditious libel—of liability based on criticism of public officials.

In language that has become the most famous line in First Amendment history, Justice Brennan declared:

> [W]e consider this case against the background of a profound national commitment to the principle that debate on public issues should be uninhibited, robust, and wide-open, and that it may well include vehement, caustic, and sometimes unpleasantly sharp attacks on government and public officials.

7.2 THE VIEW FROM THE PROS: LIBEL LAW'S EVOLUTION DURING THE CIVIL RIGHTS MOVEMENT

The law of libel changed drastically in the 1960s with a lawsuit arising from an advertisement in the *New York Times* which asked for money and support for Martin Luther King Jr. and "the struggle for freedom in the South" during the Civil Rights Movement.[1] The ad had charged police brutality against civil rights protesters in Montgomery, Alabama, but it had a handful of inconsequential errors. Those minor mistakes would have typically meant a win for the plaintiff in a libel suit in 1960. What you may not realize is that the case might have signaled the death knell for the *New York Times*, which faced several large libel suits filed by Southern public officials who were angry about coverage of civil rights issues. Southern leaders had begun using existing libel laws to craft what amounted to a sedition law to stop the press from covering the civil rights struggle in an attempt to maintain the racial status quo.[2]

1. "Heed Their Rising Voices," *New York Times*, March 29, 1960, 25.

2. Kermit L. Hall and Melvin I. Urofsky, *New York Times v. Sullivan: Civil Rights, Libel Law, and the Free Press*, Lawrence: University Press of Kansas, 2011.

However, the U.S. Supreme Court revolutionized libel law in *New York Times v. Sullivan*.[3] Shattering precedent, the nation's high court created a new standard that required public officials prove actual malice and insured that citizens were free to exercise their First Amendment right to criticize the government.

Had the Supreme Court failed to overturn *Sullivan* and create the actual malice doctrine, the case's impact on the Civil Rights Movement would have been staggering.[4] Without the world looking at the South through the lens of the national press, Southern officials and other segregationists would have been free to continue to squelch activism in their own way.[5] "The last desperate reaction of a clinging regime was to try to suppress the message itself," wrote legal scholar Rodney A. Smolla in 1986. "If one could not stop the marches, one might at least keep the marches off television and out of the newspapers."[6]

In the *Sullivan* opinion, the Supreme Court turned away from the common law tradition handed down from English courts to extend a right unique to the United States: constitutional protections of speech critical of the government, even speech that is false. By 1964, when the case was overturned, southern officials had filed at least $388 million in libel actions against newspapers, news magazines, television networks and civil rights leaders.[7] *Sullivan* and its companion cases accounted for $5.6 million, a huge sum at the time and one that threatened the financial solvency of the *Times*.[8] But it was not just the *Times* that felt the pain of the adverse libel judgment. Editors from other publications could not send a reporter or photographer into the South to cover civil rights demonstrations without fear of being sued.[9] The Supreme Court's unexpected decision thus widened the doors for the national press to cover civil rights demonstrations and activities in the South.

Northern journalists had begun swooping into the region in the 1950s to write about race, telling the story of the Civil Rights Movement as it unfolded and telling the story from the largely unheard black point of view.[10] Plaintiffs such as Sullivan and other police officers had heavy stakes in shutting down the protests. Sullivan and Birmingham police commissioner Bull Connor gave mobs of Ku Klux Klansmen time to way-lay Freedom Riders at the Montgomery and Birmingham bus stations before calling in their officers to haul the wounded demonstrators off to jail.[11] It was Connor who made an international spectacle out of Birmingham with his lunging police dogs and skin-shredding fire hoses that washed young protesters down the street and into newspapers and broadcasts around the world.[12] He filed several libel suits worth millions in response to civil rights coverage in the *Times* and on CBS News, suits that were strikingly similar to *Sullivan*.

Before *Sullivan* was overturned, similar libel suits arose out of the Ole Miss riots in 1962 as Air Force veteran James Meredith sought to desegregate the university. Mississippi police were angered by coverage of their handling of the riots as reported in the *Saturday Evening Post*.[13] A similar libel suit also arose out of coverage of the 1963 March on Washington, when yet another southern lawman, the sheriff of Etowah County, Alabama, disputed a flashback scene of his brutality of civil rights protesters in an article for *Ladies Home Journal*

---

3. 376 U.S. 254 (1964).

4. Anthony Lewis, *Make No Law: The Sullivan Case and the First Amendment*, New York: Random House, 1991. Lewis, a Pulitzer Prize winning reporter, covered the Supreme Court for the *Times* when this case was argued.

5. For a more complete analysis of civil rights-related libel cases, see Aimee Edmondson, "In Sullivan's Shadow: The Use and Abuse of Libel Law During the Civil Rights Movement," Ph.D. dissertation, University of Missouri, 2008. See also, Aimee Edmondson, "In Sullivan's Shadow: The Use and Abuse of Libel Law Arising from the Civil Rights Movement, 1960–1989," *Journalism History* 37:1 (April 2011): 27–38.

6. Rodney A. Smolla, *Suing the Press*, New York: Oxford University Press, 1986, p. 43.

7. John Herbers, "Libel Actions Ask Millions in South," *New York Times*, April 4, 1964.

8. Lewis, *Make No Law*, p. 151.

9. Harrison E. Salisbury, *Without Fear or Favor*, New York: Times Books, 1982, p. 384.

10. Gene Roberts and Hank Klibanoff, *The Race Beat, The Press, the Civil Rights Struggle, and the Awakening of a Nation*, New York: Knopf, 2006. Also see David Halberstam, *The Children*, New York: Fawcett Books, 1998, p. 293. Freedom Riders like John Lewis began counting on the national media to tell their stories, for example.

11. This point has been widely established in the literature. See for example, Howard K. Smith, *Events Leading Up to My Death: The Life of a Twentieth-century Reporter*, New York: St. Martin's Press, 1996; see also J. Mills Thornton III, *Dividing Lines: Municipal Politics and the Struggle for Civil Rights in Montgomery, Birmingham and Selma*, Tuscaloosa: University of Alabama Press, 1991).

12. William A. Nunnelley, *Bull Connor*, Tuscaloosa: University of Alabama Press, 1991.

13. *Curtis v. Birdsong*, 360 F. 2d 344.

written by the famous playwright Lillian Hellman.[14] Still more Southern police officers and public officials filed libel suits for coverage of the Freedom Summer murders of three civil rights workers in Philadelphia, Mississippi, in 1964.[15]

Scholars and other media experts agree the *Sullivan* case stopped what surely would have been an even greater onslaught of libel suits for civil rights coverage. What might be the last case came in 1988, when the film *Mississippi Burning* appeared in theaters across the nation and told a fictionalized story of the three murdered civil rights workers in Neshoba County, Mississippi. The same litigious former sheriff Lawrence Rainey sued Orion Pictures for libel, but he quickly dropped the case when lawyers for the film

company said they would prove truth, the ultimate defense in a libel suit, that Rainey was responsible for the deaths of the three civil rights workers whose bodies had been found in an earthen dam in rural Mississippi. Twenty-six years had passed since the *Sullivan* decision. Members of the media, exercising their First Amendment right and responsibility to report on events about public officials and on events of public interest, had spent millions trying to defend that right.

Aimee Edmondson is an Associate Professor at Ohio University. A newspaper reporter for a dozen years, she earned a doctorate in journalism from the University of Missouri in 2008.

---

14. *New York Times*, "Curtis Publishing Is Named in a $3 Million Libel Suit," February 27, 1964.

15. For example, *Rainey v. CBS*, Neshoba County Circuit Court, Case no. E78–0121 (1978).

This time there were 44 words. And with those words, the First Amendment sprang to life. Brennan captured the essence of freedom of expression, a principle born out of centuries of struggle.

Having set the stage for a broad interpretation of speech rights, Justice Brennan found that though some of the statements in the *Times* advertisement were false, that could not be the end of the matter, because "erroneous statement is inevitable in free debate."

Given that, even certain false statements "must be protected if the freedoms of expression are to have the 'breathing space' that they 'need . . . to survive.'"

And then, in a sweeping exercise of judicial power, Justice Brennan crafted a new rule to better protect freedom of speech and press without granting a free pass for intentional falsehoods: Public officials now would be unable to recover damages for a defamatory falsehood relating to official conduct unless the official can prove that the statement was made with "actual malice"—that is, with knowledge that it was false or with reckless disregard of whether it was false or not.

▶ DRAWING LINES

It's hard to overstate the importance of the Court's ruling in *New York Times v. Sullivan*. In a single day, laws that had been used to silence and intimidate speakers were swept aside, replaced with a new standard that better protected speech, as the nation careened toward the late 1960s, the culmination of the Civil Rights Movement, the Anti-war Movement and the Vietnam War. The stage was set for the greatest expansion of First Amendment rights in the nation's history, and the societal turmoil bubbling up ensured that the courts had plenty of cases pitting the rights of speakers against the authorities trying to keep a grip on things.

In 1971, in the famous case of *New York Times Co. v. United States*, the Court ruled that a court order instituting a "prior restraint" on news stories based on the Pentagon Papers—a top-secret history of U.S. involvement in Vietnam—was unconstitutional. In its opinion, the Court said that "Any system of prior restraints comes to this Court bearing a heavy presumption against its constitutional validity."

So we can see that some regulatory methods, like prior restraint, are all but forbidden by the First Amendment. To what extent can the government regulate speech and expression?

As the sheer number and variety of speech and expression cases began to grow, governments at all levels began to enact a variety of laws aimed at controlling the means of protest. Some of these laws seemed reasonable enough on their face, while others clearly were designed to inhibit speech. Lines needed to be drawn for lower courts to be able to make sense of it all. The result of all of this judicial activity was a pair of tests for determining whether laws interfere with free expression in ways that violate the First Amendment.

Start with this general rule of thumb: normally, the government may punish people for causing various harms, directly or indirectly. But it generally may not punish speakers when the harms are caused by what the speaker said— by the content, in other words (unless, of course, the speech falls within one of the First Amendment exceptions, such as incitement, false statements of fact, threats, obscenity or fighting words).

In order to focus on whether or not the content of the speech is what is being regulated, judges employing First Amendment analysis also focus on the form of the regulation.

The United States Supreme Court created a test for doing just that in a 1968 case, *United States v. O'Brien*. David O'Brien was a Vietnam War protester who was convicted under a federal law that made it a crime to destroy a draft card. O'Brien had set fire to his card at a protest.

The law, on its face, was pretty clear: It required all males above the age of 18 to obtain and carry a draft card, in order for the military draft to run smoothly (remember, these are in the days before the personal computer, when a paper card really was that critical to something like the draft).

The Court rejected O'Brien's arguments that the law was unconstitutional because it infringed his right to free speech. Instead, the Court looked at the purpose of the law itself and at Congressional intent, and found the sole motivation to be orderly administration of the draft.

O'Brien had plenty of ways to express himself. He just couldn't burn a draft card, because the government had a strong interest in making sure people had their draft cards on their persons.

So, having found the statute content-neutral, the Court created a new test to judge the constitutionality of such laws, ruling that the law will be upheld if: (1) it furthers an important or substantial government purpose, (2) the government purpose is unrelated to the suppression of expression and (3) the restriction is narrowly tailored to accomplish the substantial purpose.

The Court uses the *O'Brien* test to analyze regulations the government argues are not about content, but about regulating the "time, place or manner" of speech. There are lots of these laws that pass First Amendment scrutiny, such as noise ordinances regulating how loud music can be played at 2 a.m., or law regulating the size and density of billboards on the side of highways.

What if the law is about regulating content?

Then the test gets a lot stiffer.

It can be tough to see the difference, at least at first blush. One way to think about time, place, manner restrictions is by using the "Five Ws and a H" of journalism. If a law is aimed solely at how, when or to some extent, where speech is conducted, the law more likely than not has no effect on the content of speech.

On the other hand, if the law is aimed at the "why," the "who" or the "what" of speech, the law may not be content-neutral, and in fact, may be content-based.

Content-based statues face the toughest test of them all: so-called "strict scrutiny" review. Courts almost always strike down content-based laws under First Amendment challenge unless they (1) use the least restrictive means possible to (2) advance a compelling government interest.

7.3 THE VIEW FROM THE PROS: WIKILEAKS AND THE FIRST AMENDMENT

WikiLeaks is a website that publishes political and government documents, many of them classified at one level or the other. The idea behind the site is that secrecy and democracy are incompatible. Although that's hardly radical, WikiLeaks and its founder, Julian Assange, have embedded that idea in a framework somewhat at odds with the institutional ethics of journalism. Consider the backstory.

In April 2010, WikiLeaks released a classified video of a U.S. Army helicopter in Baghdad opening fire on a group of people that included a Reuters photographer. From the P.O.V. of the helicopter's gun-sight, the video clearly shows the killings. Assange titled the video "Collateral Murder," and later, as a guest on Stephen Colbert's show, Assange said he wanted the title to "create maximum possible political impact."

In July 2010, WikiLeaks published more than 75,000 classified U.S. documents about the war in Afghanistan—publishing them in cooperation with the *New York Times*, the *Guardian* and *Der Spiegel*. The documents consisted of field reports prepared by troops on the ground, giving day-to-day accounts of the war. The Pentagon condemned WikiLeaks and demanded that the website return the leaked documents. Assange refused, but by then Bradley Manning,

(now Chelsea Manning), a 20-something U.S. intelligence analyst, was sitting in a military prison, suspected of providing the classified material to WikiLeaks.

In October 2010, WikiLeaks published nearly 400,000 classified U.S. documents about the war in Iraq—again publishing them in cooperation with major newspapers around the world. Although the U.S. government accused WikiLeaks of endangering national security, one month later WikiLeaks began publishing U.S. diplomatic cables. The first batch totaled about 220, and since then WikiLeaks has published more than 2,500. They provide a he-said-she-said account of contemporary diplomacy. The *New York Times* reported that the cables give you a "look at bargaining by embassies, candid views of foreign leaders, and assessments of threats."

In response, Secretary of State Hillary Clinton said the release of the cables was "not just an attack on America's foreign policy interests; it [was] an attack on the international community." Director of National Intelligence James Clapper said the "actions taken by WikiLeaks are not only deplorable, irresponsible, and reprehensible—they could have major impacts on our national security." And then-Attorney General Eric Holder announced that the Justice Department and the Pentagon were investigating the leaks to determine if criminal charges would be filed. As of this writing, a federal grand jury empanelled in 2010 to weigh the government's evidence against WikiLeaks and Assange is still ongoing.

The possibility of prosecution brings into question the proper balance between free speech and national security. There's no one law that makes it a crime to publish classified information—no catchall that says, "Thou shalt not disclose." Instead, there's a patchwork of laws serving that function, each applying in different circumstances. Take, for example, the Espionage Act of 1917, which might be used to prosecute WikiLeaks for communicating or transmitting defense information. Such a prosecution would trigger First Amendment challenges.

The first is called "strict scrutiny," and the second is called the "clear and present danger" test. They both require the government to meet a high burden before punishing someone for publishing. It's unclear how those challenges would play out, because the government hasn't released factual findings from its investigation. One thing, however, is clear: It doesn't matter in this context whether WikiLeaks is part of the press. The First Amendment doesn't belong to the press. It protects the rights of all speakers, sometimes on the basis of the Speech Clause and other times on the basis of the Press Clause. Remember, the First Amendment says, "Congress shall make no law abridging the freedom of speech, or of the press."

To argue that the First Amendment would protect WikiLeaks and Assange, as publishers, only if they're part of the press is to assume (1) that the Speech Clause wouldn't protect them, and (2) that there's a major difference between the Speech and Press clauses. In reality, most of the freedoms that the press gets from the First Amendment are no different from the freedoms that everyone gets from the Speech Clause. This is true even for the core freedoms essential to the press. The few times the Supreme Court has decided cases using the Press Clause alone, the same results could have been reached using the Speech Clause. As a result, one commentator said not long ago that "the Press Clause today is an invisible force in the law."

So what does this mean for WikiLeaks? On the one hand, it could be a good thing for WikiLeaks and Assange. If the Justice Department prosecuted them for publishing, they wouldn't have to argue that they do journalism or deserve to be protected as members of the press. They could just call on the Speech Clause, which would trigger strict scrutiny or the clear and present danger test.

On the other hand, it could be a bad thing for the legacy press. Bill Keller, former executive editor of the *New York Times*, summed up the problem in February 2010. He said,

> It's very hard to conceive of a prosecution of Julian Assange that wouldn't stretch the law in a way that would be applicable to us. American journalists . . . should feel a sense of alarm at any legal action that tends to punish Assange for doing essentially what journalists do. That is to say, any use of the law to criminalize the publication of secrets.

Putting Keller's remarks in legal terms, unless the Supreme Court all of a sudden decided to interpret the Press Clause differently from the Speech Clause, any prosecution of WikiLeaks for publishing secrets would affect the legacy press and their rights to do the same. That would be significant because in the last 40 years, with the exception of cases targeting government employees, the Supreme Court has never upheld a prosecution for the publication of truthful information about the government.

Jonathan Peters is an assistant professor of journalism at the University of Kansas, where he specializes in First Amendment and media studies, with an affiliate research position exploring big data and Internet governance in the KU Information & Telecommunication Technology Center.

It's tough to find a compelling interest at stake where speech is concerned, at least most of the time. That's why flag-burning laws, for all the emotion invested in them, will never survive constitutional scrutiny.

Take the leading case in the area, *Texas v. Johnson.* Gregory Lee Johnson was convicted and sentenced to a year in prison and a $1,000 fine for burning an American flag during a protest at the 1984 Republican National Convention in Dallas under a Texas statute that made it a crime to "desecrate" the flag.

Johnson appealed his conviction all the way to the United States Supreme Court, which in a 5–4 decision said that the state of Texas had found no compelling interest. The state's argument that preserving the sanctity of the flag was such an interest actually constituted government picking and choosing viewpoints.

"If there is a bedrock principle underlying the First Amendment," Justice William Brennan wrote for the Court, "it is that the government may not prohibit the expression of an idea simply because society finds the idea itself offensive or disagreeable."

That's what the Court calls "viewpoint discrimination," and it's the most basic, yet also the most powerful rule under the First Amendment: When you get right down to it, viewpoint discrimination means that the government can't tell us what to think or say. And when it tries, through passing laws, to limit what we can write or say, it better have a compelling reason for doing so.

Think about that a minute: This rule, which effectively removes government from the content business, establishes a system in which the fewer people agree with a speaker's point, the greater that speaker's protection. The state is so limited in what it can do to speech that speech flourishes in the absence of regulation.

Don't take our word for it: Look at the just how powerful First Amendment law has become. The best evidence available might just be the Rev. Fred Phelps.

You might not recognize the name, but surely you remember the signs: "Thank God for Dead Soldiers," "Fags Doom Nations," "America is Doomed," "Priests Rape Boys," and "You're Going to Hell," among other similar messages, displayed at the funerals of American soldiers.

The reverend's attention-getting, highly offensive posters made him quite possibly the least popular speaker in the country, yet when one soldier's

FIGURE 7.2 New York City, September 11, 2014: Members of the Westboro Baptist Church appeared in front of Ground Zero during memorial services on the 13th anniversary of the World Trade Center attacks with signs praising the attack.
Source: a katz/Shutterstock.

family sued him for intentional infliction of emotional distress and intrusion upon seclusion, the Court wasted little time in finding that that the First Amendment protected Reverend Fred Phelps' hateful and harmful speech.

To Chief Justice Roberts, who wrote for an 8–1 majority, the issue was rather straightforward. Phelps' speech was on matters of public import; Phelps' signs were on public land next to a public street; and Phelps and his fellow protesters stayed away from the actual funeral service.

"Snyder could see no more than the tops of the signs when driving to the funeral. And there is no indication that the picketing in any way interfered with the funeral service itself," Justice Roberts wrote.

He added that states could enact reasonable content-neutral time, place, and manner restrictions on speech at funerals. These lawsuits didn't fit the bill because they sought to punish Phelps specifically because of the "what" of his speech. That Phelps is, quite possibly, the least popular speaker of our generation, speaks to the underlying value at the heart of the First Amendment: tolerance.

More than anything else, free speech requires us to tolerate speech we find repulsive, shocking, offensive, or just plain wrong. The First Amendment scholar Lee Bollinger has written eloquently of the "social ethic" created by the system of free expression, in which society learns to exercise self-restraint and recognize the intolerance in each of us. In *The Tolerant Society: Free Speech and Extremist Speech In America*, Bollinger points out an uncomfortable truth: We are often eager to repress speech we disagree with, and so we have built a legal system of protection to overcome that impulse.

Rather than look at speech like that of Phelps as the price we must pay for free speech, Bollinger sees it as an opportunity to prove our commitment to tolerance. "The free speech principle involves a special act of carving out one area of social interaction for extraordinary self-restraint, the purpose of which is to develop and demonstrate a social capacity to control feelings evoked by a host of social encounters." So it's a matter of building that tolerance, day by day, citizen by citizen. It's a massive investment, really, and one that shows just how seriously we take free speech in America.

That's not to say, however, that protection for speech is absolute, not by any means. No majority of the United States Supreme Court has ever interpreted the First Amendment as absolute, and while we enjoy broad freedom to speak and to write as we wish, the courts have been less expansive when it comes to the means by which news is gathered. This creates some real limits when it comes to the ways journalists can access government information, use anonymous sources or enter other people's property in the pursuit of news.

Courts generally hold that journalists have no greater rights than those of the general public—a principle known as "laws of general applicability."

One area where the laws of general applicability run headlong into the work journalists do is in the use of anonymous sources. Reporters sometimes make promises of confidentiality to sources in exchange for information, particularly in investigative reporting. Sources in such stories often fear retribution from those in power, yet in some stories dealing with fraud, abuse or corruption, a single source can make all the difference in the public airing of important stories. Or a grand jury investigating a crime may seek to force a reporter to reveal the source of a story. In other cases, journalists may be asked to testify at a criminal or civil trial. It's a fundamental conflict between the rights of journalists and the duty of every citizen to testify to help the courts determine justice.

▶ SECRETS, AND WHEN TO KEEP THEM

Because of the work they do, journalists often find themselves at the scene of events that are important and newsworthy. Anyone wanting the facts about an event can subpoena reporters to testify about all the details. Journalists almost always resist such orders.

Their argument is that they don't want to become a de facto arm of law enforcement. Even worse, if journalists can't honor their promises of confidentiality, what source would talk to them about a really sensitive subject, knowing that their identities or their information could end up being disclosed in court?

The United States Supreme Court ruled in the 1972 case of *Branzburg v. Hayes* that reporters have no First Amendment right to refuse to answer all questions before grand juries if they actually witnessed criminal activity.

Two justices in the deeply divided opinion recognized a qualified constitutional privilege, however, keeping hope alive for journalists. Justice Powell, while agreeing with the majority, wrote a concurrence arguing that reporters would still be able to contest subpoenas if they were issued in bad faith, or if there were no legitimate law enforcement need for the information.

Justice Stewart, dissenting, made a much stronger case for a robust privilege, arguing that anything less would allow officials to "annex" the news media as "an investigative arm of government." Two other justices joined Stewart. These four justices, together with Justice William O. Douglas, who dissented in a separate opinion, gave the notion of a qualified constitutional privilege a majority.

Since *Branzburg*, many federal and state courts have found some form of qualified constitutional privilege. Where the privilege is recognized, the courts generally use a three-part balancing test to assess whether the subpoenaed information is clearly relevant and material to the pending case, whether it goes to the heart of the case and whether it could be obtained from other sources besides the media.

In recent years, however, a growing number of federal courts have become reluctant to recognize a privilege under the First Amendment. In 2005, the U.S. Court of Appeals in the District of Columbia said a grand jury's need for information outweighed any reporter's privilege after *New York Times* reporter Judith Miller refused to testify about her sources for a story about CIA operative Valerie Plame. Miller and her bosses at the *Times* took the position that her promise to hold confidential her sources' names was not one she could break. The U.S. Supreme Court refused to hear her appeal. Although her imprisonment inspired bills in Congress calling for a federal shield law, Congress has not yet passed such a law. Miller spent 85 days in jail before agreeing to testify.

At the state level, legislatures picked up Justice Stewart's three-part test and passed "shield laws" providing some protection for journalists facing orders to testify or provide notes, photographs or other reporting work product. By 2015, 49 states and the District of Columbia had some form of shield laws in place.

The lack of any federal shield law protection demonstrates just how important the laws can be for journalists. In 2001–02, Vanessa Leggett, a freelance journalist in Houston, Texas, spent a record 168 days in jail for refusing a federal grand jury's command to hand over notes and tapes of interviews she had made while writing a book about the murder of a Houston socialite.

▶ WHEN REPORTING BECOMES PRYING, THERE ARE CONSEQUENCES

Journalists also face limits created by the law of privacy. Almost every state recognizes some right of privacy, either by statute or under common law—the traditional court-made law that U.S. courts adopted long ago from the English standards.

A right of privacy can be violated by any means of communication, including spoken words. This tort, or civil action, is usually divided into four categories: intrusion, publication of private facts, false light and misappropriation.

The basis of privacy law is what the courts call a "reasonable expectation of privacy." In some settings—the home, for example—individuals have a right to expect some measure of privacy. That expectation is not nearly as strong in the middle of a public street.

Although private individuals usually can claim privacy rights, that right is not absolute. For example, if a person who is normally not considered a public figure is thrust into the spotlight because of her participation in a newsworthy event, her claims of a right of privacy may be limited. Courts will allow some leeway in the name of newsworthiness, in other words.

◄ INTRUSION: Intentionally intruding, physically or otherwise, upon another person's seclusion or solitude or another person's private affairs.

Intrusion claims against the media often center on the behavior of journalists in the newsgathering process, such as the intrusive use of recording devices, cameras or other intrusive equipment. Trespass also can be a form of intrusion. Entering another person's property without permission frequently gives rise to intrusion cases.

Journalists can also find themselves in legal trouble for publishing truthful information if that information is about the private life of a person that would be both highly offensive to a reasonable person and not of legitimate public interest.

◄ PUBLICATION OF PRIVATE FACTS: The publication of information about someone's personal life that has not been previously revealed to the public, is not a matter of public concern, and the publication of which would be offensive to a reasonable person.

This can be a real legal wild card, because liability often is determined by a jury after examination of how the information was obtained and its newsworthiness.

Another privacy tort, false light invasion of privacy, occurs when information is published about a person that is false or places the person in a false light, is highly offensive to a reasonable person, and is published with knowledge or in reckless disregard of whether the information was false or would place the person in a false light.

False light privacy is a close cousin of defamation, but has a couple of key differences. Most importantly, the report need not be defamatory to be

▶ **FALSE LIGHT INVASION OF PRIVACY:** Giving publicity to a matter concerning another person that portrays that person falsely if the portrayal would be highly offensive to a reasonable person.

▶ **MISAPPROPRIA-TION:** The use of one's name or likeness for personal or commercial gain without consent or compensation.

actionable as false light. False light can be created by embellishment (the addition of false material to a story, which places someone in a false light), distortion (the arrangement of materials or photographs to give a false impression) or fictionalization (references to real people in fictitious articles or the inclusion in works of fiction of disguised characters that represent real people).

Those in advertising and other media fields should be aware that the use of a person's name or likeness for commercial purposes without consent gives rise to a privacy tort called misappropriation. The key here is whether the use has an overriding commercial purpose. Incidental references to real people in books, films, stories or other works, generally are not misappropriations. Even the use of a photograph to illustrate a newsworthy story is not misappropriation. The use of the same photograph to sell products in an advertisement is a different matter, as that overriding commercial purpose kicks in.

Use of a celebrity's name or likeness, without consent, to sell a product is usually misappropriation. However, other unauthorized uses of celebrities' images may violate their publicity rights. Trading on a celebrity's fame and popularity even for noncommercial purposes, including public relations campaigns or other promotions, is an unauthorized use of the famous person's name or likeness that could violate his or her right of publicity. The bottom line: If you want to use someone's image, get permission.

▶ CONCLUSION

In the spring of 2011, the eyes of the world were fixed on the Middle East as civil unrest gave way to revolution in Egypt, Tunisia and Libya. We watched, transfixed, as monarchies staggered and fell under popular resistance fueled by a mix of smartphones, handheld video cameras and tweets. We then watched, amazed, as some of the same notions of civic participation and public unrest landed right in the United States in the form of the Occupy movement.

What did those events teach us? For starters, that the days of tidy authoritarian controls, where states can lean on journalists and silence the public through official means, are coming to an end. The repressive response to the

Egyptian protests are a fine example: Given the ubiquity of smartphones, the universal use of Twitter and Facebook to pass along scenes of violence and police misconduct and military overreach, the Arab Awakening fed on itself. The government's ham-handed attempts to silence a technologically enabled populace just led to more posts, more tweets, more pictures . . . the inescapable conclusion is that it has become nearly impossible to control speech. Non-democratic governments still manage, but not without spending a lot of time and money on the effort, and even then, with uneven results (remember the Iranian protests of 2009?).

America still claims the most protection for speech and expression in the world. The First Amendment is just different—it protects a lot of speech that other nations ban outright. Hate speech, for example—speech that denigrates the race or religion of others—is banned in England, Canada, France, Germany and in just about every other democratic nation in the world. Rev. Phelps wouldn't make it out of his garage with those signs he carries around in any of those countries.

We deplore Rev. Phelps' speech, but the First Amendment protects it. We learn, in turn, to tolerate speech that offends us. There is a tradeoff in all of this: By broadly protecting such hatred, we avoid the risks of suppressing valuable speech on the basis that someone finds it offensive. Think about it: Every few weeks someone in the United States wants to ban a book, for some reason or another. By establishing such broad protections, we avoid these fights, or at least greatly reduce the odds that they will succeed. And by doing so, we make it possible to think, to write, to opinionate.

"The right to think is the beginning of freedom, and speech must be protected from the government because speech is the beginning of thought," wrote Justice Anthony Kennedy.

If the right to think is the beginning of freedom, then we risk suffering the harms of speech like Rev. Phelps' protests because that it is a better choice than offering the potential for the risk of suppressing valuable speech.

Why do we go to such lengths to protect freedom of speech? The First Amendment scholar Zechariah Chafee Jr. said the First Amendment protects two interests in free speech: the individual interest we have in expressing ourselves, and a societal interest in the attainment of truth. Both are crucial. In fact, people free to follow their political thoughts generate the societal change. That's the essential magic of the First Amendment and the role it performs in our democracy.

Chapter Seven Review

Chapter Summary

Activities

Discussion/Debate Questions

Read More

▶ **CHAPTER SUMMARY**

The First Amendment provides an amazing amount of protection for journalists and citizens alike to express themselves just about any way they like. While limits do exist, the courts generally protect speech against attempts by government to regulate it unless the government has extraordinarily powerful reasons to restrict it. The courts have created a number of judicial tests for evaluating First Amendment disputes, and have created a number of areas in which media practitioners face potential legal liability for harm caused by the work they do, especially in the area of libel and privacy.

▶ **ACTIVITIES**

1. Conduct a moot court hearing in your class. The class should split up into teams (ranging from three to six members). One team will defend a First Amendment regulation—one that works well is a local noise ordinance—and the other team will argue against it. Many cases involving noise ordinances can be found online at the First Amendment Center at www.firstamendmentcenter.org/tag/noise-ordinance. If you have a larger class, two other groups can debate "free speech zones" on campuses. An article from the University of Alabama's *Crimson White* on this issue can be found at http://cw.ua.edu/2010/09/26/free-speech-on-campus-raises-concerns/.

2. Create a First Amendment Storify project. Select a key First Amendment case from the many discussed on the First Amendment Center's site (www.firstamendmentcenter.org/category/press), then search for and gather elements from social media about that case. Ensure you include several Facebook posts, tweets and pictures—all of the things that Storify allows you to assemble from across the web, in one place. Add your own narrative too. (Go to Storify.com to see examples.) You can then share the project on Facebook or on a class website.

3. Have a conversation with a First Amendment "user." Of course, we're all users of the First Amendment, but many of us don't come in daily contact with someone who really leans on their right to free speech. Invite to class (in person or through Skype) a member of a group in your community who really speaks out on issues. Examples might include a drive-time radio host, a member of your local newspaper editorial board, a representative of a local or state political party office, a leader of the ACLU or an official of the NRA. What are their views on freedom of expression? Have their rights ever been challenged? If so, how did they respond?

4. To reinforce the information in the chapter, watch a nine-minute video about the *New York Times v. Sullivan* case produced by Thinkwell Videos: www.youtube.com/watch?v=FtqQWt7aoZ0&feature=related. What new information does this video provide? Discuss the Doctrine of Incorporation in particular to explain how the First Amendment applies to state government. Review the history of U.S. press freedom, the three-part standard for libel for public officials and the concept of actual malice. How do legal rights to publish and the public tolerance of journalistic practice conflict?

5. Visit the Student Press Law Center online at www.splc.org/. Under "Classroom Resources," locate the First Amendment quiz. The quiz has 30 questions and takes 10 minutes to complete. The last screen will report your score and tell you how you did. Take a screen capture of that result and e-mail it to your instructor with a brief note highlighting one or two things you were surprised to learn about the First Amendment.

▶ DISCUSSION/DEBATE QUESTIONS

1. What impact do you think the context in which the American press operated under British rule had on those drafting the First Amendment? Some have argued that the authors put this amendment first in the Bill of Rights for a reason. Do you agree?

2. Think about criticisms leveled against President Barack Obama (or earlier, against President George W. Bush) on social networks, blogs, talk shows and other platforms. Think of the worst of these that you can recall. Now, view those through the context of U.S. First Amendment policy and law toward starting in 1798 and going through 1969. In which eras might these statements have landed the authors in jail? How did the thinking of lawmakers and judges change over this time period?

3. About half of those responding to a First Amendment Center/American Journalism Review survey said the First Amendment goes too far in the rights it guarantees. Do you agree? Why do you think so many people believe the First Amendment should be curtailed? What can and should journalists do to help audiences understand the need for a strong First Amendment?

4. State shield laws protect journalists. What issues arise in defining who is entitled to this protection? If you have a blog, are you a journalist? What if you routinely share information of public interest through a Twitter or Facebook page?

5. We read regularly reports of celebrities and politicians engaged in extra-marital affairs. The lines between publications like the *National Enquirer* and the *Washington Post* began to change in the 1980s and 1990s on reporting these types of stories. Think of this news in relation to the definition of "publication of private facts" included in this chapter. Are these matters of public concern? Would they be offensive to a reasonable person? Why are these reports protected under current law? Why might reputable news organizations publish this material?

▶ READ MORE

Lee Bollinger, *The Tolerant Society: Free Speech and Extremist Speech In America*, New York: Oxford University Press, 1986.

Anthony Lewis, *Make No Law*, New York: Random House, 1991.

Kent R. Middleton and William Lee, *The Law of Public Communication*, 8th ed. New York: Longman, 2011.

Don R. Pember and Clay Calvert, *Mass Media Law*, 16th ed. Dubuque, Iowa: McGraw-Hill, 2009–2010.

www.firstamendmentcenter.org: Significant historical events, court cases, and ideas that have shaped our current system of constitutional First Amendment jurisprudence, presented by the Freedom Forum. Also stories, commentaries and roundups of First Amendment disputes.

www.rcfp.org: The Reporters Committee for Freedom of the Press maintains online "publications and topical guides on First Amendment and Freedom of Information issues." Current stories, plus archives and much more.

8

A Declaration
of Journalistic
Independence

Edward Snowden has been described lots of different ways, but the labels generally fall into one of two categories: whistleblower or traitor. In 2013, the former CIA employee and National Security Agency contractor leaked a massive trove of classified documents to journalists who have since published articles revealing the existence of the NSA's wide-ranging mass surveillance program. Among the more shocking revelations: The telephone calls, texts and e-mails of tens of millions of average Americans were collected and tracked, an apparent violation of Constitutional protections against unreasonable search and seizure. While the revelation about such domestic spying was explosive, the leaked materials also include intelligence files of some U.S. allies, as well as information about the existence and operation of global surveillance programs. The documents also include evidence that the U.S. eavesdropped on the phone calls of world leaders and tapped the computer networks of the European Union and China. No one's secrets were spared.

It's hard to overstate the significance of Snowden's disclosures or to predict just how far and wide the ripple effects will be felt. Indeed, journalists from

LEARNING OBJECTIVES

Understand the central importance of "independence" in journalism;

Explore and critique the concept of "objectivity";

Bring together concepts from this and earlier chapters to create a deeper understanding of journalism's mission.

the *Washington Post*, the *Guardian* and other news organizations who continue to process the leaked material and publish new, often alarming stories won't run out of material any time soon. While the exact number of documents Snowden disclosed isn't known, the U.S. government puts the number at more than 1 million.

Depending on one's perspective, Snowden is either a whistleblower, who brought information of grave public concern to light at considerable personal risk, or a traitor who endangered national security. Or maybe to some people he's a little of both. But one thing Snowden is *not* is a journalist. He is a source and a subject of news who sought out journalists to tell the stories that those top secret documents contain. He could have taken a cue from Julian Assange, the founder of Wikileaks, and simply posted everything to a website and let the chips fall where they might. Instead, he reached out to Laura Poitras and Glenn Greenwald, a documentary filmmaker and journalist respectively, to disclose the documents—a decision that made his name public and contributed to the gray area of temporary asylum in Russia in which he currently lives. The question is, why leak to journalists? More specifically, what is it about journalists that Snowden believed was important to accomplishing his goals in disclosing the information?

This entire book is an answer to that question.

You've read a lot about what it is journalists are supposed to do and the things—economic, legal, and technological—that affect whether and how they do it. You've even been introduced to a process for helping journalists make ethical decisions, when confronted with these and other kinds of barriers to doing their jobs. What we want to emphasize now is how independence sits right at the intersection of the journalist's job and the things standing in the way of doing it. Think about it. When we talk about barriers to good journalism, we are essentially talking about people, policies and institutions that compromise journalistic independence: The push for profits that can push journalists to do fewer tough and expensive stories in favor of more easy and cheap ones; competitive pressures that sacrifice a journalist's independent judgment to the judgment of the crowd; powerful sources or advertisers who seek to steer journalists toward one kind of story or away from another.

In this chapter we are revisiting and summarizing basic principles of journalism's purpose and practices as a way to champion independence and draw conclusions about their central role in journalism's ability to engage in those practices and fulfill that purpose. What does all of this have to do with Edward Snowden? Well, he chose to leak to journalists. Why? He was counting on the ability of journalists to dig, verify, and answer to no one but the public on a story that very powerful people would have preferred remained a secret. Snowden was banking quite a lot, in fact, on journalistic independence.

Independence, as you learned in Chapter 2, means journalists operate with the public foremost in their minds and avoid splitting their loyalty to the public with loyalties to other "factions." Those factions might be political parties or religions, charitable organizations or businesses—any entity that might try to get between a journalist and the public. The chief obligation of Poitras, Greenwald and Ewen MacAskill, the *Guardian* reporter who joined them, wasn't to the NSA or the U.S. government or the British government, though of course they had ethical duties to them. Their obligation, and the obligation of the other reporters who joined the story, was to report what they thought the public ought to know.

Just as important, in leaking to journalists, Snowden was submitting the information to the verification process, the objective *method* of journalism. Doing so would enhance the credibility and therefore the power of the information as well as ensure that some sort of filtering of such highly sensitive information would take place. Here's how Janine Gibson, another *Guardian* reporter working with the NSA documents, explained it on Reddit's "Ask Me Anything" forum:

► **INDEPENDENCE:** An essential component of journalism practice in which journalists are free to pursue truth with loyalty only to citizens, and not particular interests, causes or other pressures, in mind.

> We have a process that we run with every story where we approach the administration, tell them what we're doing and identify any documents that we might quote from or publish. We invite them to share any specific national security concerns that would result from those disclosures. What happens next varies. Sometimes they respond with redaction requests (and sometimes we agree and sometimes not). Sometimes just a statement. Sometimes we ask questions. Sometimes they answer. Much of the time, we've already made some decisions ourselves on redactions of obviously sensitive operational detail or people's names etc. As we've gone on, working this story has become closer to journalistic standard practice (or at least, how we practice it). In terms of the news cycle—obviously we try and make sure each story has as much impact as possible, but we tend to publish when we've found a story, worked it up to our satisfaction, determined that it's in the public interest and it's ready.

FIGURE 8.1 The Edward Snowden affair highlights the tension between government secrecy and the public's right to know.
Source: Mike Mozart (Jeepersmedia) via Flickr. Reprinted via Creative Commons license (CC BY 2.0).

Notice that Gibson is describing not only the process of verification, but also of ethical decision-making in a fast-paced, competitive environment—the "news cycle" she mentions—from the perspective of an independent journalist with the public interest solidly in mind. We couldn't have described better ourselves how all the pieces we've been describing in this book fit together.

▶ INDEPENDENCE, POWER AND RISK

The Snowden story is one more example of the kind of power journalism has, power that must be exercised responsibly. It's also an example of the kind of work journalists are supposed to do in a democracy. A story about secrets and surveillance that raises Constitutional questions certainly counts as information of consequence to citizens. Without the kind of independence journalists like Gibson, MacAskill, Greenwald and Poitras enjoy, it simply wouldn't be possible. But even with that independence, many of these journalists face enormous personal risks in getting the story out. Poitras and Greenwald, for example, felt unable to return to the United States for nearly a year after meeting Snowden out of fear the authorities would try to seize the information Snowden passed on to them and, perhaps, arrest them as well. MacAskill has experienced difficulties at passport control every time he returns to the United Kingdom from traveling abroad.

As terrible as that might sound, it pales in comparison to the story of Lasantha Wickramatunga, the Sri Lankan newspaper editor we told you about in Chapter 1, whose approach to journalism captured the concepts of the watchdog, mirror and marketplace of ideas so well. Remember, Wickramatunga paid the price of doing independent journalism with his life. While the (mostly) American and British journalists reporting the surveillance story almost certainly do not face a lethal threat, their experiences say quite a lot about why independent journalism, though powerful, can be so hard to come by sometimes. On that Reddit AMA forum, Glenn Greenwald said:

> All good journalism entails risk, by definition, because all good journalism makes someone powerful angry. It's important to be rationally aware of those risks and take reasonable precautions, but not fixate on them or, under any circumstances, allow them to deter you in doing what you think should be done. Fearlessness can be its own form of power.

But before we break out the champagne to celebrate this instance of independent reporting in the face of formidable obstacles, we need to note the reaction of other journalists to the story. Journalists are in no way unanimous in their feelings about Snowden or the reporters to whom he released the documents or the subsequent reporting they and other journalists have done with the leaked material. And, really, why should we expect unanimity? The situation is the very definition of "complex."

8.1 THE VIEW FROM THE PROS: INDEPENDENCE OUTSIDE THE U.S.

Journalism takes many different forms around the world. From the early1960s until the late 1980s, many journalists in Africa (particularly Eastern and Southern Africa) thought of journalism primarily as a form of protest for social justice and as a way of seeking freedom from the vestiges of colonial rule. This type of journalism was rooted in the expression of dissent, and it's a far cry from Western notions of independence and distance from faction.

It is a pity that many practicing journalists are not impartial about either the government or those who oppose it. It is not in the DNA of many African journalists to be as fair and impartial on matters such as human rights protection, responsible national governance and socioeconomic equality. It is also pretty clear that the universal ethical standards—such as truth or accuracy or responsibility—in Africa's journalism have different meanings under oppressive governments. For instance, many young journalists chronicle the activities of state actors and simply promote state propaganda. That is their understanding of journalism, which they define as *developmental journalism*. These journalists might think of themselves as being truthful when they accurately report on government business, but in most cases they are providing little more than public relations for the state instead of reflecting good checks and balances.

But an even more significant difference lies in the state of investigative journalism in many African nations. Even privately owned media never report corruption in top government offices that are closely connected to the presidency. They only investigate and expose junior politicians and mid-level civil servants. Thus, the media report what is principally "truthful" and "accurate" about African governments. But it is also irresponsible journalism because their coverage of news tends to favor government leaders and friends of media owners and the government.

I should point out here that the challenge is that journalists fear retribution from some of the dictatorial governments. Yet, it is the independent media (media that are neither owned/controlled by the government nor a government official) which are more crucial to mobilizing and politically energizing citizens to de-legitimize dictatorships. It is my contention that government leaders try to tear down the adversarial role of the press when coverage is aimed at state institutions because such coverage gives citizens the information they need to make the right decisions in a democratic society.

Even in this new millennium, independent journalists in Africa can easily be co-opted by their governments or national leaders due to the culture of state patronage. Throughout the 1990s and the 2000s, governments appointed journalists they patronized or compromised in order to destabilize independent voices in the news media. For instance, I write in my book *African Media and Democratization* (2011) that in the mid-to-late 1990s and 2000s, independent journalists were ferried in and out of police detention on weekends so regularly in parts of Africa that their wives automatically recognized a peculiar jail scent.

Here are a few examples of why the concept of journalism and journalism practice is a daunting challenge in many African nations.

- In late 2007, journalist Mathias Manirakiza, director of Radio Isanganiro, was detained for the third time in five years on charges of authorizing his station to broadcast information capable of breaching national security.
- In Ethiopia, two editors and countless journalists were also prosecuted simply for writing about non-threatening topics such as music that exposes government corruption. For example, Amare Aregawi, the editor-in-chief of the *Reporter*, Ethiopia's leading independent newspaper, was imprisoned in connection with published stories addressing criticisms about the management of a brewery linked to the government.
- In many African nations journalists can be charged with treason for inciting "disaffection with the government" for their reporting. The risk of going to prison poses the greatest threat to independent journalists. A few independent newspapers also face financial constraints that prohibit them from managing a news organization. For instance, the state-run *New Times* is the only daily newspaper in Rwanda. Just like the other East African nations, the Rwandan government does not advertise with any independent news organization that is perceived to be criticizing the regime and its government.

The list of problems for the practice and understanding of journalism in Africa is endless! Yet the courage and energy of African journalists is astonishing under such difficult conditions.

LEARN MORE: Students in the United States often take for granted the First Amendment freedoms of press, speech, religion, assembly and petition. Visit the website of the Committee to Protect Journalists (www.cpj.org) and read more about the challenges faced by journalists in Africa and other parts of the world.

Yusuf Kalyango Jr. is a faculty member at the E. W. Scripps School of Journalism at Ohio University. Before earning a doctorate, he spent 13 years as a journalist for East African and U.S. news outlets.

Journalists using the Snowden trove risk making mistakes in the actual act of disclosure, which can lead to serious unintended consequences. The *New York Times,* for example, did not adequately block out the name of an NSA agent in reporting on documents related to the agency's use of smartphone game apps to track someone's location, identity and other information. It's probably obvious, but we'll spell it out anyway: Revealing the identity of an NSA agent and naming his target is dangerous to the agent and potentially damaging to the agency's ability to track terrorists.

Aside from the potential for such errors, there is some disagreement about the judgment journalists have exercised in determining what is appropriate to disclose and report on. Consider, for example, the perspective of Dan Murphy, a reporter for the *Christian Science Monitor*:

> To me it's always seemed clear that Snowden's revelations have done two things. First, he has exposed NSA programs that improperly targeted US citizens and represent enormous government surveillance overreach in the post-9/11 era. Second, and more frequently, he has brought to light entirely legal and appropriate NSA programs aimed toward foreign intelligence targets (which is after all the NSA's remit from Congress). I often try to point out on my Twitter feed that many Snowden revelations have nothing to do with protecting the US Constitution and have the effect of helping foreign intelligence targets of the NSA.

Murphy is saying that the leaked documents and the reporting about them include stuff that should have remained secret. That's a fair point, right? Snowden himself said he gave the documents to journalists rather than publicly releasing them himself so that they could be properly vetted and filtered. So questions about those vetting and filtering decisions are—or ought to be—legitimate. That's not what happened to Murphy, however. In raising those questions he also raised the ire of Greenwald, who used his own Twitter feed to make a very unflattering comparison. As Murphy writes:

> I was furious that he compared me to Joe McCarthy, the mid-20th century charlatan who led an ideological witch-hunt against legions of Americans for their political beliefs. My crime? Taking what, to me at least, is the uncontroversial position that NSA disclosures about fully legal overseas intelligence operations are not a form of whistle-blowing and help US foreign intelligence targets.

Contrary to what Greenwald's tweets seem to suggest, independence doesn't grant journalists immunity from criticism, nor should it. Indeed, independence is important for press critics as well as practitioners if there is to be any accountability in journalism at all. But note that there's a big difference between critiquing the judgments of independent journalists and arguing that journalists should not be the ones making those judgments. Reasonable people, after all, can and do sometimes disagree. For all the controversy the Snowden disclosures have stoked in journalism, few would prefer a system in which journalists did not exercise independent judgment in the public interest.

It's the *public* part we need to revisit a bit here. Greenwald has been called an advocate or even activist when it comes to government secrecy and national security issues. The same is true of Poitras, whose documentary *Citizenfour* leans far more toward "whistleblower" than "traitor" in portraying Snowden. How might we understand their approach to the public interest in this situation? Are Greenwald and Poitras exhibiting independence from faction? Is believing that openness is generally preferable to secrecy a bias? If it is a bias, is it necessarily bad?

So many questions. Time to tackle the objectivity issue head on.

▶ FACTS, VALUES AND THE OBJECTIVITY TRAP

Independence is the core value of journalism—the value from which all of the other values that form journalism's core functions come to life. Public communication without such independence wouldn't be journalism, it would be something more client- or agenda-driven—something that one expects a good public relations practitioner, not a journalist, to do. Why? Because journalism must retain the ability to address difficult questions in tough circumstances to people who'd rather not have to answer them.

When the story is easy, its conclusions apparent, anyone can play journalist. But when the story is difficult, the sources are reluctant and maybe even deceptive, when the partisan knives are drawn and the truth is hiding behind spin and money, journalists must be able to approach the story free from the baggage of perceived conflicts. That's not to say that the critics still won't attack: in fact, it's the inevitable attempts to shoot the messenger that make independence so important. Critics have seized on charges of bias and used the objectivity trap time and time again, and no amount of journalistic excellence is going to change that. The motivation for such criticism is all too often to squelch rather than improve journalism.

Fortunately, journalists can best neutralize their critics by hewing to the time-honored principles that differentiate the craft from the bread-and-circus mass media. And to do so, they must begin and end with the pursuit of truth for truth's sake, a task complicated by the many things that get between journalists and the pursuit of truth these days, from the speed of the news cycle to the creep of partisan infotainment to the economic pressures of the digital era.

The *New York Times* seems as good a place as any to highlight just how confused even journalists can be about the very nature of journalism. The paper's then public editor, Arthur S. Brisbane, created an Internet maelstrom in 2012 with a seemingly innocent question: Should journalists challenge "facts" that are asserted by newsmakers they write about? The blog post was prompted by reader questions like this one, which Brisbane quoted:

> My question is what role the paper's hard-news coverage should play with regard to false statements—by candidates or by others. In general, the Times sets its documentation of falsehoods in articles apart from its primary coverage. If the newspaper's overarching goal is truth, oughtn't the truth be embedded in its principal stories? In other words, if a candidate repeatedly utters an outright falsehood [. . .], shouldn't the Times's coverage nail it right at the point where the article quotes it?

In other words, this reader wondered, why are demonstrably false statements not corrected, or really even addressed, in news stories that purport to offer the truth? Good question! And Brisbane answered it with more questions—"How can *The Times* do this in a way that is objective and fair? Is it possible to be objective and fair when the reporter is choosing to correct one fact over another?"—before inviting readers to share their thoughts on the subject.

And share, they certainly did. The response to Brisbane's blog post ricocheted all over the blogosphere, punctuated by an angry, snarky tone. One typical comment, from "Fed Up" in Brooklyn, summarized the debate: "The fact that this is even a question shows us how far mainstream journalism

◀ **OBJECTIVITY:** Commonly used to describe a person's (alleged) ability to completely detach from, and have no opinion or perspective on, a given issue. Because people can't really be objective, what we advocate here is seeing objectivity as a quality of the methods journalists employ in their work, not of the journalists themselves.

has fallen." The vast majority of the comments, excellently summarized by the Nieman Journalism Lab blog, converge on a common theme: Readers' disgust with the notion that reporting that calls out falsehoods somehow offends the unwritten rule of "objectivity."

Here lies the disconnect between what citizens expect of journalism, and what journalism, all too often, has come to be. As preeminent journalism observer and historian Michael Schudson has written, the "objectivity norm guides journalists to separate facts from values, and report only the facts." As if "facts" mean much when stripped of their context. As if "facts" somehow equal "truth."

It's a trap, really. As Kovach and Rosenstiel so eloquently illustrate in *The Elements of Journalism*, the idea that a journalist can, through some purity of thought, "be" objective holds them to an unachievable standard. It substitutes the unanswerable ("Is this *individual* objective?") for the answerable ("Is this *reporting* verifiable and replicable?") and by doing so, makes every work of journalism ultimately suspect.

Way back in Chapter 2, we offered a mini-overview of the scientific method to make a point about how the kind of verification process and transparency essential to the scientific method are similarly essential to the journalistic method. Scientists have to be open about how they collect and analyze their data, so that others can assess the validity of what they did; journalists likewise have to be open about the sources they consult and the observations they make, so that the public can evaluate the credibility of their reporting. And just as scientists have to be open to the prospect of their experiments failing, to the idea that their hypotheses were just, plain wrong, so do journalists have to be open to alternative explanations and new information that might change what they thought they knew about a given story or event.

But is all this really necessary? Why aren't scientists or journalists simply trusted at their word? Why don't we just take it on faith that a scientist's conclusions are based on a rigorously designed study, or that a journalist's story is based on a discipline of verification? Because scientists and journalists are human, that's why. Because they can't help but have opinions and experiences that could affect how they approach an experiment or a news story. One of the biggest benefits of the method each kind of investigator,

FIGURE 8.2 The public should be able to get information on all sides of an issue—but that doesn't mean that all sides of the issue deserve equal weight.
Source: Courtesy of Understanding Science (undsci.berkeley.edu).

whether scientist or journalist employs is that it is objective. *The method is objective, because the person cannot be.*

What's weird—yes, weird—is that this narrow and misguided definition of objectivity persists even as journalism has shifted and expanded to include practices that appear to fly directly in the face of that definition. Take that fact-checking Brisbane was so worried about. Not only are there entire organizations devoted to it—FactCheck.org, PolitiFact, Fact Checker—those organizations operate in partnership with and are sometimes financially supported by news organizations. (Fact Checker is part of the *Washington Post*.) As scholars Lucas Graves, Brendan Nyhan and Jason Reifler point out in a study of the spread of fact-checking in journalism, these organizations have become widely and rapidly accepted in professional journalism, their work considered complementary, not contradictory, to the kind of accountability reporting journalism is supposed to do. PolitiFact has even been awarded a Pulitzer Prize. And one of the first things Margaret Sullivan,

Brisbane's successor as public editor at the *Times*, wrote about? The importance of fact-checking. She said:

> Whatever the conclusions, whatever the effectiveness, of challenging facts, the idea that we have to debate the necessity of doing so strikes me as absurd. What is the role of the media if not to press for some semblance of reality amid the smoke and mirrors?

More broadly, scholars like Kevin Barnhurst, Michael Schudson and Katherine Fink have traced journalism's steadily increasing embrace of analysis and interpretation. It's not "just the facts, ma'am," and it hasn't been for a long time. While this, too, flies in the face of some popular though misguided understandings of what objectivity requires, it also resonates with the Hutchins Commission's recommendations we mentioned in Chapter 1. You may recall that the Commission linked the survival of a free press to its performance in serving the needs of democracy. One of those services: "A truthful, comprehensive, and intelligent account of the day's events *in a context which gives them meaning.*" There is no way around offering the kind of judgment, analysis and interpretation—the very stuff that seems ripe for charges of bias—providing that context requires.

Bias. Yep, we said it. But what does it really mean in journalism?

▶ JOURNALISM'S BUILT-IN (NOT NECESSARILY BAD) BIASES

Journalists can't "be" objective any more than anyone else can, and the critics who decry the "mainstream media" know that. It's a bludgeon—a political one, in every sense of the word—in the form of an unreachable ideal, and a frequent companion of "bias," another over- and misused term. One of the most frequently heard critiques of journalism is that it has a liberal bias, that it favors liberal viewpoints over conservative ones. You may have noticed that Fox News has built its whole identity (and marketing strategy) on offering an alternative to that alleged bias.

We could write a whole book on bias—indeed, many people already have—but we will spare you the gory details. We'll just say this: Political bias is probably the least useful lens through which to examine journalism. What people see as bias in the news is very much rooted in their pre-existing beliefs about the world. Research shows that people not only seek out news and viewpoints from sources that agree with them, but also that people with opposing beliefs who are shown the same news story are likely to say the story is biased in favor of the other viewpoint. One story, two opposing charges of bias. Crazy, right?

If political bias or liberal/conservative bias doesn't explain much about the news, what does? Is there a better set of lenses through which to examine journalism, to explain why news emphasizes the things it does? The good news is yes. The even better news is that you have already established a foundation for understanding them from your reading of earlier chapters. We can elaborate on what you learned by pointing you to the work of journalism scholar Andrew Cline, who has developed a list of nine structural biases in the news. By "structural," Cline means biases that are built into journalistic practice. As structural, or inherent, biases, these are almost invisible to us. They seem to be the "natural" order of things even though there are other practices that journalism arguably *could* adopt.

The list of biases includes "temporal" and "bad news," which easily connect back to some of the news values covered in Chapter 3, such as timeliness and conflict. And the "commercial" and "expediency" biases Cline describes certainly harken back to the cheap and easy news that journalism in the U.S. is under pressure to produce, as you learned in Chapter 4. Of the five remaining biases on Cline's list—visual, fairness, narrative, status quo and glory—fairness is most relevant to our concerns here. But how, exactly, can fairness, which is a *good* thing, be a bias?

When we call something a structural bias, we aren't necessarily saying it's bad. Sure, "bias" has come to have a pretty negative connotation, particularly when you put the word "political" or "liberal" in front of it as we mentioned earlier. But we (and Cline) are using it in a more neutral, descriptive way here to understand how certain practices tend to favor one kind of presentation of news over other possible kinds of presentations. Fairness bias, for example, shows up in the news in a couple different ways. It refers to that common journalistic practice of offering one "side" a chance to comment on news generated by the other "side." Seems fair, hence the name "fairness bias." What's biased about it? Here's Cline's explanation:

> This creates the illusion that the game of politics is always contentious and never cooperative. This bias can also create situations in which one

◄ **STRUCTURAL BIAS:** A type of frame or approach, inherent to journalism practice, which favors certain kinds of news topics and presentations over others. For example, visual bias in news refers to relatively greater emphasis, especially in television news, on stories that are visually interesting over those that are not.

faction appears to be attacked by the press. For example, politician
A announces some positive accomplishment followed by the press
seeking a negative comment from politician B. The point is not to
disparage politician A but to be fair to politician B. When politician A
is a conservative, this practice appears to be liberal bias.

From our perch here in 2015, when the public is very politically polarized,
the idea that politics isn't "always contentious and never cooperative" might
be hard to imagine. Fairness bias probably makes polarization worse by
setting up every issue as a battle. What's more, this impulse toward a certain kind of fairness also gives equal weight to perspectives or "sides" even
when one side has a lot more evidence behind it than the other. Fairness
bias is a way journalists avoid being seen as taking sides, even when the evidence indicates there's really only one side to be taken. The Earth orbits the
Sun, right? Do we need to note that Random Guy, who failed all his science
courses, has a contrary opinion on how the solar system works? You get the
idea. A variety of opinions is great. What would the marketplace of ideas be
without such variety? But journalism's purpose to inform can't be made to
suffer in the name of providing a platform for opinion. This "on-the-other-
hand-it is" hinders journalism's truth-telling mission, because it misleads
the public about the very issues on which they must make decisions or elect
representatives to make them on their behalf. It also illustrates why "fairness," "balance," "neutrality" and "detachment" are no better than "objectivity" at describing the stance journalism in the public interest must take.

Avoiding the pitfalls of fairness bias is an ethical, not just technical, issue.
As we explained in Chapter 6, it's a matter of getting all the facts you can,
identifying all of your duties, and *weighing* them. The ethics handbook that
guides the journalists at National Public Radio, for example, confronts fairness bias directly:

> At all times, we report for our readers and listeners, not our sources.
> So our primary consideration when presenting the news is that we
> are fair to the truth. If our sources try to mislead us or put a false
> spin on the information they give us, we tell our audience. If the
> balance of evidence in a matter of controversy weighs heavily on
> one side, we acknowledge it in our reports. We strive to give our
> audience confidence that all sides have been considered and
> represented fairly.

Which brings us back to Arthur Brisbane, the former public editor of the *New York Times*, and his question about the press acting as a "truth vigilante." Brisbane was worried about fairness and objectivity—but not necessarily the kind of fairness or objectivity of method we've been promoting in this chapter. The response from readers, the wider blogosphere and, even, Brisbane's successor? Correcting errors and falsehoods *is* fair—it's fair to the truth and to *us*.

But what about Poitras and Greenwald? Does their pro-Snowden bias get in the way of their fairness to the truth? Maybe their favorable opinion of Snowden and his motivations for leaking all that information influences how they portray *Snowden*. But that's not really the main issue, is it? Looking through the objectivity-as-method lens means considering whether their reporting on that leaked material is fair to the truth, regardless of whatever feelings—positive or negative—they might have about the person who leaked it.

8.2 A VIEW FROM THE PROS: WHY JOURNALISTS SHOULD BE ACTIVISTS

Two months ago, a *New York Times* journalist, investigative reporter James Risen, went on Twitter to denounce the Obama administration's attitude toward the press. The administration, he said, was the "greatest enemy of press freedom in a generation."

Risen's tirade became a topic of conversation among the community of people who watch and comment on journalism. Some said a reporter shouldn't be expressing such thoughts publicly, because it might cause readers to question his—and his newspaper's—commitment to objective reporting. But the newspaper's editor in charge of of journalism standards told Margaret Sullivan, the *Times*' public editor, that Risen had done the right thing.

"In general," this editor said, "our reporters understand that they don't and shouldn't editorialize on issues we cover . . . I would put this in a different category."

What category? Freedom of the press, of course. And he was right.

This was an important moment in the history of the *New York Times*. It was officially admitting that it is not neutral—isn't pretending to be neutral—on this topic. The *Times*, as an organization, was taking an activist stance—far from its traditional role of observer and reporter.

I'm here to suggest to you today that all journalists need to think of themselves as activists in the world we now live in.

Before I explain this further, let me first explain what I mean by journalism and activism. Journalism can include so many things, ranging from deep investigative work to fluffy entertainment, but for our purposes I think of it as helping people understand the world they live in, so they can make better decisions about how they live. This often involves telling truth to the rich and powerful, and uncovering things that the rich and powerful would prefer to keep secret. It also involves being thorough, accurate, fair, independent and—this is not done enough—transparent. Journalism is vital to liberty, because it is a cornerstone of free speech.

For activism, I'll simply use the dictionary definition: "the policy or action of using vigorous campaigning to bring about political or social change." I'd add to that—sometimes activism is campaigning to stop things from happening.

In many parts of this world, doing real journalism is activism—because truth telling in some societies is an act designed to bring about change. I'm humbled by the people who risk their freedom, and sometimes their lives, to tell their fellow citizens and the rest of the world what is happening where they live. You will be hearing from one of them in the next talk.

In the western democracies with a more robust tradition of free speech and a free press, the idea of journalists as activists is often seen as taking sides in contravention of journalistic norms. But there's a long and honorable history of what we call "advocacy journalism"—we could easily call it "activist journalism"—exposing injustices with the absolute goal of stirring public anger, and then public action to bring about change. In America, the people we called muckrakers in the early 20th century did brilliant journalism of this kind. Today filmmaker Laura Poitras, who'll be speaking here by video this evening, and her colleagues are among many others who are carrying on that tradition. (Do see *Citizenfour*, by the way; it's brilliant.)

Also today, we have a new category of journalism in this realm—journalism being done by people who are advocates first, and media producers second. I'm talking about Human Rights Watch, which consistently does brilliant reporting on human rights issues around the world.

I'm talking about the American Civil Liberties Union, an organization in my own country that consistently does some of the best journalism—in several senses of the word—about threats to our fundamental liberties. In the interest of transparency, I should mention that my fantastically talented nephew, Daniel Kahn Gillmor, works with the ACLU.

In the past, these organizations and NGOs like them around the world were doing the journalism. But to get it seen they had to persuade traditional media organizations to care about, and then to publish or broadcast, reports based on the information the NGOs had collected. Now, in the digital age, every organization of any kind is also a media enterprise, and can go more directly to the public. Collaborations with traditional journalists are still helpful, but no longer as absolutely necessary as they were. We journalists should be welcoming the advocates to the journalism ecosystem—and recognizing them for their work. By the way, the American Civil Liberties Union probably litigates more open-records cases on issues related to liberty, using the U.S. Freedom of Information Act, than all traditional news organizations put together.

Now, I'm not saying all advocates are doing journalism—far from it. In many cases we're getting untrue, unfair propaganda. We need know the difference, as journalists and as members of the public—that's another talk entirely.

So we have a baseline of journalistic activism—all around us and often incredibly valuable—on a variety of topics. It makes many traditional journalists, especially in my country, uncomfortable. Why? Because we're told, again and again, that one of journalism's core values is objectivity and/or neutrality.

But even those journalists who worship at the altar of objectivity should recognize that on at least some issues, they cannot possibly be objective. Or at least, they should not be. On some issues we have to take stands, even though those stands may put us at policy odds with the people and institutions we cover.

What are these issues? The *New York Times* has picked one: freedom of the press. I hope no one here would dispute the need to take a stand for press freedom.

But I'd suggest this is only one of several policy issues where journalists who do not take activist stands are unfit to call themselves journalists. They all come under larger topics that are at the core of liberty, among them: freedom of expression, freedom to associate, freedom to collaborate, freedom to innovate.

We can't be neutral here. We should be openly biased toward openness and freedom. Period.

Powerful governments and corporations are leading the attack against these core values, usually in the name of protecting us or giving us more convenience. In the process, these powerful entities are creating a host of choke points. They're doing their best to lock down a lot of our computing and communications, and creating a system of control by others over what we say and do online.

This is a betrayal of the Internet's decentralized promise, where speech and innovation and collaboration would often start at the edges of this network of networks, where no one needed permission to do those things. Choke points mean we have to ask permission.

What are these choke points? The most obvious is what's happening to the Internet itself. Start with direct censorship, a growing trend in far too many parts of the world. I can't imagine anyone here would object to journalistic activism on this front.

Surveillance, too, has become a method for government—often working with big companies—to keep track of what journalists and activists are doing—going way beyond the mission of stopping terrorism and solving major crimes. Surveillance is having a measurable chilling effect on freedom of expression, and no society that exists under pervasive surveillance can claim to enjoy basic liberty. We know from history that it deadens innovation and culture. If we don't actively oppose mass surveillance, we're not fit to call ourselves journalists.

Another choke point is the telecommunications industry. In America and many other countries—and often in concert with governments—big telecoms say they should have the right to decide what bits of information get to people's devices in what order and at what speed, or whether they get there at all. This is what the network neutrality debate is all about in the U.S.: whether we, at the edges of the networks, or the telecom companies that provide the access to the Internet, get to make those decisions. If we don't campaign for open and truly competitive networks, we're not fit to call ourselves journalists.

"Intellectual property" is a valuable concept, but it's also a choke point. Hollywood and its allies try to lock down or control innovative technologies that threaten incumbent companies' business models. They're abusing the patent and copyright systems, among other tactics. And they never, ever quit. The latest sneak attack from this crowd comes in a secretly negotiated treaty called the Trans Pacific Partnership and is the latest attempt by the intellectual property cartel to prevent innovation, and speech, that it can't control—among many other bad effects. (We know about some of this because Wikileaks has published drafts of several chapters of this immense treaty.) If we don't explain to the public what is happening, and then campaign for a more open process and for the right to innovate, we are unfit to call ourselves journalists.

Speaking of Wikileaks, let's mention another choke point: the major payment systems like Mastercard, Visa and PayPal. They almost shut down Wikileaks with a funding blackout. Only a few news organizations noticed, much less complained. Yet if you can't get paid for your work, how do you plan to put food on your table? The centralized payment industry holds enormous power, by proxy, over journalists' ability to make a living. If we don't campaign against its arbitrary decisions, we're not fit to call ourselves journalists.

Now let's be honest about something: We've helped create some of the choke points—by choosing convenience over liberty in relying centralized Internet platforms like Facebook and Twitter and Google. I have to note that these companies do provide useful services. And they are often trying to be advocates for free speech, though not consistently.

But do journalists understand that the Internet is getting new editors, namely the people who work for some of those companies? Do journalists understand that by feeding Facebook they are feeding a company that will be their biggest financial competitor? If this was only a business issue I wouldn't raise it. But it's much more than that. This is about whether the terms of service at a tiny number of giant companies, as opposed to the First Amendment and other laws like it, will effectively determine our free speech rights. If we aren't activists for open, decentralized technology and communications, we are unfit to call ourselves journalists.

The corporate online powers are also spying on us. It's their business model. Journalists are waking up to this, more so in Europe than in the U.S., but we all need to be thinking harder about how companies can use and abuse big data. If we aren't campaigning for privacy from corporations, not just governments, we are unfit to call ourselves journalists.

I'm not asking journalists to ignore nuances in any of this; life and business and policy truly are complicated. But when it comes to things that directly threaten perhaps our most fundamental liberties—without which journalism is vastly more difficult if not impossible—there's no excuse for failing to explain what's at stake. Nor is there any excuse for failing to take more direct action.

Core freedoms—of expression, association, and more—should be everyone's right. Journalists have a duty to be their defenders.

So I ask this of my journalism friends: Take stands, loudly and proudly. Be activists. Unless you prefer a world of choke points and control by others, this is part of your job.

Dan Gillmor is a leading thinker on journalism in the digital age. Author of *Mediactive* and *We the Media: Grassroots Journalism by the People, for the People*, Gillmor teaches at the Walter Cronkite School of Journalism and Mass Communication at Arizona State University. This is the text of a speech Gillmor gave at the International Journalism Festival in Perugia, Italy, in April 2015.

▶ THE NO-SURPRISES SCHOOL OF JOURNALISM

When disaster strikes, the American Red Cross is often one of the first relief organizations on the ground. Perhaps you've even texted a donation to them in the aftermath of a hurricane or tornado, trusting that your money will help them help others. People feel good about giving to charity and good about the organizations helping those in need. So if it weren't for independence, objectivity of method and a rejection of the fairness bias, it's at least possible that our warm feelings about charities like the Red Cross could get in the way of fair coverage of their work, right? And, given the Red Cross' size and reputation, without an independent, objective and fair approach to covering them, a journalist might find it difficult to defend her reporting.

Let's take a look at how reporters for ProPublica and NPR exercised their independence in putting together a story revealing serious problems with Red Cross relief efforts, and in handling the Red Cross' complaints about that reporting. First, the story. Here are the first few paragraphs of the coverage, published in the fall of 2014.

> In 2012, two massive storms pounded the United States, leaving hundreds of thousands of people homeless, hungry or without power for days and weeks.
>
> Americans did what they so often do after disasters. They sent hundreds of millions of dollars to the Red Cross, confident their money would ease the suffering left behind by Superstorm Sandy and Hurricane Isaac. They believed the charity was up to the job.
>
> They were wrong.
>
> The Red Cross botched key elements of its mission after Sandy and Isaac, leaving behind a trail of unmet needs and acrimony, according to an investigation by ProPublica and NPR. The charity's shortcomings were detailed in confidential reports and internal emails, as well as accounts from current and former disaster relief specialists.
>
> What's more, Red Cross officials at national headquarters in Washington, D.C. compounded the charity's inability to provide relief by "diverting assets for public relations purposes," as one internal report puts it. Distribution of relief supplies, the report said, was "politically driven."

We'll cut to the chase: The series is pretty devastating. In document after document, interview after interview, a picture emerges of the Red Cross failing to get food and supplies to storm victims, to direct volunteers to the places where victims needed help, and even to account for how much of the donated funds went to disaster relief. On top of that, the charity seemed more worried about public relations than providing relief. As you might imagine, the Red Cross was not amused. In a 12-page, single-spaced letter sent a few months later, the charity asked for corrections of what it called "10 serious problems" with the reporting. To offer just one example, the Red Cross disputed the reporters' claim that they could not find many people who had positive things to say about the Red Cross:

> While an investigative journalist may not want to print it, obviously it's not difficult to find someone with positive observations about the Red Cross. And we have shown you in this document that on numerous occasions, we provided comment and this team claimed that we did not. As demonstrated by the following examples of positive statements regarding the Red Cross' operations, the absence of balanced reporting indicates a troubling bias on the part of the reporters.

Well, that's interesting. A powerful organization asserting that the reporters covering it were biased, that their reporting wasn't balanced, because they hadn't included as many positive as negative comments about the Red Cross. No, your eyes aren't deceiving you. The Red Cross is actually upset that the journalists had *not* succumbed to the fairness bias. *Why* the reporters might be biased is not addressed, but note that it's the *reporters* and not their *reporting* whose objectivity is being called into question. All of this would be funny if such tangled understandings of objectivity, balance and fairness didn't present a threat to journalistic independence.

So how did the reporters respond? They published both the Red Cross' letter and their own point-by-point rebuttal of the letter's claims. They also came right out and said, "The Red Cross is wrong" to say the story was incomplete and inaccurate. In a podcast explaining the decision to publicly issue such a detailed response, reporter Justin Elliott described the "no-surprises philosophy" he and most other investigative reporters worth their salt follow. No surprises means that the information in a story has been checked and rechecked with the sources so many times that nothing in the final, published version will come as a surprise to those sources. That sort of verification process is a way to be fair both to the sources in letting them respond to allegations as the reporting process is under way and fair to the truth in giving weight to the claims that are backed up by the most evidence.

We highly recommend looking at the entire response as it serves as a sort of primer on the discipline of verification. For now, though, let's just see how the reporters handled the Red Cross' claim regarding the lack of positive comments.

> In our dozens of interviews it was quite rare to hear positive assessments of the Red Cross' storm responses from people who do not currently work for the Red Cross' public affairs office.
>
> In fact, we did not include in our story many of the *negative* experiences we heard about the Red Cross.
>
> For example, the Red Cross writes in its complaint that "the reporters spoke with the Head of the Mississippi office of Emergency Management, who discussed our response to Isaac in what we understand was positive terms, and none of that was included."
>
> It's accurate that ProPublica reporter Justin Elliott interviewed Robert Latham, executive director of the Mississippi Emergency Management Agency. But Latham was quite critical of the Red Cross' response. Echoing others we interviewed, Latham told us that the Red Cross' reorganizations had alienated experienced disaster responders, contributing to an anemic Isaac response.

It boils down to this: The Red Cross says there are lots of people with nice things to say about its relief efforts, and the biased reporters didn't include them in the story. The reporters say that—outside of people whose job it is to say nice things about the Red Cross—few people had nice things to say. In other words, the reporters weren't just interested in tallying up positive and negative comments, but in evaluating the authority and motivation of the people making the comments. Fairness bias led one direction; the reporters went in the other direction.

Beyond this illustration of an ethically grounded discipline of verification process, the tale of the Red Cross story also circles us back to key issues of independence and objectivity. It might not be entirely obvious to you, but by journalism standards, the reporters' rebuttal was a bit unusual and dramatic, a sort of "mic drop" of a response. When approached about a potential correction, journalists typically go back and recheck their information

FIGURE 8.3 Disasters represent one of the news media's greatest challenges, and offer important lessons for coverage.
Source: Photo by Andrea Booher—Nov 08, 2012 / Courtesy of FEMA.

and, when necessary, publish a correction. But when no correction is warranted, they don't go into much detail, saying something like "we stand by our reporting" and leaving it there. In publicly pointing out the errors in the Red Cross' complaints, the ProPublica and NPR reporters were sidestepping the objectivity trap that says journalists shouldn't make themselves part of the story, shouldn't stray from reporting "just the facts." In doing so, they offer us some hope that the objectivity trap might finally, if slowly, be losing its bullying power.

▶ ENGAGEMENT OR DETACHMENT?

Media scholar Jay Rosen, relying on the work of philosopher Thomas Nagel who coined the phrase "the view from nowhere," describes journalists' anxiety about being seen as taking sides as "a bid for trust that advertises the viewlessness of the news producer." In a polarized political world, it places the journalist in a desperate position, trying to gain the trust of the public not by truth-seeking, but by pandering to the critics that, inevitably and somewhat ironically, won't like the results of that truth-seeking anyway. It's a losing game, every time, because every piece of serious, policy-oriented journalism is bound to make some people happy and others less so. It's an age-old attempt to secure a kind of legitimacy by making everyone happy through false equivalency.

Can the "cult of balance," as some have called it, do real damage to our collective understanding of the world? Certainly it can, and does. Let's be clear: Viewless-ness is not objectivity, and it's certainly not independence. Sure, to have no particular view might make it look like a journalist is independent from faction. But where, if one has no view, does the view of the public interest fit in? There is always one side a journalist must take, and that's the public's side. Another way of thinking about it? Truth-seeking doesn't *have* a point of view; it *is* a point of view.

Taking the public's side means practicing what Kovach and Rosenstiel call "engaged independence." Rather than try to play the detached, neutral observer, an engaged, independent journalist lets the facts take her where they may, demands answers to questions sources would rather not answer, and presses the powerful for the truth. We also agree with many prominent journalists like James Risen and Dan Gillmor that engaged independence includes a duty to defend that independence. (See Gillmor's sidebar (8.2) for more details.) Taking a position on press freedom issues is indeed taking a side, but it's the public's side. After all, independence is what enables the press to do the things the public needs it to do.

We may all agree that good journalists understand that objectivity isn't about refusing to take sides—it is about reporting the facts as they are, even when that means making one side look bad. But just because many understand that, it doesn't make methods-based objectivity the norm.

That approach to reporting has taken quite a beating over the years, as a host of well-paid critics in institutions ranging from corporations to think tanks on the left and right repeatedly set the objectivity trap, and as structural biases in journalistic practice shape stories in ways that often don't serve citizens very well. To serve citizens by giving them meaningful information they need to run their lives and make democracy function, we must focus our efforts on our methods—on verification and transparency—and challenge the assertion that good journalism doesn't have a point of view.

▶ UNCHANGING PRINCIPLES FOR A CHANGING WORLD

In a world awash in information, in which old business models are failing and in which new disruptive technologies emerge seemingly daily, as you learned in Chapter 5, it's easy to panic and follow the herd, substituting quantity for quality and succumbing to a mishmash of celebrity gossip and viral videos. The shackles of an artificial "view from nowhere" may contribute to the decline of the mainstream press as the public turns to other sources in the information tide who—right, wrong or otherwise—don't really worry about taking a stand.

We don't know the magic answer to saving journalism. No one does. We do believe that abandoning the values of independence, of accuracy through verification, of transparency of practice, of objectivity-as-method, is precisely the wrong way to go. The key, to us, lies in a return to the principles outlined in this book.

To preserve some segment of the broader world of mass communication dedicated to newsgathering in the independent pursuit of functional truth, is to us the most important challenge facing journalism today. To remain a viable part of a democracy, journalism must return to its past to discover its future.

That might seem a bit simplistic, but it's not. Preserving those principles requires courage too often lacking in today's corporate newsrooms. It demands no less than a sustained effort to encourage aggressive, inquisitive, watchdog journalism that marked the rise of the American press, and that will fuel its rise again. That, in turn, demands investment in reporting, in boots on the ground and eyes on City Hall. Traditional news outlets may or may not rise to the challenge, but rest assured, someone will, for the society's innate need to inform itself does not depend upon any media-specific channel.

We've moved from an era of few media producers and a mass audience to an era in which anyone can be a media producer and have an audience, even if just a tiny one. This tells us that now, more than ever, journalism must return to its core mission to differentiate itself. That core mission—informing the members of a community so that they might better live their lives—has remained the beating heart of journalism, while everything else has changed.

Chapter Eight Review

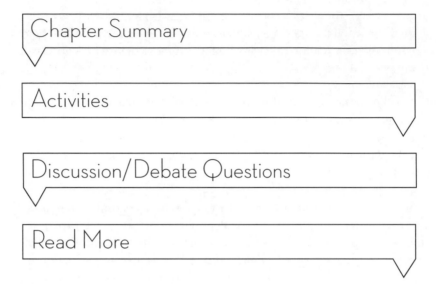

Chapter Summary

Activities

Discussion/Debate Questions

Read More

▶ CHAPTER SUMMARY

Independence is a crucial element of journalism that makes the truth-seeking work of journalists possible. But it's an ongoing fight to preserve it. Many forces are arrayed against journalistic independence, from economic pressures to do or not do certain kinds of reporting to the objectivity trap used by all kinds of political actors to squelch the publication of uncomfortable information. Even within journalism, there's not always as much agreement on how to exercise independence as one would hope. Independence, combined with an approach to objectivity that focuses on sound methods such as verification and transparency, is the key to journalism's enduring mission to provide truthful information of consequence to citizens in a democracy.

▶ ACTIVITIES

1. Journalism scholar Andrew Cline talks about nine structural biases. These, of course, are closely aligned with the news values and the way journalists do their jobs as discussed in Chapter 3. Split into small groups of 2 or 3 and choose a bias to explore. For about five minutes look online, on your smartphone, or in a printed daily newspaper to find one or two examples of your bias. Briefly present your findings to the class.

2. How forceful are journalists and news outlets at declaring their independence? Working independently or in small groups, pick a major news outlet. Can you find statements about the organization's stance on being objective or independent? These might be on the organization's website or might be found on another source (for example, a Q&A interview with a publisher or news executive). Share their experiences with the rest of the class. How hard were these statements to find? What did they say? If you couldn't find a statement of this type, what perception might that leave in the minds of the audience?

3. Invite a reporter either via Skype or in person to discuss with the class how he or she works to be "fair" to all sides when reporting a political issue. Prepare questions based on the chapter. Questions could include: Are there times when fairness gets in the way of the "truth" and accuracy? Do stories have to always include two or more sides? What if one side is clearly dominant in the debate? How much space should be given to minority opinion, if any? What is your response when reader or source charges you with political bias?

4. Reflect on the criticism of Edward Snowden for leaking top-secret documents. Compare this with the criticism leveled at Daniel Ellsberg, the source of the Pentagon Papers, in the early 1970s. Ellsberg and the Pentagon Papers are the subject of many movies and documentaries.

Watch a clip of *The Most Dangerous Man In America*, a documentary by First Run Features, starting around the 51:45 mark. While Ellsberg suffered greatly for leaking the papers, the decision by the *Washington Post* and *New York Times* to publish them has been lauded. How might we look back on the Snowden affair in 20 years? How might history treat both Snowden and the journalists to whom he leaked the documents?

5. Political bias has been debated ever since printing presses started running in the American colonies. In fact, early newspapers were based on having a political bias. While most news outlets strive to present objective versions of events, sometimes even the inclusion of one word can project subtle forms of bias. Find an example of a news report online that could be perceived as biased from someone with a firm stance on the issue. Include a link to the story on the class discussion board and detail what could be considered biased in the report. Next, address how the journalist, editor or producer might have altered the presentation to avoid this appearance.

▶ DISCUSSION/DEBATE QUESTIONS

1. Wikileaks became famous before Edward Snowden for obtaining and posting to the Internet a large set of top-secret documents. The person who leaked those documents, former Army private Chelsea Manning, was sentenced to a 35-year prison term for violating the Espionage Act, the longest prison term for a leaker in U.S. history. She is appealing her conviction. Compare and contrast the actions of Wikileaks and its founder, Julian Assange, with the actions of Edward Snowden, especially when it comes to the involvement of journalists. Are all of these documents newsworthy? Can you think of circumstances where a journalist might not report on the contents of top-secret documents? What might decisions on whether to do such reporting depend on? Does it depend on the people involved? The consequences? When are situations like this news?

2. Fox News' slogan is "Fair and Balanced." Is it really possible for journalists to be completely fair *and* balanced? Can you think of times where balance doesn't equal fairness in the reporting of a story?

3. Do you agree with James Risen and Dan Gillmor that journalists ought to be activists when it comes to press freedom? What might that activism look like? What, if any, limits on that activism should there be?

4. Watch this clip (a trailer for the HBO series *Newsroom*): www.youtube. com/watch?v=lgFZbrwmndA&feature=relmfu. The premise of the series is a retooling of a network news program into one modeled after Kovach and Rosenstiel's "engaged independence." What pressures might this type of news 2.0 program face from owners, shareholders, audiences and newsmakers?

5. What do you think is the future of American journalism? Are you optimistic that journalism can continue to perform a vital role in U.S. democracy? What challenges do you think are ahead? What solutions will you bring to the table when you graduate—as an audience member, a voter, a policy maker or a working journalist?

▶ READ MORE

Kevin Barnhurst, "The Interpretive Turn in News," *Journalism and Technological Change: Historical Perspectives, Contemporary Trends*, pp. 111–114, Eds. Clemens Zimmerman and Martin Schreiber, Chicago: University of Chicago Press, 2014.

Andrew Cline, "Media/Political Bias," http://rhetorica.net/bias.htm.

Justin Elliott and Jesse Eisinger, ProPublica and Laura Sullivan, "The Red Cross' Secret Disaster," NPR, 2015, https://www.propublica.org/article/the-red-cross-secret-disaster.

Justin Elliott and Jesse Eisinger, ProPublica and Laura Sullivan, "Red Cross Demands Corrections to Our 'Misleading' Coverage. Here's Our Response," NPR, 2015, https://www.propublica.org/article/red-cross-demands-corrections-to-our-coverage-our-response.

Justin Elliott and Jesse Eisinger, ProPublica and Laura Sullivan, "Special Report: The American Red Cross," NPR, 2015, www.npr.org/series/377506201/special-report-on-the-american-red-cross.

Justin Elliott and Jesse Eisinger, ProPublica and Laura Sullivan, "10 Serious Problems With ProPublica NPR Reporting on Red Cross," NPR, 2015, https://www.propublica.org/documents/item/1669928–10-serious-problems-with-propublica-npr.html.

Katherine Fink and Michael Schudson, "The Rise of Contextual Journalism, 1950s–2000s," *Journalism: Theory, Practice and Criticism* 15(1): 3–20 (2014).

Lucas Graves, Brendan Nyhan and Jason Reifler, "Why Do Journalists Fact-Check? The Role of Demand- and Supply-Side Factors," Midwest Political Science Association, March 30, 2015.

Dan Murphy, "Joe McCarthy, Glenn Greenwald and Me," *Christian Science Monitor*, January 16, 2014. www.csmonitor.com/World/Security-Watch/Backchannels/2014/0116/Joe-McCarthy-Glenn-Greenwald-and-me.

National Public Radio, "This is NPR. And These Are the Standards of Our Journalism," *NPR Ethics Handbook*, ethics.npr.org.

Laura Poitras, director, *Citizenfour*, Praxis Films, 2014. https://citizenfourfilm.com/.

Reddit.com, "We're Glenn Greenwald and Janine Gibson of the Guardian US, and We've Been Breaking Stories on the NSA Files since June. AUA!" https://www.reddit.com/r/IAmA/comments/1nisdy/were_glenn_greenwald_and_janine_gibson_of_the/.

A.O. Scott, "Intent on Defying an All-Seeing Eye," New York Times, October 23, 2014. www.nytimes.com/2014/10/24/movies/citizenfour-a-documentary-about-edward-j-snowden.html?_r=0.

Margaret Sullivan, "Facts, Truth . . . and May the Best Man Win," *New York Times*, September 4, 2012. http://publiceditor.blogs.nytimes.com/2012/09/04/facts-truth-and-may-the-best-man-win/?_r=0.

Appendix
Codes of Ethics

▶ **SOCIETY OF PROFESSIONAL JOURNALISTS CODE OF ETHICS**

Preamble   Members of the Society of Professional Journalists believe that public enlightenment is the forerunner of justice and the foundation of democracy. Ethical journalism strives to ensure the free exchange of information that is accurate, fair and thorough. An ethical journalist acts with integrity.

The Society declares these four principles as the foundation of ethical journalism and encourages their use in its practice by all people in all media.

Seek Truth and Report It   Ethical journalism should be accurate and fair. Journalists should be honest and courageous in gathering, reporting and interpreting information.

Journalists should:

- ▶ Take responsibility for the accuracy of their work. Verify information before releasing it. Use original sources whenever possible.

- ▶ Remember that neither speed nor format excuses inaccuracy.

- ▶ Provide context. Take special care not to misrepresent or oversimplify in promoting, previewing or summarizing a story.

- ▶ Gather, update and correct information throughout the life of a news story.

- ▶ Be cautious when making promises, but keep the promises they make.

▶ Identify sources clearly. The public is entitled to as much information as possible to judge the reliability and motivations of sources.

▶ Consider sources' motives before promising anonymity. Reserve anonymity for sources who may face danger, retribution or other harm, and have information that cannot be obtained elsewhere. Explain why anonymity was granted.

▶ Diligently seek subjects of news coverage to allow them to respond to criticism or allegations of wrongdoing.

▶ Avoid undercover or other surreptitious methods of gathering information unless traditional, open methods will not yield information vital to the public.

▶ Be vigilant and courageous about holding those with power accountable. Give voice to the voiceless.

▶ Support the open and civil exchange of views, even views they find repugnant.

▶ Recognize a special obligation to serve as watchdogs over public affairs and government. Seek to ensure that the public's business is conducted in the open, and that public records are open to all.

▶ Provide access to source material when it is relevant and appropriate.

▶ Boldly tell the story of the diversity and magnitude of the human experience.

▶ Seek sources whose voices we seldom hear.

▶ Avoid stereotyping. Journalists should examine the ways their values and experiences may shape their reporting.

▶ Label advocacy and commentary.

▶ Never deliberately distort facts or context, including visual information.

▶ Clearly label illustrations and re-enactments.

▶ Never plagiarize. Always attribute.

Minimize Harm Ethical journalism treats sources, subjects, colleagues and members of the public as human beings deserving of respect.

Journalists should:

▶ Balance the public's need for information against potential harm or discomfort. Pursuit of the news is not a license for arrogance or undue intrusiveness.

▶ Show compassion for those who may be affected by news coverage. Use heightened sensitivity when dealing with juveniles, victims of sex crimes, and sources or subjects who are inexperienced or unable to give consent. Consider cultural differences in approach and treatment.

▶ Recognize that legal access to information differs from an ethical justification to publish or broadcast.

▶ Realize that private people have a greater right to control information about themselves than public figures and others who seek power, influence or attention. Weigh the consequences of publishing or broadcasting personal information.

▶ Avoid pandering to lurid curiosity, even if others do.

▶ Balance a suspect's right to a fair trial with the public's right to know. Consider the implications of identifying criminal suspects before they face legal charges.

▶ Consider the long-term implications of the extended reach and permanence of publication. Provide updated and more complete information as appropriate.

Act Independently   The highest and primary obligation of ethical journalism is to serve the public.

Journalists should:

▶ Avoid conflicts of interest, real or perceived. Disclose unavoidable conflicts.

▶ Refuse gifts, favors, fees, free travel and special treatment, and avoid political and other outside activities that may compromise integrity or impartiality, or may damage credibility.

- ▶ Be wary of sources offering information for favors or money; do not pay for access to news. Identify content provided by outside sources, whether paid or not.

- ▶ Deny favored treatment to advertisers, donors or any other special interests, and resist internal and external pressure to influence coverage.

- ▶ Distinguish news from advertising and shun hybrids that blur the lines between the two. Prominently label sponsored content.

Be Accountable and Transparent   Ethical journalism means taking responsibility for one's work and explaining one's decisions to the public.

Journalists should:

- ▶ Explain ethical choices and processes to audiences. Encourage a civil dialogue with the public about journalistic practices, coverage and news content.

- ▶ Respond quickly to questions about accuracy, clarity and fairness.

- ▶ Acknowledge mistakes and correct them promptly and prominently. Explain corrections and clarifications carefully and clearly.

- ▶ Expose unethical conduct in journalism, including within their organizations.

- ▶ Abide by the same high standards they expect of others.

The SPJ Code of Ethics is a statement of abiding principles supported by additional explanations and position papers (at spj.org) that address changing journalistic practices.

It is not a set of rules, rather a guide that encourages all who engage in journalism to take responsibility for the information they provide, regardless of medium. The code should be read as a whole; individual principles should not be taken out of context. It is not, nor can it be under the First Amendment, legally enforceable.

Source: www.spj.org/ethicscode.asp

▶ RADIO TELEVISION DIGITAL NEWS ASSOCIATION CODE OF ETHICS

Guiding Principles   Journalism's obligation is to the public. Journalism places the public's interests ahead of commercial, political and personal interests. Journalism empowers viewers, listeners and readers to make more informed decisions for themselves; it does not tell people what to believe or how to feel.

Ethical decision-making should occur at every step of the journalistic process, including story selection, news gathering, production, presentation and delivery. Practitioners of ethical journalism seek diverse and even opposing opinions in order to reach better conclusions that can be clearly explained and effectively defended or, when appropriate, revisited and revised.

Ethical decision-making—like writing, photography, design or anchoring—requires skills that improve with study, diligence and practice.

The RTDNA Code of Ethics does not dictate what journalists should do in every ethical predicament; rather it offers resources to help journalists make better ethical decisions—on and off the job—for themselves and for the communities they serve.

Journalism is distinguished from other forms of content by these guiding principles:

Truth and Accuracy Above All

- ▶ The facts should get in the way of a good story. Journalism requires more than merely reporting remarks, claims or comments. Journalism verifies, provides relevant context, tells the rest of the story and acknowledges the absence of important additional information.

- ▶ For every story of significance, there are always more than two sides. While they may not all fit into every account, responsible reporting is clear about what it omits, as well as what it includes.

- ▶ Scarce resources, deadline pressure and relentless competition do not excuse cutting corners factually or oversimplifying complex issues.

- ▶ "Trending," "going viral" or "exploding on social media" may increase urgency, but these phenomena only heighten the need for strict standards of accuracy.

- ▶ Facts change over time. Responsible reporting includes updating stories and amending archival versions to make them more accurate and to avoid misinforming those who, through search, stumble upon outdated material.

- ▶ Deception in newsgathering, including surreptitious recording, conflicts with journalism's commitment to truth. Similarly, anonymity of sources deprives the audience of important, relevant information. Staging, dramatization and other alterations—even when labeled as such—can confuse or fool viewers, listeners and readers. These tactics are justified only when stories of great significance cannot be adequately told without distortion, and when any creative liberties taken are clearly explained.

- ▶ Journalism challenges assumptions, rejects stereotypes and illuminates—even where it cannot eliminate—ignorance.

- ▶ Ethical journalism resists false dichotomies—either/or, always/ never, black/white thinking—and considers a range of alternatives between the extremes.

Independence and Transparency

- ▶ Editorial independence may be a more ambitious goal today than ever before. Media companies, even if not-for-profit, have commercial, competitive and other interests—both internal and external—from which the journalists they employ cannot be entirely shielded. Still, independence from influences that conflict with public interest remains an essential ideal of journalism. Transparency provides the public with the means to assess credibility and to determine who deserves trust.

- ▶ Acknowledging sponsor-provided content, commercial concerns or political relationships is essential, but transparency alone is not adequate. It does not entitle journalists to lower their standards of fairness or truth.

▶ Disclosure, while critical, does not justify the exclusion of perspectives and information that are important to the audience's understanding of issues.

▶ Journalism's proud tradition of holding the powerful accountable provides no exception for powerful journalists or the powerful organizations that employ them. To profit from reporting on the activities of others while operating in secrecy is hypocrisy.

▶ Effectively explaining editorial decisions and processes does not mean making excuses. Transparency requires reflection, reconsideration and honest openness to the possibility that an action, however well intended, was wrong.

▶ Ethical journalism requires owning errors, correcting them promptly and giving corrections as much prominence as the error itself had.

▶ Commercial endorsements are incompatible with journalism because they compromise credibility. In journalism, content is gathered, selected and produced in the best interests of viewers, listeners and readers—not in the interests of somebody who paid to have a product or position promoted and associated with a familiar face, voice or name.

▶ Similarly, political activity and active advocacy can undercut the real or perceived independence of those who practice journalism. Journalists do not give up the rights of citizenship, but their public exercise of those rights can call into question their impartiality.

▶ The acceptance of gifts or special treatment of any kind not available to the general public creates conflicts of interest and erodes independence. This does not include the access to events or areas traditionally granted to working journalists in order to facilitate their coverage. It does include "professional courtesy" admission, discounts and "freebies" provided to journalists by those who might someday be the subject of coverage. Such goods and services are often offered as enticements to report favorably on the giver or rewards for doing so; even where that is not the intent, it is the reasonable perception of a justifiably suspicious public.

▶ Commercial and political activities, as well as the acceptance of gifts or special treatment, cause harm even when the journalists involved are "off duty" or "on their own time."

▶ Attribution is essential. It adds important information that helps the audience evaluate content and it acknowledges those who contribute to coverage. Using someone else's work without attribution or permission is plagiarism.

Accountability for Consequences

▶ Journalism accepts responsibility, articulates its reasons and opens its processes to public scrutiny.

▶ Journalism provides enormous benefits to self-governing societies. In the process, it can create inconvenience, discomfort and even distress. Minimizing harm, particularly to vulnerable individuals, should be a consideration in every editorial and ethical decision.

▶ Responsible reporting means considering the consequences of both the newsgathering—even if the information is never made public—and of the material's potential dissemination. Certain stakeholders deserve special consideration; these include children, victims, vulnerable adults and others inexperienced with American media.

▶ Preserving privacy and protecting the right to a fair trial are not the primary mission of journalism; still, these critical concerns deserve consideration and to be balanced against the importance or urgency of reporting.

▶ The right to broadcast, publish or otherwise share information does not mean it is always right to do so. However, journalism's obligation is to pursue truth and report, not withhold it. Shying away from difficult cases is not necessarily more ethical than taking on the challenge of reporting them. Leaving tough or sensitive stories to non-journalists can be a disservice to the public.

A growing collection of coverage guidelines for use on a range of ethical issues is available on the RTDNA website—www.rtdna.org.

Source: Revised Code of Ethics adopted June 11, 2015. See more at: www.rtdna.org/content/rtdna_code_of_ethics#sthash.c5ZofYK5.dpuf.

▶ SOCIETY OF AMERICAN BUSINESS EDITORS AND WRITERS CODE OF ETHICS

Statement of Purpose   As business and financial journalists, we recognize we are guardians of the public trust and must do nothing to abuse this obligation.

It is not enough that we act with honest intent; as journalists, we must conduct our professional lives in a manner that avoids even the suggestion of personal gain, or any misuse of the power of the press.

It is with this acknowledgment that we offer these guidelines for those who work in business and financial journalism:

Personal Investments and Relationships

- ▶ Avoid any practice that might compromise or appear to compromise objectivity or fairness.

- ▶ Never let personal investments influence content. Disclose investment positions to your superior or directly to the public.

- ▶ Disclose personal or family relationships that might pose conflicts of interest.

- ▶ Avoid active trading and other short-term profit-seeking opportunities, as such activities are not compatible with the independent role of the business journalist.

- ▶ Do not take advantage of inside information for personal gain.

Sources

- ▶ Insure confidentiality of information during the reporting process, and make every effort to keep information from finding its way to those who might use it for gain before it is disseminated to the public.

- ▶ Do not alter information, delay or withhold publication or make concessions relating to news content to any government.

Gifts and Favors

▶ In the course of professional activity, accept no gift or special treatment worth more than token value.

▶ Accept no out-of-town travel paid for by outside sources.

▶ Carefully examine offers of freelance work or speech honoraria to assure such offers are not attempts to influence content.

▶ Disclose to a supervisor any offer of future employment or outside income that springs from the journalist's professional activities or contacts.

▶ Accept food or refreshments of ordinary value only if absolutely necessary, and only during the normal course of business.

Editorial Integrity

▶ Publishers, owners and newsroom managers should establish policies and guidelines to protect the integrity of business news coverage.

▶ Regardless of news platform, there should be a clear delineation between advertising and editorial content.

▶ Material produced by editorial staff should be used only in sections, programming or pages controlled by editorial departments.

▶ Content, sections or programming controlled by advertising departments should be distinctly different from news sections in typeface, layout and design. Advertising content should be identified as such.

▶ Promising a story in exchange for advertising or other considerations is unethical.

Using Outside Material

▶ Using articles or columns from non-journalists is potentially deceptive and poses inherent conflicts of interest. This does not apply to content that is clearly labeled opinion or viewpoint, or to

> submissions identified as coming directly from the public, such as citizen blogs or letters to the editor.

► Submissions should be accepted only from freelancers who abide by the same ethical policies as staff members.

Technology

► Business journalists should take the lead in adapting professional standards to new forms of journalism as technologies emerge and change.

The business journalist should encourage fellow journalists to abide by these standards and principles.

Source: http://sabew.org/about/codes-of-ethics/sabews-code-of-ethics/.

► NATIONAL PRESS PHOTOGRAPHERS ASSOCIATION CODE OF ETHICS

Preamble   The National Press Photographers Association, a professional society that promotes the highest standards in visual journalism, acknowledges concern for every person's need both to be fully informed about public events and to be recognized as part of the world in which we live.

Visual journalists operate as trustees of the public. Our primary role is to report visually on the significant events and varied viewpoints in our common world. Our primary goal is the faithful and comprehensive depiction of the subject at hand. As visual journalists, we have the responsibility to document society and to preserve its history through images.

Photographic and video images can reveal great truths, expose wrongdoing and neglect, inspire hope and understanding and connect people around the globe through the language of visual understanding. Photographs can also cause great harm if they are callously intrusive or are manipulated.

This code is intended to promote the highest quality in all forms of visual journalism and to strengthen public confidence in the profession. It is also meant to serve as an educational tool both for those who practice and for those who appreciate photojournalism. To that end, The National Press Photographers Association sets forth the following.

Code of Ethics   Visual journalists and those who manage visual news productions are accountable for upholding the following standards in their daily work:

1.   Be accurate and comprehensive in the representation of subjects.

2.   Resist being manipulated by staged photo opportunities.

3.   Be complete and provide context when photographing or recording subjects. Avoid stereotyping individuals and groups. Recognize and work to avoid presenting one's own biases in the work.

4.   Treat all subjects with respect and dignity. Give special consideration to vulnerable subjects and compassion to victims of crime or tragedy. Intrude on private moments of grief only when the public has an overriding and justifiable need to see.

5.   While photographing subjects do not intentionally contribute to, alter, or seek to alter or influence events.

6.   Editing should maintain the integrity of the photographic images' content and context. Do not manipulate images or add or alter sound in any way that can mislead viewers or misrepresent subjects.

7.   Do not pay sources or subjects or reward them materially for information or participation.

8.   Do not accept gifts, favors, or compensation from those who might seek to influence coverage.

9.   Do not intentionally sabotage the efforts of other journalists.

Ideally, visual journalists should:

1.   Strive to ensure that the public's business is conducted in public. Defend the rights of access for all journalists.

2.   Think proactively, as a student of psychology, sociology, politics and art to develop a unique vision and presentation. Work with a voracious appetite for current events and contemporary visual media.

3. Strive for total and unrestricted access to subjects, recommend alternatives to shallow or rushed opportunities, seek a diversity of viewpoints, and work to show unpopular or unnoticed points of view.

4. Avoid political, civic and business involvements or other employment that compromise or give the appearance of compromising one's own journalistic independence.

5. Strive to be unobtrusive and humble in dealing with subjects.

6. Respect the integrity of the photographic moment.

7. Strive by example and influence to maintain the spirit and high standards expressed in this code. When confronted with situations in which the proper action is not clear, seek the counsel of those who exhibit the highest standards of the profession. Visual journalists should continuously study their craft and the ethics that guide it.

Source: https://nppa.org/code_of_ethics.

▶ AMERICAN SOCIETY OF NEWS EDITORS STATEMENT OF PRINCIPLES

ASNE's Statement of Principles was originally adopted in 1922 as the "Canons of Journalism." The document was revised and renamed "Statement of Principles" in 1975.

Preamble   The First Amendment, protecting freedom of expression from abridgment by any law, guarantees to the people through their press a constitutional right, and thereby places on newspaper people a particular responsibility. Thus journalism demands of its practitioners not only industry and knowledge but also the pursuit of a standard of integrity proportionate to the journalist's singular obligation. To this end the American Society of Newspaper Editors sets forth this Statement of Principles as a standard encouraging the highest ethical and professional performance.

Article I—Responsibility   The primary purpose of gathering and distributing news and opinion is to serve the general welfare by informing the people and enabling them to make judgments on the issues of the time.

Newspapermen and women who abuse the power of their professional role for selfish motives or unworthy purposes are faithless to that public trust. The American press was made free not just to inform or just to serve as a forum for debate but also to bring an independent scrutiny to bear on the forces of power in the society, including the conduct of official power at all levels of government.

Article II—Freedom of the Press   Freedom of the press belongs to the people. It must be defended against encroachment or assault from any quarter, public or private. Journalists must be constantly alert to see that the public's business is conducted in public. They must be vigilant against all who would exploit the press for selfish purposes.

Article III—Independence   Journalists must avoid impropriety and the appearance of impropriety as well as any conflict of interest or the appearance of conflict. They should neither accept anything nor pursue any activity that might compromise or seem to compromise their integrity.

Article IV—Truth and Accuracy   Good faith with the reader is the foundation of good journalism. Every effort must be made to assure that the news content is accurate, free from bias and in context, and that all sides are presented fairly. Editorials, analytical articles and commentary should be held to the same standards of accuracy with respect to facts as news reports. Significant errors of fact, as well as errors of omission, should be corrected promptly and prominently.

Article V—Impartiality   To be impartial does not require the press to be unquestioning or to refrain from editorial expression. Sound practice, however, demands a clear distinction for the reader between news reports and opinion. Articles that contain opinion or personal interpretation should be clearly identified.

Article VI—Fair Play   Journalists should respect the rights of people involved in the news, observe the common standards of decency and stand accountable to the public for the fairness and accuracy of their news reports. Persons publicly accused should be given the earliest opportunity to respond. Pledges of confidentiality to news sources must be honored at all costs, and therefore should not be given lightly. Unless there is clear and pressing need to maintain confidences, sources of information should be identified.

These principles are intended to preserve, protect and strengthen the bond of trust and respect between American journalists and the American people, a bond that is essential to sustain the grant of freedom entrusted to both by the nation's founders.

Source: http://asne.org/content.asp?pl=24&sl=171&contentid=171.

Index